imperial archipelago

Writing Past Colonialism is the signature book series of the Institute of Postcolonial Studies, based in Melbourne, Australia. By postcolonialism we understand modes of writing and artistic production that critically engage with and contest the legacy and continuing mindset and practices of colonialism, and inform debate about the processes of globalization. This manifests itself in a concern with difference from the Euro-American, the global, and the norm. The series is also committed to publishing works that seek "to make a difference," both in the academy and outside it.

OUR HOPE IS THAT BOOKS IN THE SERIES WILL
  • engage with contemporary issues and problems relating to colonialism
      and postcolonialism
  • attempt to reach a broad constituency of readers
  • address the relation between theory and practice
  • be interdisciplinary in approach as well as subject matter
  • experiment with new modes of writing and methodology

ipcs

INSTITUTE OF POSTCOLONIAL STUDIES | WRITING PAST COLONIALISM

imperial archipelago

REPRESENTATION AND RULE IN THE INSULAR TERRITORIES UNDER U.S. DOMINION AFTER 1898

Lanny Thompson

 University of Hawai'i Press   Honolulu

Publication of *Imperial Archipelago* was assisted through a grant by
the Office of the Dean of Graduate Studies and Research,
University of Puerto Rico, Río Piedras.

Library of Congress Cataloging-in-Publication Data
Thompson, Lanny.
  Imperial archipelago : representation and rule in the insular territories
under U.S. dominion after 1898 / Lanny Thompson.
    p.   cm.—(Writing past colonialism)
  Includes bibliographical references and index.
  ISBN 978-0-8248-3401-2 (hardcover : alk. paper)
  ISBN 978-0-8248-3488-3 (pbk. : alk. paper)
  1. United States—Insular possessions—History.   2. United States—
Colonial question.   3. Imperialism in literature.   4. Colonies in
literature.   I Title.   II. Series: Writing past colonialism series.
  F970.T48 2010
  973.8—dc22

                              2009050519

Series design by Leslie Fitch

CONTENTS

ILLUSTRATIONS

Map

Figures

Tables

PREFACE

THIS BOOK BEGAN many years ago as a monograph, a short study of the symbolic construction of a colonial people in the many popular travelogues illustrated with photographs that appeared after the acquisition of Puerto Rico following the Spanish-American War of 1898. That monograph, *Nuestra isla y su gente*, published by the Center for Social Research at the University of Puerto Rico, is now in its second edition. The current book, however, is considerably different, thanks to the critical comments and perceptive observations made by my colleagues, as well as my own reflections regarding the limitations of the monograph.

First, some criticized the monograph because, after all was said and done, the popular books were just erroneous fantasies about foreign peoples that the authors and photographers didn't even know and about whom they knew even less. This criticism led me to trace the complex and extensive connections among the widespread representations of Puerto Rico that could be found in widely disparate and significantly different kinds of documents: popular travelogues, official reports, the census, congressional debates, Supreme Court decisions, and the laws that established the colonial state of Puerto Rico.

Second, while researching the representations of Puerto Rico in the popular travelogues, I compiled a bibliography of all the books from 1898 to 1914 that contained photographs and descriptions of it. Shortly after the completion of the monograph, it occurred to me that more than half of the volumes that I had examined included other sites as well, especially Cuba, Hawai'i, and the Philippines. It seemed as if the authors had engaged in spontaneous comparisons of the areas recently obtained or controlled by the United States. At the same time, these books understood these areas, at least implicitly, as a group, defined by their subordinate relation to the United States. I also began to think comparatively and to conceptualize these differences in the context of the U.S. overseas expansion. Puerto Rico, my original point of departure, became part of a larger comparative framework, a piece in the puzzle. By this method, I was able to identify particularities of places immersed in a wider process and thus to understand why things turned out the way they did. Later, I added Guam for comparative purposes, although it is almost absent from the popular travelogues.

I now had a systematic comparative project that sought to demonstrate that the representations of colonial peoples were discourses that were fundamental to the conceptualization, redaction, and justification of the legal documents that determined, in part, the political trajectories of each of the sites in the "imperial archipelago." On the one hand, the representations were not simply fantasies, but rather imaginaries to be acted upon. On the other hand, to understand the particular political status of Puerto Rico historically, it was necessary to contextualize and compare. Indeed, the understanding of each of the sites in the imperial archipelago required the same contextualization and comparison.

The research and writing of this book have been supported principally by the University of Puerto Rico, Río Piedras campus. The College of Social Sciences provided a one-year sabbatical, and the dean, Dr. Carlos Severino, approved many course leaves. The Office of the Dean of Graduate Studies and Research provided invaluable support through institutional research grants (FIPI), and the dean, Dr. Ana Guadalupe, was especially generous in her financial support for the artwork of this book. Special attention goes to the Center for Social Research and the Department of Sociology and Anthropology. Also, at crucial moments the Department of History has provided invaluable support and encouragement. Among the past administrators of these offices who have graciously extended their support are Luis Agrait, Jorge Duany, David Hernández, José Luis Méndez, Emilio Pantojas, Ethel Ríos, and Mayra Rosario Urrutia. The university has provided a number of research assistants throughout the years, and I thank them for their dedication: Yamel Arvelo, Wilma Maldonado, Vionex Martí, Benjamín Rivera, and Olga Rosas.

In the library, I would like to thank María E. Ordóñez, director of the Colección Puertorriqueña and guardian of the rare books and a host of other materials that make up this special collection. Manuel Martínez, the librarian of interlibrary loans, was a valuable resource for locating and providing bibliographic sources unavailable at the university library. He always responded above and beyond the call of duty. In addition, Axel Santana shared with me his knowledge of old photographs and how to reproduce them; more recently, Luis Joel Donato Jímenez taught me how to digitalize, and José A. Rodríguez helped with the scanning process in LabCad. Anne Catesby Jones loaned me her antique volumes for scanning. Finally, outside of Puerto Rico I am especially indebted to William Weurch of the Micronesian Area Research Center for photocopies of the official reports from Guam.

Several of my colleagues at the University of Puerto Rico have been especially supportive: Juan Giusti, Fernando Picó, and Efrén Rivera. Special thanks go to Juan José Baldrich, my office mate for many years, who graciously listened to my research updates and offered feedback. My most treasured colleague is also my wife, María del Carmen Baerga, an outstanding scholar in the History Department at the University of Puerto Rico. She patiently listened to the first drafts of my ideas and read the various versions of my chapters. Her suggestions, comments, and challenges have enriched the content of this volume beyond measure.

Throughout the years I have attended a number of conferences and seminars in Spain, the Philippines, Puerto Rico, Cuba, and the United States in which I have presented earlier versions of some of the arguments developed in this book. After considerable revision, two of my conference papers were published in *Pacific Historical Review* and *American Studies Asia*. I thank the editors of those two fine journals and the anonymous reviewers for their comments and suggestions. Special recognition goes to Virginia Dominguez and Jane Desmond, who organized a superb two-week faculty seminar at the University of Iowa. Among the colleagues I have met in these various conferences, the following stand out as inspirations: Oscar Campomanes, Vicente Díaz, Julian Go, Paul Kramer, Gary Okihiro, Annie Santiago, Bartholomew Sparrow, and David Wilkins. Finally, although this volume is not inspired directly by world-systems theory, I owe a great deal to my teachers, Immanuel Wallerstein, the late Terence K. Hopkins, and the late Giovanni Arrighi, who taught me to look beyond conventional boundaries and to creatively reconceptualize.

Introduction

THIS BOOK IS ABOUT the connections between representations, both textual and photographic, and rule in the U.S. imperial archipelago—that is, island territories under U.S. military and political dominion after 1898, namely, Cuba, Guam, Hawai'i, the Philippines, and Puerto Rico. After the United States took control over these diverse and wide-ranging islands, many turn-of-the-century authors used the term "new possessions" to refer to them, and it was commonplace for popular books, periodicals, pamphlets, legal discussions and recommendations, official reports and studies, congressional speeches and debates, and political platforms to mention all, or any combination, of these distinct, and in many ways incomparable, places. Nevertheless, scholarly literature, especially in the last fifty years or so, has completely lost sight of this historical aggregation. Instead, we have national histories, which disassociate the islands, or area studies, which create other combinations, such as the Caribbean, the Atlantic, Polynesia, Southeast Asia, and the Pacific Rim.

At present, there is no generally accepted, theoretically informed term to refer to the overseas territories under the control of the United States; hence, "imperial archipelago."[1] First, the adjective "imperial" refers to an empire, which is a "relationship, formal or informal, in which one state controls the effective sovereignty of another political society" by means of "force," "political collaboration," and "economic, social, or cultural dependence."[2] More specifically, imperialism entails the creation of colonies—that is, the establishment of new, dependent political organizations built upon local historical conditions.[3] Theories of imperialism have either slighted or completely ignored the analysis of representations and their effects in favor of economic and political processes. Indeed, all of the principal theories of imperialism construe representations of colonial subjects both as ideology, in the sense of a specious justification after the fact, and as social pathology—that is, as epiphenomenal as well as deviant.[4] In contrast, this book will demonstrate that representations, not only textual but also photographic, both constituted and normalized imperial rule. In this sense, it deploys recent conceptualizations that theorize ideologies as the confluence of cognition (the symbolic field of thought and belief), discourse (communication and linguistic expression), and society (group interests and conflicts); in short, ideologies are the social representations put into practice by members of social groups.[5]

Second, the word "archipelago" evokes an image of numerous proximal islands occupying an expansive sea. In the case of the imperial archipelago, however, the islands in question did not share a geographic oceanic space, but rather the military, political, and discursive space constituted through the overseas expansion of the United States. A fundamental characteristic of the imperial archipelago, construed as an object of study, was the paucity of autonomous lateral connections and the dominance of the imperial network. In other words, the islands were not so much related to one another as they were all joined to the United States. There was relatively little movement of people, products, technology, or even ideas among the islands during the period under study, roughly 1898 to 1903. Certainly some countries, such as Cuba and Puerto Rico, enjoyed close connections throughout the nineteenth century, due in part to geographical proximity and shared Spanish dominion.[6] As a whole, however, the islands of the imperial archipelago were connected principally to the United States, not to each other, through centralized chains of empire: local elites were linked to the on-site colonial administrators, who were responsible to the executive authorities in the metropole.[7] Likewise, the United States was the most important trading partner of each; there was relatively little inter-island commerce.

Another characteristic of the imperial archipelago was the diversity of complex social formations throughout the islands as a whole. The archipelago was an assemblage of multiple contact zones, each profoundly different and unique.[8] These islands would not be a focus for comparison were it not for the U.S. intervention, which made possible the same kind of questions to be directed to different kinds of places: what kinds of people were these and how should they be ruled? Thus, the most important characteristic of the imperial archipelago was that it comprised a "colonial project," an attempt to transform local populations by means of strategies that were both imaginative and practical, both conceptualized and realized in complex ways with varied results and unintended consequences.[9] This colonial project was comparative in the sense that it attempted to address the specificities of each place and its particular conditions.

This book is premised on the idea that the imperial archipelago is an object worthy of study in that it allows us to pose relevant questions that can be fruitfully addressed through comparisons of these sites. Its overarching research problem is derived from the general field of postcolonial studies—specifically colonial discourse theory, which poses the following fundamental interlocking and overlapping questions: What are the connections between knowledge and power, between discourse and governmentality, between representation and rule?[10] One specific question guides the exposition of this book: What were the connections between the descriptions (textual and photographic) of the islands and the specific forms of rule in the imperial archipelago that the United States acquired in 1898? Furthermore, why did each site have a different political relationship with the United States? This book, then, will address the issue of the relationship between representation and rule, between the descriptions of subject peoples and the creation of governments for them. The term "representation" refers to the process by which material reality, concepts, and signs become integrated and articulated as descriptions and depictions. Representations are further understood as discourses—that is, as language practices that effect subjects and produce strategic knowledge.[11] The term "rule" is understood specifically as the concrete forms of government established throughout the imperial archipelago. More generally, these governments are understood as instances of governmentality—that is, as the establishment of institutions, procedures, knowledge, strategies, and techniques that effect the management of populations. In turn, subject populations find ways to resist and accommodate govermentality.[12]

"Colonial discourse," the principal object of analysis of this book, refers to those representations, comprised of symbols, meanings, and propositions, that create subject peoples and justify imperial rule over them. This concept is borrowed from the work of Edward Said, who, in his exemplary book *Orientalism*, defined a new object of study (colonial discourse), a theoretical framework (representations that created colonial subjects), and a methodological orientation (discourse analysis).[13] In this book, Said adapted the archeological and genealogical methods of Michel Foucault to the study of imperial texts. A defining feature of Said's model was the use of a wide variety of textual genres in order to elucidate the underlying discursive formation. The bureaucratic report, the census, the scientific treatise, the scholarly work, the travelogue, the diary, the literary creation were all manifestations of discursive practices. In addition to texts, many authors have shown how photographs, exhibits, and museums also expressed colonial discourses.[14] In addition, Said incorporated the notion of hegemony, originally developed by Antonio Gramsci, as a way of understanding the processes of legitimation of colonial rule as distinct from the blatantly coercive aspects of colonial rule.[15]

In *Orientalism* Said stated, "To say simply that modern Orientalism has been an aspect of both imperialism and colonialism is not to say anything very disputable. Yet it is not enough to say it; it needs to be worked through analytically and historically."[16] However, it was precisely at this point that his analysis faltered: it did not make any specific connection between Orientalism and the particular forms of colonial or imperial rule. In other words, Said did not produce a historical analysis that was attentive to differences in the particular forms of imperial or colonial domination. This resulted in a rather mechanical portrayal of the relationship between a discourse of the "other" and consequent subjugation. Likewise, for the most part, postcolonial studies in general, and colonial discourse analysis in particular, have overlooked the study of concrete forms of rule.

More specifically, colonial discourse studies have inherited three problems from Said's Orientalist paradigm. First, the hypothesis of alterity has proposed that colonial discourses suppress cultural differences and produce homogenous colonial subjects under the sign of a fundamental and generalized inferiority. Generally, the literature on colonial discourses has criticized the incessant repetition of gendered, racialized, and infantilized images to portray the subject peoples and, in turn, to justify imperial dominion. According to this perspective, colonial discourses have suppressed a wide variety of historical differences among peoples in favor of broad abstract generalities regarding inferiority; they posit a homogeneous "other"—childlike, feminine, and colored—as a means of creating and governing subject peoples.[17]

Likewise, most traditional historical scholarship of U.S. expansion has emphasized the issue of differences *between* the new possessions and the older states and territories but has ignored the issue of differences *among and within* the new possessions.[18] No doubt, the culture of imperialism in the United States drew upon and extended the continental colonial experience in the elaboration of the fundamental alterity of the subject peoples in general. Nevertheless, it would seem that the cultural representations of the period—photographic and textual—demonstrated an acute awareness of the exceptional diversity of the peoples newly under U.S. dominion. Thus, alterity was not only a homogeneous notion, as most of the literature has suggested, but was simultaneously a thoroughly differentiated and hierarchical one. Indeed, the general proposition that colonial discourses constructed a homogeneous colonial subject is not entirely adequate for understanding the representations of subject peoples of the imperial archipelago. More precisely, the proposition of the homogeneous "other" fails to explicate the connections between particular representations of subject peoples and the specific patterns of imperial rule. This is due to the impossibility of addressing *differences* in imperial rule based upon a theory of the *homogeneous* construction of the colonial "other."

Second, the colonial discourse model is unclear and ambiguous regarding the issue of representation: most of the time Said treated discursive representations as essentially arbitrary creations, yet at times he criticized them as misrepresentations of concrete realities. The definition of Orientalism systematically eliminated any reference to concrete historical relations, whether economic, political, or social, and Said presumed the virtual autonomy of the text, except for context of colonialism in its most abstract and general sense. Yet Said sought to refute its incorrectness and belie its stereotypes. On balance, his notion of empire was a seamless, unified text devoid of the messy materiality of history, and he tended to treat representations as linguistic phenomena almost independent of concrete historical contexts.[19] However, it is not possible to explain variations in imperial rule without a consideration of historical context and the concrete consequences of discursive practice. I will not treat the descriptions of the subject peoples as simply misrepresentations of a fundamental cultural reality. For this reason, I will avoid any attempt to describe "native peoples" authentically. I do not seek to refute the imperial descriptions, but rather to see what historical processes produced them and how they in turn produced governments. The colonial discourse of the imperial archipelago was composed of pragmatic strategies that articulated economic and geopolitical interests, as well as knowledge and value judgments of local conditions—in particular the pattern of colonial settlement, the development of national consciousness, and the history of armed anticolonial rebellion. In addition, colonial administrators directly engaged local elites, so their historical formation; political aspirations; and forms of resistance, accommodation, and collaboration were important.[20] Discursive strategies responded to historical conditions and contended with local elites; this complex process produced new forms of rule.

Finally, proponents of colonial discourse analysis have disdained systematic claims of etiology and have relied on rather vague suggestions of correspondences between representations and imperial domination.[21] Consequently, the notion of colonial discourse often remained at an excessively high level of generality and abstraction. It appeared as if imperial domination were a power that created colonial subjects discursively and yet was devoid of any colonial governments as such. Despite the insistence of colonial discourse on the relationship between knowledge and power, few authors ever connected this relationship to any particular strategies of rule.[22] Most authors have emphasized the cultural, literary, or discursive elements of imperial rule and have either ignored or questioned the primacy of economic and geopolitical determinants. Although textual approaches vary, they share a disdain toward any ultimate referent conceived as extratextual or "beyond" the text. The overwhelming tendency of postcolonial theory has been to characterize colonial discourses as indeterminate, ambiguous constructions and then to deconstruct or decenter them as a means of contradicting or confronting their repressive dimensions. A consequence of these textual approaches has been the lack of interest in any notion of causality. As a part of the critique of historicism, discourse theory looked askance at etiology, in all of its hermeneutic, positivist, and Marxist variants, and systematically avoided all questions of "Why?" This fundamental question has been largely excluded from discourse analysis and theory in general.[23]

My argument is that contrary to the postulate of indeterminacy, representations were historically connected to the concrete and specific forms of rule. They were not entirely accidental nor arbitrary nor indeterminate, but rather "causal" in a historical sense. That is, variations in representations explain why rule was organized in certain particular ways and not others.[24] Rather than the methodological postulate of indetermination, this book will show that discourses were strategic textual deployments in response to particular local situations, which in turn shaped discursive practices. In this sense, colonial discourses and local conditions were co-determinant: their interaction produced and legitimized diverse forms of government in the imperial archipelago. That is, discursive practices, in response to local factors (which I will elaborate below), resulted in the creation of new governments and subject peoples. In this way, discourses were neither arbitrary nor indeterminate: rather they articulated knowledge about local conditions in a way that not only justified but also produced certain effects: colonial governments and subjects. Furthermore, since discursive practices both produce and legitimate (but are not mere reflections), they exist both prior to and simultaneously with the creation and implementation of the governments. Therefore, the exposition of representations in this book will include texts and images that are prior to and simultaneous with the establishment and early implementation of the following governments: Cuba (1902), Guam (1899), Hawai'i (1900), the Philippines (1902), and Puerto Rico (1900).

It has been widely documented that during the end of the nineteenth century, economic and geopolitical interests coalesced to form an expansionist impulse inspired by the ideas of John Fiske, Brooks Adams, Frederick Jackson Turner, Alfred Thayer Mahan, and Theodore Roosevelt. The expansionist mentality arose from the effective combination of several overlapping and reinforcing doctrines: manifest destiny (Fiske), social evolution (Adams), the end of the frontier (Turner), the importance of sea power (Mahan), and the strenuous life (Roosevelt). The expansionists had a deep interest in market expansion and sought outlets for new capital investment, in part a reaction to the economic downturns of the 1890s. As interest turned to the consolidation of national markets and the search for foreign trade, geopolitical concerns also took center stage. Driving much of the discussion was an evolutionary interpretation of the past, present, and future of the nation. The following short narrative, expressed in the terminology of the day, informed the expansionist mentality. By the end of the nineteenth century, the manifest destiny of the American people to grow economically, mature democratically, and expand geographically had reached the limits of the continent. The frontier, fundamental to the formation of the national character, was finally consumed and consummated. But without a frontier for continuous expansion, the nation faced a crisis of identity and a weakening of character that transcended the purely economic. In order to continue to evolve and develop, in order to avoid the decadence of refined, established civilization, the nation needed to turn its attention to manly, adventurous pursuits overseas: just wars, naval dominance, canal building, foreign trade, and sowing the seeds of liberty. The development of sea power would guarantee international status and protect market expansion. In turn, sea power depended upon a modern navy; the control of maritime routes, ports, and coaling stations; and the construction of a trans-isthmian canal.[25]

A central element of this grand vision was the trans-isthmian canal, which was conceived long before its initiation in Panama in 1904 and its completion in 1914. The canal would cut the distance between the east and west coasts of the United States in an unprecedented manner. In addition, the control of foreign commerce required the control of the seaways traversing the Pacific Ocean, the Atlantic Ocean, the Caribbean Sea, and the Gulf of Mexico.[26] However, the dominance of those seaways, which the canal itself made possible, required the control of additional strategic insular sites for coaling stations, protected harbors, and naval fortifications, all to be distributed throughout the great oceanic expanses. Before 1898, the United States had already begun to establish footholds in the Pacific. In 1856 it claimed sovereignty over several Pacific "guano islands" (Jarvis, Baker, and Howland), and in 1867 it claimed Midway. The sovereignty of the Samoan islands was disputed for two decades among the United States, Great Britain, and Germany until the three countries established a tripartite protectorate in 1899, with the United States gaining control of the valuable Pago Pago harbor. In 1877, the United States acquired the exclusive use of Pearl Harbor by means of treaties with the Kingdom of Hawai'i and later the Republic of Hawai'i. In the Caribbean, the United States enjoyed much commerce and influence but did not possess any territory. In 1898, it took advantage of the independence revolution in Cuba to challenge and defeat the Spanish empire in the Spanish-American War. It then made the most of the opportunity to seize control, by means of the Treaty of Paris with Spain, of four highly strategic locations, the last remnants of the once vast Spanish empire: Cuba, Guam, the Philippines, and Puerto Rico. That same year it annexed Hawai'i. One year later (1899), Roosevelt affirmed, "We must build the isthmian canal, and we must grasp the points of vantage which will enable us to have our way of deciding the destiny of the oceans of the East and the West."[27] These "points of vantage" were Cuba, the Philippines, and Puerto Rico. The canal and the imperial archipelago were inextricably connected.[28]

Most of U.S. historiography has been written as the "great triumph" of this potent combination of influential ideas, strategic plans, and economic interests that ushered in the "American century."[29] The literature of U.S. history does not usually get into the details of the colonies, except for military history of the "war with Spain" and the "Philippine Insurrection." Of course, there is a vast library of studies that treats the histories of the individual island groups, much of it produced by local historians. However, very little of this research has ventured into the area of comparative studies. As a result, the history of each island group is portrayed as entirely unique yet situated equally within a context of the expansionary interests and vision of the United States. Read in isolation, the history of each island group seems to be simply a result of the expansion of the United States and the expression of its economic and geopolitical interests. The problem is that although ideology, economic interests, and geopolitical strategy are, in the most general sense, determinants of expansionary impulse overseas, these factors are not sufficient to explain the varied forms of rule throughout the imperial archipelago. They are too general and too vague to be determinants of the specific forms of rule. Although this general process provided the overall context and general conditions, it cannot explain the specific results in each of the areas under U.S. control. One must look at both local conditions and the discursive practices of imperial officials, which interacted within the general expansionary impulse in the determination of the forms of rule.[30] On the one hand, one must explain why one territory (Hawai'i) was annexed while the others were not. On the other hand, one must explain why one country (Cuba) gained formal independence quickly but the rest did not. Both Cuba and Hawai'i were of utmost strategic importance, and both were important trading partners and locations of capital investment during the 1890s and after. Why, then, was their political trajectory diametrically opposite? Between these two "extremes"—an incorporated territory and a formally independent country—there are three territories that became possessions, each in its own way. Puerto Rico received limited local self-government with considerable economic and judicial integration to the United States. The Philippines had similar limited local self-government in some provinces (with direct rule in others) but with economic and judicial exclusion from the United States. Guam did not have local self-government at all, with very little formal integration to the United States except through the presence of the U.S. Navy. In general, it is not at all apparent that these political differences correspond precisely to economic and strategic interests.

Rather than focus on the general processes of U.S. expansion, I propose to emphasize the local (or pericentric) conditions that affected the discursive strategies that led to the particular political outcomes in each site. A complex interplay of the following sociohistorical factors was determinate: the history of settlement; clear manifestations of compact nationhood; and the forms of resistance, especially the existence of sustained armed rebellion or collaboration. Of course, these historical conditions were not independent of representations; indeed, they were articulated as fundamental elements in the discursive narrative about the past, present, and future. The narrative representations constituted the means of evaluating the particular local conditions, understanding the unfolding state of affairs, recommending a course of action, implementing governance, and then justifying the forms of political dominion.

A fundamental determinant of Hawaiian annexation was its previous colonization by European Americans. None of the other islands were colonized in this manner, and none were annexed: Cuba, Guam, the Philippines, and Puerto Rico were all former *Spanish* colonies. Its unique historical experience was one of the central elements in the principal narrative of Hawai'i. Contrary to this narrative, however, there was considerable political and some armed resistance to the takeover of the Hawaiian monarchy by the European American elite. In addition, Hawaiian culture was still strong and vibrant in spite of missionary and political attempts to assimilate it.[31] Nevertheless, the history of hegemonic European American settlement, when narrated as a natural, political evolution from native monarchy to constitutional republic, was the overriding and deciding factor.

In contrast, in Cuba the long history of sustained armed rebellion and the unmistakable ideological manifestation of compact nationhood worked together in the determination of the political trajectory there. When articulated through the discourse of masculine honor and values, these two combined elements resulted in the formal independence of Cuba. With a standing army and a promise of independence from the United States, the Cuban elites were in a fairly good position to bargain. However, at first they did not control the state

apparatus, and the whole country was economically devastated. Given these conditions, they were forced to disband the revolutionary army, collaborate with the
provisional military government, and eventually accept less than full sovereignty
as a protectorate.[32]

Compact nationhood plus armed struggle was not predominant in Puerto
Rico, notwithstanding the incipient national consciousness in the late nineteenth century. The leading political currents in Puerto Rico were autonomist
and nonviolent. Indeed, Spain had granted an autonomist government to Puerto
Rico shortly before the outbreak of the war with the United States.[33] The local
elites shared with their new rulers the ideology of civilization and democracy
and believed a U.S. territorial government would be advantageous both politically and economically. In Puerto Rico, we find much more collaboration than
resistance, which took political, rather than military, forms as the elite sought
expanded local autonomy and influence in a new civil government.[34] The colonial discourse on Puerto Rico characterized the population as an abused people
neither willing nor capable of defending itself, with only limited experience in
self-government, and in desperate need of economic development.

Likewise, Guam evidenced neither strong national consciousness nor
emphatic political will for sovereignty backed up by the force of arms. Under
Spanish rule, the island had been a distant military outpost with little development of political institutions. Following the change of sovereignty, the U.S. Navy
quickly established a government over the whole island and its inhabitants. The
predominant representations of Guam were static and ahistorical; its people
appeared as simple, hospitable Pacific islanders.[35] Residents adopted a tactic of
appeal; they pointed out the paradox of military rule of the insular possession of
a republic. They petitioned Congress for political rights and civilian government
to no avail.

The situation in the Philippines was somewhat more complex.[36] Armed
struggle against the Spanish certainly did take place but was recent, beginning
only in 1896, and short-lived, leading to exile of the Filipino leaders. In the wake
of the U.S. attack on the Spanish fleet in the Philippines, exiled leaders returned
and armed resistance resumed, spreading quickly throughout the provinces and
effectively containing the Spanish forces. In 1899, conscious of the imperial
designs of the United States, the Philippine Army refused to disband, and a long
and bitter war ensued. This armed struggle for independence certainly contributed to the notion that assimilation of the Philippines to the United States was
impossible. Congress did not formally promise independence until 1916, but
the idea of independence at some time in the distant future was often explicit in
the discussions of Philippine political destiny from the very beginning. There-

fore, additional factors must have impeded the immediate independence of the Philippines. One of those factors was the anticipated weakness of an independent Filipino state in the face of the threat of European or Japanese intervention. A second was that the Philippines was by far the most culturally heterogeneous of all the areas under U.S. control, and Congress did not recognize any tradition of cohesive and compact national consciousness; the people were characterized as an aggregate of tribes of different races, religions, and levels of civilization. Likewise, the estimation of their capacity for local self-government was decidedly unfavorable.

After armed resistance ended, the elites settled in for the long political struggle for local autonomy and independence by means of collaboration and accommodation. They actively participated in the new regime and sought acknowledgment of their fitness to rule from the colonial administrators who were their supervisors or "tutors," in the language of colonial discourse. Congress organized a centralized colonial state with limited self-government, and depending upon religion and the level of civilization, provincial and municipal governments were also established. Participation of the elites was central to this organization and functioning, especially at the municipal and provincial levels. Most provinces had limited self-government and would later send representatives to the legislative assembly in Manila. However, paternalistic colonial administrators governed as special provinces those areas deemed especially backward. Therefore, the crucial sociohistorical factor in the eventual independence of the Philippines was the armed struggle. Independence was delayed because of the perceived weakness of the nation and the decidedly negative evaluation by U.S. officials of the considerable cultural diversity and the especially low levels of civilization in some provinces.

This book expands upon the thesis that representations of inferior alterity were a means to conceive, mobilize, and justify imperial rule. I argue that the elaboration of cultural difference became fundamental in the organization of different governments for the new U.S. possessions. In general terms, this book suggests that colonial discourses distinguish multiple "others" with the intent to rule them differently. I argue that representations were part of a discursive formation—that is, a complex of rhetorical figures directly related to and constitutive of material practices of imperial rule. In order to demonstrate this, it will be necessary to explicate the differences among the representations within the imperial archipelago and then to discover the connections among these distinct representations and the established governments. The principal sources will be the numerous popular books (illustrated with photographs) about the "new possessions"; the many official reports, censuses, and legal studies produced by the U.S. government and its colonial administrators; the legal debates that took place in the leading law journals of the day; the congressional debates and the laws that established civil governments; and the decisions of the Supreme Court that validated these laws. In chapter 1, I will show that these different sources all articulated a common colonial discourse, which I identify as the "imperial problem." In chapters 2–4, I will differentiate the representations of the islands by means of a comparison of the fundamental symbols and their insertion into narratives. In other words, I will show that within the context of a general colonial discourse, different rhetorical devices and narratives served to establish differences within the imperial archipelago and project particular political trajectories.[37] These chapters will also address the impact of historical conditions—namely, the pattern of European settlement, the development of national consciousness, and the forms of resistance and collaboration. Chapter 5 will discuss the legislative process, the laws that created civil governments, and their validation by the Supreme Court. The establishment of military rule in Guam is the subject of chapter 6. In the final chapter, I will present a systematic comparative analysis that summarizes the connections among historical conditions, narrative representations, and the forms of rule established throughout the imperial archipelago.

This book spans several academic fields of study; it is not a work confined to any particular discipline. Above all, its reliance on a critical reworking of colonial discourse analysis places it firmly within the growing, complex field of postcolonial studies. In addition, it engages, in an oblique and critical fashion, the field of American Studies, addressing those aspects of the "culture of U.S. imperialism" that had a direct impact in the governance of the overseas territories.[38] As such, this study places the history of the United States within the boundaries of imperial history, usually dedicated to the English, French, and Spanish overseas empires, and within the field of postcolonial studies, usually focused on the textual and specifically literary production of those same European empires and their colonies. Despite the recurrent criticism of "American exceptionalism," we frequently overlook the U.S. imperial archipelago, composed of those oft-forgotten territories of the first overseas "American empire," and relegate the whole experience to an unsettling chapter of turn-of-the-century expansion. Yet the issues of that empire have not been entirely resolved. The relationship between Cuba and the United States has been problematic for more than a century after its independence in 1902. The Philippines did not gain formal independence until 1948 and continues to be marked by its recent colonial history. Hawai'i became a state of the republic in 1959, yet not long ago the United States formally apologized for the undemocratic proceedings that led to annexation in 1898, and indigenous rights organizations have flourished in recent years. Puerto Rico and Guam are still unincorporated territories of the United States and therefore are among the "oldest colonies in the world," despite the formal establishment of the "commonwealth" of Puerto Rico (1952) and civil government in the Territory of Guam (1950).[39]

Notes

1. I first used this term in 1995 in a short article that accompanied an exposition of historical photographs that traversed Spain and Puerto Rico. See Lanny Thompson, "'Estudiarlos, juzgarlos y gobernarlos': Conocimiento y poder en el archipiélago imperial estadounidense," in *La nación soñada: Cuba, Puerto Rico y Filipinas ante el '98*, ed. Consuelo Naranjo Orovio et al. (Aranjuez, Spain: Ediciones Doce Calles, 1995). More recently, I published preliminary versions of some of the arguments developed in this book. See "The Imperial Republic: A Comparison of the Insular Territories under U.S. Dominion after 1898," *Pacific Historical Review* 71, no. 4 (2002): 535–574, and "Representation and Rule in the Imperial Archipelago: Cuba, Puerto Rico, Hawai'i, and Philippines under U.S. Dominion," *American Studies Asia* (Manila) 1, no. 1 (2002): 3–39. Javier Morillo Alicea used the term "imperial archipelago" to describe the late-nineteenth-century Spanish empire. He argued that in the Spanish empire, connections between islands tended to be weak and tenuous, with the important exception of Cuba and Puerto Rico. See "Uncharted Landscapes of 'Latin America': The Philippines in the Spanish Imperial Archipelago," in *Interpreting Spanish Colonialism: Empires, Nations, and Legends,* ed. Christopher Schmidt-Nowara and John Nieto-Phillips (Albuquerque: University of New Mexico Press, 2005).

2. Michael Doyle, *Empires* (Ithaca, N.Y.: Cornell University Press, 1986).

3. Jürgen Osterhammel, *Colonialism: A Theoretical Overview* (Princeton, N.J.: Markus Wiener, 1997).

4. This problem is evident in the earliest theories of imperialism. For example, Hobson emphasized the economic causes of empire and viewed racism as shameless justification of crass exploitation. He considered these justifications of imperialism to be "wanton exhibitions of hypocrisy . . . based on a falsification of facts and a perversion of the motives that actually direct the policy." Thus, for Hobson, the racialist arguments for imperialist expansion were but an ideology that justified foreign domination and covered up the worst forms of exploitation. He spoke out against the racialist justifications of economic exploitation, exposing the falsehood and hypocrisy of this ideology. J. A. Hobson, *Imperialism: A Study* (Ann Arbor: Anchor Books, 1965), 208; originally published 1902. Many theorists, especially Lenin, ignored the ideological issue altogether, concentrating their efforts on the economic causes of imperialism. V. I. Lenin, *Imperialism: The Highest Stage of Capitalism* (New York: International

Publishers, 1939), 89; originally published 1917. Beginning with Joseph Schumpeter, a number of influential authors disputed the primacy of economic causes and argued for the importance of "non-economic" factors in European imperialism—namely, archaic ruling classes; jingoism and public opinion; national security and prestige. In addition, "pericentric" theories emphasized the particular characteristics of the peripheries that led to imperial domination. The pericentric perspective focused upon the processes of collaboration or resistance to European expansion by peripheral groups and social classes. For a review of late-nineteenth- and twentieth-century theories, see Wolfgang Mommsen, *Theories of Imperialism* (New York: Random House, 1980), and David Healy, *Modern Imperialism: Changing Styles in Historical Interpretation* (Washington: American Historical Association, 1967). Even more recent authors underestimate the importance of "colonialist thought"; for example, see Osterhammel, *Colonialism*. Those few authors who are attuned to the importance of discursive strategies fault postcolonial theory for stressing the supposed binary categories of modern imperialism and for subsequently adopting a deconstructive tactic of resistance. Joel Kahn has suggested that a "postcolonial empire"—that is, one based upon difference—is logically possible if not empirically evident. In a similar fashion, Michael Hardt and Antonio Negri have also argued that the new structure of "empire" encompasses postmodern difference as a fundamental element of its dominion. See Joel Kahn, *Culture, Multiculture, Postculture* (London: Sage, 1995), and Michael Hardt and Antonio Negri, *Empire* (Cambridge, Mass.: Harvard University Press, 2000).

5. Teun van Dijk has formulated a new theory of ideology that is consistent with "critical discourse analysis." Unlike Michel Foucault, who distanced himself from the Marxian concept of ideology, van Dijk argues that discourses—that is, linguistic practices—are a fundamental part of ideologies. He moves away from Foucault's abstract analysis of the discursive formations to the close study of the content and context of communications. Teun van Dijk, *Ideology: A Multidisciplinary Approach* (London: Sage, 1998). Although van Dijk is interested in racialist ideologies in contemporary Europe, he doesn't locate his work with respect to the field of postcolonial studies.

6. Compare Morillo, "Uncharted Landscapes."

7. The phrase "chains of empire" is borrowed from Julian Go, "Chains of Empire, Projects of State: Political Education and U.S. Colonial Rule in Puerto Rico and the Philippines," in *The American Colonial State in the Philippines: Global Perspectives,* ed. Julian Go and Anne Foster (Durham, N.C.: Duke University Press, 2003).

8. The concept of "contact zone" is from Mary Louise Pratt, *Imperial Eyes: Travel Writing and Transculturation* (London: Routledge, 1992), 6–7.

9. The concept of "colonial project" is from Nicholas Thomas, *Colonialism's Culture: Anthropology, Travel, and Government* (Princeton, N.J.: Princeton University Press, 1994), 105–106.

10. For an overview of postcolonial theory, see Bart Moore-Gilbert, *Postcolonial Theory: Contexts, Practices, Politics* (London: Verso, 1997).

11. Stuart Hall, "The Work of Representation," in *Representation: Cultural Representations and Signifying Practices,* ed. Stuart Hall (Thousand Oaks, Calif.: Sage Publications, 1997).

12. Foucault proposed this notion of governmentality, although he shifted the analysis away from the institutional structures of government in favor of a more abstract discursive analysis. In contrast, the present work seeks to connect discourses with the creation of institutional structures. For a comprehensive view of Foucault's concepts, see Edgardo Castro, *El vocabulario de Michel Foucault: Un recorrido alfabético por sus temas, conceptos y autores* (Buenos Aires: Universidad Nacional de Quilmes, 2004). For an approach similar to mine, see, Thomas, *Colonialism's Culture,* 42–43.

13. Edward Said, *Orientalism* (New York: Pantheon, 1994). The publication of *Orientalism* was a defining moment in the constitution of "postcolonial studies," comprised of "postcolonial theory" and "postcolonial criticism." Postcolonial theory may be defined as the introduction of "high theory" (discourse analysis, deconstruction, psychoanalysis) into the study of colonial relations, while postcolonial criticism has devoted most of its attention to literatures produced by postcolonial subjects. Indeed, the bulk of postcolonial studies has been devoted to literary creation, both imperial and postcolonial. Theoretical debates have focused on the issues of agency, resistance, and the literature of postcolonial subjects. This definition of postcolonial studies is based on Moore-Gilbert, *Postcolonial Theory.* Regarding Said's legacy, see also Robert Young, *White Mythologies: Writing, History and the West* (London: Routledge, 1990).

14. The classic study is Edward Said, *Culture and Imperialism* (New York: Vintage Books, 1994). David Spurr, in *The Rhetoric of Empire* (Durham, N.C.: Duke University Press, 1993), has shown that narrative tropes were found in official documents and reports as well as in travel writing and journalism, and he classified a number of fundamental tropes that circulated among a wide range of documents. His book is especially useful in that it comprises a compendium of rhetorical tropes organized by type. Its main weakness is that in a compilation of tropes from widely different contexts, the specific historical contexts are lost. Many authors have analyzed photographs in the context of colonial discourses. For an outstanding study of the connections between photography and anthropology, see Elizabeth Edwards, ed., *Anthropology and Photography, 1860–1920* (New Haven, Conn.; and London: Yale University Press in association with the Royal Anthropological Institute, 1992). The classic study of colonial postcards is Malek Alloula, *The Colonial Harem* (Minneapolis: University of Minnesota Press, 1986). For a critical study of the *National Geographic Magazine,* see Catherine Lutz and Jane Collins, *Reading National Geographic* (Chicago: University of Chicago Press, 1993). The classic study of exhibitions is Robert Rydell, *All the World's a Fair: Visions of Empire*

at American International Expositions, 1876–1916 (Chicago: Chicago University Press, 1984). An excellent study of both exhibitions and photographs is by Anne Maxwell, *Colonial Photography and Exhibitions: Representations of the "Native" and the Making of European Identities* (London: Leicester University Press, 2000). Two excellent studies of images of Filipinos in a variety of contexts, including the census, travelogues, memoirs, and world's fair exhibitions, are Benito Vergara, *Displaying Filipinos: Photography and Colonialism in Early 20th Century Philippines* (Quezon City: University of the Philippines Press, 1995), and Elizabeth Mary Holt, *Colonizing Filipinas: Nineteenth-Century Representations of the Philippines in Western Historiography* (Honolulu: University of Hawai'i Press, 2002).

15. Said explicitly acknowledges Foucault and Gramsci as theoretical sources in the introduction to *Orientalism*. He elides the possible conflicts between the two perspectives, especially the theoretical incompatibility of "ideology" and "discourse." See Dennis Porter, "*Orientalism* and Its Problems," in *Colonial Discourse and Post-Colonial Theory: A Reader*, ed. Patrick Williams and Laura Chrisman (New York: Columbia University Press, 1994).

16. Said, *Orientalism*, 123.

17. The following authors are examples of this point. Homi Bhabha, *The Location of Culture* (London: Routledge, 1994); Partha Chaterjee, *The Nation and Its Fragments* (Princeton, N.J.: Princeton University Press, 1993); and Abdul JanMohamed: "The Economy of Manichean Allegory: The Function of Racial Difference in Colonialist Literature," *Critical Inquiry* 12, no. 1 (1985): 59–87, and *Manichean Aesthetics: The Politics of Literature in Colonial Africa* (Amherst: University of Massachusetts Press, 1983). Kelvin Santiago, the first to use postcolonial theory to analyze Puerto Rico, also suffers from this problem. See Kelvin Santiago-Valles, "*Subject People*" and Colonial Discourses: Economic Transformation and Social Disorder in Puerto Rico, 1898–1947* (Albany: State University of New York Press, 1994). For an excellent theoretical critique of the "other" as an undifferentiated totality that is combined with an empirical study, see Thomas, *Colonialism's Culture*. For a recent study that also addresses this problem, see Julian Go, "Racism and Colonialism: Meanings of Difference and Ruling Practices in America's Pacific Empire," *Qualitative Sociology* 27, no. 1 (2004): 35–58.

18. Countless scholars have argued that the cultural and racial descriptions of the island peoples frequently used analogies to both African Americans and American Indians to justify political domination in the overseas possessions. The following authors have all argued, or implied, that home-grown racism was extended, without much complication or modification, to the former Spanish islands: Rubin Weston, *Racism in U.S. Imperialism: The Influence of Racial Assumptions on American Foreign Policy, 1893–1946* (Columbia: University of South Carolina Press, 1972); Richard Slotkin, *Gunfighter Nation: The Myth of the Frontier in Twentieth-Century America* (New York:

Atheneum, 1992); Walter Williams, "United States Indian Policy and the Debate over Philippine Annexation: Implications for the Origins of American Imperialism," *Journal of American History* 66 (1980): 810–831; Gail Bederman, *Manliness and Civilization: A Cultural History of Gender and Race in the United States, 1880–1917* (Chicago: University of Chicago Press 1995); and Lisa Marcus, *Tender Violence: Domestic Visions in the Age of U.S. Imperialism* (Chapel Hill: University of North Carolina Press, 2000). On the widespread use of feminine and childhood metaphors, see John Johnson, *Latin America in Caricature* (Austin: University of Texas Press, 1980); Kristin Hoganson *Fighting for American Manhood: How Gender Politics Provoked the Spanish-American and the Philippine-American Wars* (New Haven, Conn.: Yale University Press, 1998); and Holt, *Colonizing Filipinas*. The childhood metaphor was the most common way to portray the dependent peoples of the imperial archipelago. It has a long tradition in U.S. history; even Thomas Jefferson used such a metaphor to justify autocratic governments in the U.S. territories at the beginning of the nineteenth century. See Peter Onuf, *Statehood and Nation: A History of the Northwest Ordinance* (Bloomington: Indiana University Press, 1987), 69–72.

19. Said, *Orientalism*, 5. One of Said's most systematic materialist critics is Aijaz Ahmad, *In Theory: Classes, Nations, Literatures* (London: Verso, 1992).

20. Two outstanding works on the elites of the Philippines and Puerto Rico are Paul Kramer, *The Blood of Government: Race, Empire, the United States, and the Philippines* (Chapel Hill: University of North Carolina Press, 2006), and Julian Go, *American Empire and the Politics of Meaning: Elite Political Cultures in the Philippines and Puerto Rico during U.S. Colonialism* (Durham, N.C.: Duke University Press, 2008). Both authors skillfully combine historical and discourse analysis.

21. True to its kinship with poststructuralist and postmodern theory, postcolonial theory has opposed most varieties of historical method and consequently has repudiated notions of causality in favor of indeterminism. The avoidance of the issue of causality is linked to the studied rejection of "historicism," an irregular notion that had at least two distinct meanings. On the one hand, historicism referred to the notion that historical periods must be understood in their own terms rather than those imposed by historians. This notion is related to the German historical school, which emphasized subjects (whether individual or collective, such as the nation), their actions, and motivations and employed a hermeneutic approach to understanding. This perspective was empiricist in its approach to primary documents yet adopted a narrative approach to the reconstruction of historical events. On the other hand, historicism referred to the position that there were general patterns of historical change. Karl Popper was the first to define historicism in this novel way. There were two important variants. First, the positivist version of this kind of historicism, formulated by Carl Hempel, argued that transhistorical "covering laws" determined the actions and

events of the past. Second, the Marxist version stressed the economic determination of history through the development of a series of modes of production, the consequent formation of social classes, and the inevitable conflict among these classes. This methodological perspective, whether of positivist or Marxist persuasion, sought to theoretically construct conceptual schemes that would explain history in terms of general laws rather than simply narrate singular events. In general, postmodern perspectives have been critical of both major variants of historicism. On the one hand, the postmodern critique has argued that hermeneutic historicism was simplistic in its naïve acceptance of empirical evidence as revealing the way things really were. In addition, it posited the notion of an autonomous subject whose intentional, voluntary actions were the "causes" of historical events. Finally, historicism utilized the most superficial hermeneutic approach to understand actions and events in their own terms. On the other hand, postmodern perspectives have criticized both the scientific positivist method and the Marxist materialist concept of history for their proclivity to construct "metanarratives" of universal historical tendencies, whether expressed in terms of progress toward modernity or the dialectic of class struggle. Confusingly, many of the rival textual approaches that challenged the hermeneutic and the scientific varieties of historicism were known as the "new historicism." For a discussion of the varieties of historicism, see Alun Munslow: *The Routledge Companion to Historical Studies* (London: Routledge, 2000), 130–131, and *Deconstructing History* (London: Routledge, 1997). See also the excellent summary in Norman J. Wilson, *History in Crisis? Recent Directions in Historiography* (Upper Saddle River, N.J.: Prentice Hall, 1999), 13–15.

22. Said adapted Foucault's notion of power to the colonial context. Foucault was primarily interested in the discursive formations of power/knowledge that produced subjects as individuals. Although his notion of "biopower" alluded to the efforts of the state to control populations by demographic means, Foucault had little interest in the structures of government. In contrast, Said's notion of the subject is less individual and more collective and political; his interest is in the formation of *colonial* subjects. Nevertheless, Said also showed little interest in the government per se of these subjects.

23. Go also emphasizes the importance of causal analysis; see *American Empire*, introduction.

24. I am paraphrasing Max Weber: "We wish to understand, on the one hand, the relationships and cultural significance of individual events in their contemporary manifestations and, on the other, the causes of their being historically *so* and not *otherwise.*" Max Weber, *The Methodology of the Social Sciences,* translated and edited by Edward Shils and Henry Finch (New York: Free Press, 1949), 72. It has become fashionable of late to treat sociology in general, including Weberian sociology, as a hopelessly modernist project. However, the Weberian perspective should not be confused with either Dur-

kheimian positivist sociology or Marxist metanarratives. While perfectly comfortable with economic or material determinants, Weberian sociology is equally at home with the study of the impact of culture and ideas. Weberian sociology also has the advantage of posing, at the level of its fundamental methodology, the question of "why" in a historical context. It does not necessarily allude to either universal or middle-range laws. It simply asks why things are historically this way and not another, seeking meaningful explanations of particularities. Weber was a stern critic of his contemporaries, both the Marxists for their mono-causality and the positivists for their attempt to formulate general laws of history. His idea of an interpretative social science included the understanding of connections among historical phenomena and their cultural meanings, as well as the exploration of the particular reasons for their manifestations. He argued that social sciences should stress the unique and specific character of sociocultural phenomena. It should be noted, however, that Weber was responsible for Orientalist expressions and arguments; see, for example, the introduction to *The Protestant Ethic and the Spirit of Capitalism* (New York: Charles Scribner's Sons, 1958).

25. Alexander Missal, *Seaway to the Future: American Social Visions and the Construction of the Panama Canal* (Madison: University of Wisconsin Press, 2008), 26–42.

26. Ibid., 38–47.

27. Theodore Roosevelt, "The Strenuous Life," speech presented at the Hamilton Club, Chicago, 10 April 1899. Retrieved on 14 September 2001 from the Theodore Roosevelt Association Web page: www.theodoreroosevelt.org. Roosevelt did not mention the acquisition of Hawai'i, presumably because its retention as a territory was unquestionable. He is also silent about Guam. I will discuss this speech in detail in chapter 2.

28. This connection suggests that the Panama Canal Zone might be considered to be part of the imperial archipelago as I have defined it. My interpretation of Missal's book, however, suggests that the Canal Zone was substantially different from the imperial archipelago. First, it was literally and figuratively carved out of a country and so did not impose directly on an existing political society. Second, the administration was openly autocratic and had no pretense of promoting local self-government. Third, the residents were mostly transient, immigrant employees and not citizens of the Canal Zone. Fourth, it was more an "American utopia" than a colonial encounter. See Missal, *Seaway to the Future*, ch. 4.

29. Warren Zimmerman, *First Great Triumph: How Five Americans Made Their Country a World Power* (New York: Farrar, Straus and Giroux, 2002); David Traxel, *1898: The Tumultuous Year of Victory, Invention, Internal Strife, and Industrial Expansion That Saw the Birth of the American Century* (New York: Alfred A. Knopf, 1999). Louis Pérez argues that the U.S. historiography of the "war of 1898" repeats the same themes and arguments of the original expansionist authors and that the "proposition of empire has

not fared well." See Louis Pérez, Jr., *The War of 1898: The United States and Cuba in History and Historiography* (Chapel Hill: University of North Carolina Press, 1998), xii.

30. Julian Go has published an excellent article on the importance of local conditions in determining the outcome of colonial rule. He emphasizes the contrast between Puerto Rico and the Philippines, both of which had the beginnings of local self-government under Spanish rule, and Guam and Samoa, which did not. His causal factors and mine partially overlap. See Julian Go, "The Provinciality of American Empire: 'Liberal Exceptionalism' and U.S. Colonial Rule, 1898–1912," *Comparative Studies in Society and History* 49 (2007): 74–108. For a more general theory of the influence of local factors in colonial regimes, see Doyle, *Empires*.

31. The standard history of Hawai'i is Gavan Daws, *Shoal of Time: A History of the Hawaiian Islands* (Honolulu: University of Hawai'i Press, 1974). A more recent history of haole hegemony is Jonathan Kay Kamakawiwo'ole Osorio, *Dismembering Lāhui: A History of the Hawaiian Nation to 1887* (Honolulu: University of Hawai'i Press, 2002). On Hawaiian resistance to the republic and annexation, see Noenoe Silva, *Aloha Betrayed: Native Hawaiian Resistance to American Colonialism* (Durham, N.C.: Duke University Press, 2004).

32. Louis Pérez, Jr., *Cuba between Empires, 1878–1902* (Pittsburgh: University of Pittsburgh Press, 1983).

33. For an excellent sociohistorical analysis of the dominant political movements in Puerto Rico, see Astrid Cubano, *El hilo en el laberinto: Claves de la lucha política en Puerto Rico (siglo XIX)* (Río Piedras: Ediciones Huracán, 1990). Cubano's analysis includes several interesting contrasts between Puerto Rico and Cuba. By the same author see "El autonomismo en Puerto Rico, 1887–1898," in Naranjo Orovio et al., *La nación soñada,* and "Visions of Empire and Historical Imagination in Puerto Rico under Spanish Rule, 1870–1898," in Schmidt-Nowara and Nieto-Phillips, *Interpreting Spanish Colonialism.* Julian Go presents a superb analysis of the elite in Puerto Rico in *American Empire.*

34. Gervasio Luis García, "I Am the Other: Puerto Rico in the Eyes of North Americans, 1898." *Journal of American History* 87, no. 1 (2000): 39–64, and Go, *American Empire.*

35. For an excellent discussion of the importance of romanticized images of Guam and Samoa for their political outcome, see Go, "Racism and Colonialism." The standard history of Guam is Robert Rogers, *Destiny's Landfall: A History of Guam* (Honolulu: University of Hawai'i Press, 1995).

36. O. D. Corpuz, *The Roots of the Filipino Nation,* 2 vols. (Quezon City: AKLAHI Foundation, 1996); Luis Camara Dery, *The Army of the First Philippine Republic and Other Historical Essays* (Manila: De La Salle University Press, 1995); Kramer, *The Blood of Government.*

37. Edward Said has stressed the importance of narratives in *Culture and Imperialism*. Spurr, *The Rhetoric of Empire*, also showed how tropes (and not only symbols) were important elements of imperial rhetorical strategies. Therefore, it seems necessary to consider not only the semiotics of photographs, but also the rhetorical figures created by sequences of photographs and their insertion within descriptive and prescriptive texts. This approach will require both an analysis of the content of individual photographs and the contextualization of each within the larger narratives of the colonial discourse. Laura Chrisman outlines a methodology for the study of colonial narratives in historical context in "The Imperial Unconscious? Representations of Imperial Discourse," in P. Williams and Chrisman, *Colonial Discourse*.

38. For an excellent collection of articles on many different facets of U.S. culture in the context of empire, see Amy Kaplan and Donald Pease, eds., *Cultures of United States Imperialism* (Durham, N.C.: Duke University Press, 1993). More recently, Amy Kaplan has turned her attention to the impact of empire in the making of U.S. culture; see *The Anarchy of Empire in the Making of U.S. Culture* (Cambridge, Mass.: Harvard University Press, 2002).

39. I have borrowed the phrase "oldest colonies in the world" from José Trías Monge, *Puerto Rico: Trials of the Oldest Colony in the World* (New Haven, Conn.: Yale University Press, 1997).

Chapter 1

The Imperial Problem and the New Possessions

How to Rule?

In 1898, the United States began to build an imperial archipelago, constructed from the remnants of the Spanish empire and the erstwhile Republic of Hawai'i. In April of that year, the United States declared war on Spain, with the expressed intent of liberating Cuba from the vestigial Spanish empire, which was fragmented and vulnerable. However, the war began in the Philippines, far from the epicenter of the Cuban revolution, when, in May, the U.S. Navy attacked and roundly defeated the decrepit Spanish fleet in Manila Bay. Filipino revolutionaries quickly established control throughout the northern provinces, leaving the Spanish garrison in Manila surrounded by land and sea. The Pacific theater of war highlighted the strategic importance of Hawai'i, where local political leaders had been vying for annexation to the United States since the founding of the Pacific republic in 1895. In June, even before the short war with Spain was finished, Congress approved a joint resolution annexing the Republic of Hawai'i. Following the conclusion of the war, the Treaty of Paris (signed in December 1898 and approved by the Senate the following February) ceded to the United States the Philippines, Puerto Rico, and Guam. Although the treaty acknowledged the right of Cuban independence, the United States quickly established a provisional military government in Cuba. In a few short months, the United States had imposed control over five overseas island territories scattered throughout the Pacific and the Caribbean. This vast archipelago shared not geography, language, history, or culture, but rather the still ambiguous status of "possessions" or "dependencies" of the United States.

The Treaty of Paris provoked a flurry of ruminations and recommendations regarding the future governments of the new acquisitions. At the time,

Cuba was under temporary military rule as it awaited its formal establishment as an independent country. Congress had just annexed Hawai'i and would soon provide it with a territorial government. A temporary military government in a foreign country presented no constitutional problem, nor did the upcoming organization of a territorial government according to well-established continental precedents. But Puerto Rico, the Philippines, and Guam were somehow different. Legal scholars raised constitutional issues as early as 1898, and a debate soon ensued in the *Harvard Law Review,* the *Yale Law Journal,* and (to a lesser extent) the *Columbia Law Review* and the *American Law Register.* In addition, several books were published on the problem of imperial rule; among the first were James Fernald's *The Imperial Republic* (1898) and Horace Fisher's *Principles of Colonial Government* (1899).[1] Elihu Root, the secretary of war, solicited a report on the legal status of the islands from Charles Magoon, law officer of the War Department. Senator Henry Cabot Lodge requested that the chief bibliographer of the Library of Congress prepare an annotated bibliography on the history and political theory of colonization to accompany a House of Representatives report on the same topic.[2] Special commissioners visited Puerto Rico and the Philippines in order to study local conditions and make recommendations regarding the establishment of civil government.[3] The republic faced a legislative quandary that would entail long debates on the floor of Congress. Moreover, the legislation that it produced would provoke a constitutional problem that required a series of decisions—later known as the Insular Cases—by the Supreme Court.

What had provoked such a commotion? The United States possessed a well-established tradition of territorial expansion and had ample experience in the subjugation of racial minorities on the continent. By the end of the nineteenth century, African Americans had been socially segregated and effectively excluded from political participation, in spite of the Fourteenth Amendment. Furthermore, American Indians had been decimated, expelled from their lands, and moved to Indian Territory and other reservations. At the time, they were considered wards of the U.S. government. Moreover, Congress had just annexed Hawai'i—a group of tropical islands inhabited by peoples of diverse races, customs, and languages—and it would organize a conventional territorial government there in 1900. The reason for the commotion was the following. Historically, all U.S. territories had been intended as European American settler colonies, if not at the time of initial acquisition, at least by the time Congress had organized a territorial government. By the end of the nineteenth century, most of these areas had already been organized as territories, settled by European American immigrants, and admitted as states. Hawai'i was one of the outlying frontiers of European American settlement.[4]

With the acquisition of Puerto Rico, the Philippines, and Guam, the United States had surpassed the limits of its settler expansion and now faced what Frederic Coudert called the "imperial problem." These new "dependencies" were "inhabited by a settled population *differing from us* in race and civilization to such an extent that assimilation seems impossible, and *varying among themselves* in race, development, and culture to so great a degree as to make the application of any uniform political system difficult if not impractical."[5]

In this succinct description, Coudert identified two fundamental dimensions of the imperial problem. First, since peoples of different cultures inhabited the dependencies, they required political systems different from those of the states and territories of the United States. Second, significant cultural differences among the dependencies made any uniform political system unworkable. How, then, were the new possessions to be ruled, and what would be the political status of their inhabitants? According to Coudert, previous experience in continental territories acquired from France, Spain, or Mexico did not prepare the United States for the current imperial problem. In the continental territories, "a growing stream of immigration soon made the new lands thoroughly American." Of course, these settlers had met previous inhabitants in the continental territories. They had dealt with the "Indian problem" by removing the indigenous people from the land. In addition, the Spanish, Mexican, or French populations in the continental territories had been easily assimilated because they were few in number and were of "Caucasian race and civilization." In contrast, the imperial problem referred specifically to "the domination over men of one order or kind of civilization by men of different and higher civilization." Coudert stated that the "problem of to-day cannot be solved either by extermination, as in the case of the Indian, nor by assimilation, as in the case of the few Frenchmen and Spaniards."[6] The imperial problem, as Coudert defined it, was how to establish political rule over the islands whose "alien" inhabitants could not, and likely never would be, proper citizens of the United States and whose faraway shores would never see extensive European American settlement.

The imperial problem was much more than a narrow legal issue of government and citizenship. Coudert's specific formulation was but a part of a pervasive discourse composed of two related dimensions: (1) descriptions of the islands and their peoples; and (2) discussions of the political status and forms of rule most appropriate for them. The two dimensions were very much connected since the descriptions of "differences in race, development, and culture" elicited the question of how to rule. In turn, the question of how to rule raised the issue of what kinds of peoples inhabited the islands. This attention to differences among subject peoples was also central to the legal and legislative dis-

cussions regarding the specific forms of rule to be established in the new possessions. Horace Fisher was quite clear in his formulation: "It seems inevitable
that our body politic must be enlarged by the creation of a new legal status—that
of 'Colonial Dependencies,' for the reason that they cannot be governed by the
same uniform laws as our Territories, on account of their radical differences in
condition and political capacity, not only when compared with our Territories,
but when compared with each other."[7] Here Fisher clearly distinguished the
principles applied to "our Territories" (and states) and those applied to "Colonial Dependencies." Specifically, he sought to define Cuba, Puerto Rico, and the
Philippines as colonial dependencies of the United States. The principles of government for these dependencies were not to be same as that of the territories,
such as Hawai'i, or the states. However, these dependencies also differed among
themselves and consequently would require distinct governments according to
their particular "condition and political capacity."

The ardent imperialist from Indiana, Senator Albert Beveridge, articulated
the issue in a similar fashion in a speech before the Senate. In his discussion
of the Foraker bill for Puerto Rico, he argued as follows: "The needs of Porto
Rico are peculiar to Porto Rico; we must administer to them as good judgment
may demand. The needs of Hawaii are peculiar to Hawaii. The needs of the
Philippine Islands are peculiar to the archipelago. The needs of all are unlike
the needs of our American States when they were Territories."[8] While Fisher
grouped Hawai'i with the continental territories, Beveridge suggested in this
speech that Hawai'i was unlike them. Regardless of this divergence, both men
were articulating the same imperial problem: the new territories were unlike
the previous continental territories and were different from each other as well.
Only a careful determination of their particular conditions and needs could
establish the appropriate forms of rule for each. This minor divergence of judgment regarding Hawai'i did not detract from their like-mindedness regarding
the overall problem at hand.

The War Department also took up the issue of how to rule when it took
charge of civilian affairs in the former Spanish colonies immediately after the
conclusion of hostilities between Spain and the United States. Officers of the
U.S. Army began collecting taxes and customs revenues, governing municipalities, enforcing sanitary measures, establishing schools, and so forth.[9] In 1898,
the War Department created the Division of Customs and Insular Affairs to deal
specifically with the issues of civil administration. In 1901, this office became the
Division of Insular Affairs and continued to deal with the civilian affairs in the
two areas that remained under jurisdiction of the War Department, Cuba and
the Philippines.[10] Shortly thereafter, the Division of Insular Affairs became the

Bureau of Insular Affairs, which continued to serve as a source of information for
the president, the secretary of war, and Congress. The bureau continued to com-
pile a library, composed primarily of official documents, regarding U.S. dominion
in the entire imperial archipelago, including Hawai'i. This library was thoroughly
indexed for the use of Congress.[11] In 1902, the chief of the bureau, Clarence
Edwards, explained the difficulties involved in the administration and governance
of the areas under military, and later civilian, control from the beginning:

> Different civilizations, different systems of law and procedure, and different
> modes of thought brought into contact have evolved a great crowd of difficult
> questions for determination. New facts ascertained and changed conditions
> have called for the interpretation and application of our own rules of policy and
> the establishment of further rules. Different views as to the scope of authority
> under the distribution of powers have required reconciliation. The application
> of the law of military occupation to rights and practices existing under the laws
> of Spain and the process of overturning inveterate wrongs have brought about
> frequent appeals to the highest authority, which, being made in the name of
> justice, have required consideration. The work undertaken has been the build-
> ing up of government from the foundation upon unfamiliar ground. We have
> had no precedents, save the simple and meager proceedings under the occupa-
> tion of California and New Mexico, more than half a century ago, and it has
> been necessary to decide every question upon its own merits and to make our
> own precedents for the future.[12]

The functions of the Division of Customs and Insular Affairs and its later
manifestations centered upon the problem of knowledge associated with "the
building up of government from the foundation upon unfamiliar ground." This
formulation expressed, in a complex and contradictory way, the imperial problem. On the one hand, it expressed a profound cultural prejudice: it assumed
that the local peoples had no experience in government and so local institutions
were to be built without any previous "foundation." On the other hand, it posed
the problem of the "unfamiliar ground" upon which the local governments were
to be established. This ground was understood as "different civilizations, different systems of law and procedure, and different modes of thought." Thus, the
justification of imperial rule alluded to the local incapacity for self-government
due to the *absence* of political and legal frameworks, but the problems actually
confronted were attributed to the *presence* of different "civilizations," "systems of
law," and "modes of thought." Thus, a common characteristic of U.S. imperial
discourse was this tension between the justification of imperial rule, based upon

the premise of absence of political and legal frameworks, and its practical considerations, which arose precisely from the existence of these varied frameworks.[13]

Popular illustrated books and magazines also took up the issue of the "imperial problem" with great interest. Trumbull White, in his popular book *Our New
Possessions,* was quite explicit regarding the relation between his descriptions of
the islands and imperial rule: "If we are to be successful in our dealings with
alien people who are coming under our domination, it is necessary for us to study
them, judge them and rule them by methods which fit them instead of those
which appeal to us."[14] The language of this passage was notable for its expressed
coordination of strategies: knowledge, judgment, and government. Imperial
knowledge of "them" provided the basis of judgment to determine which methods of rule were appropriate for "them." The knowledge of these "alien people"
was integral to the process of imperial rule. Although this passage suggested a
simple dichotomous distinction between "us" and "them," this would be only
half the story. White was also attentive to the differences among the new possessions. Regarding Cuba, Puerto Rico, Hawai'i, and the Philippines, he noted that
the people, the geography, the resources, and the industries were so different that
"no one need feel that his information concerning one is sufficient to make him
acquainted with the other."[15] In White's text, alterity was certainly a homogeneous
notion, but it was simultaneously a thoroughly differentiated and hierarchical
one. Indeed, I will show that the principal photographic and textual representations in the illustrated books of the period demonstrated an acute awareness of
the exceptional diversity of the peoples under U.S. dominion at the turn of the
century and dedicated substantial effort to document it. It would seem, then, that
the imperial problem was expressed in two modalities, one of dichotomous difference, the other of hierarchical difference. The cartoons in figures 1.1 and 1.2
articulated the two modalities separately rather than simultaneously.

In one of the many political cartoons published in the United States in
1898, we observe a circus scene from the *Philadelphia Inquirer* (figure 1.1).[16]
Uncle Sam, in an acrobatic demonstration of fitness and balance, is holding up
five dark little figures, identified as the Philippines, Ladrones (Guam), Cuba,
Hawai'i, and Puerto Rico. The figures are stereotypical "blackies" or "pickaninnies": seminude infantile figures with kinky hair, black skin, and thick lips. Four
of these figures hold flags that vaguely resemble the U.S. flag. The caption reads,
"Holding His End Up." The audience, composed of various European countries,
is watching intently while John Bull (England) comments, "It's really extraordinary what training will do. Why, only the other day I thought that man unable
to support himself." This cartoon refers to the new island possessions and the
newfound imperial capacity, based on the navy and the army, of the United

Figure 1.1. Holding His End Up (cartoon). *Philadelphia Inquirer,* 1898.

States, which has gained prestige in the international context. The figures representing the islands are identical; they are indistinguishable except for their labels. Indeed, they are no different from any other "pickaninnies," whether foreign or domestic. They are all alike yet markedly different from Uncle Sam and his European audience.

In figure 1.2, a cartoon that appeared on the front page of *Harper's Weekly* in 1898, we see Uncle Sam teaching a class in the principles of self-government.[17] His students represent four sites: the Philippines, Cuba, Hawai'i, and Puerto

Figure 1.2. Uncle Sam's New Class (cartoon). *Harper's Weekly,* 1898.

Rico. Guam is entirely absent. Unlike the previous cartoon, the representations of the sites are different. Hawai'i and Puerto Rico appear as two young women; they are pleasant, pretty, well dressed, and very studious. Emilio Aguinaldo, Filipino nationalist and commander of the Army of the Republic of the Philippines, wears a dunce cap and sulks in the corner. His skin is dark and he appears recalcitrant; he is an ignorant and rebellious child. Máximo Gómez, Cuban patriot and general of the Liberation Army of Cuba, appears as a proper gentleman. He reads a book on self-government that he has authored himself. However, the other dark-skinned Cubans, identified as "ex-patriots" and "guerrillas," are fighting among themselves while Uncle Sam attempts to establish order. Except for the similarity between Hawai'i and Puerto Rico, each site is represented differently with respect to its capacity for self-government. In addition, the cartoon establishes internal conflicts in Cuba; it distinguishes between its cooperative, well-behaved inhabitants and those who are contentious and disorderly.

These two cartoons, exemplifying the two modalities of colonial discourse, appear here in a somewhat isolated fashion. The first exemplified a strategy of dichotomous representation of difference: the construction of alien peoples as homogeneous, generally inferior "others," appropriate subjects of imperial rule. The second exemplified a strategy of hierarchical differentiation: the elaboration of distinctions among the subject peoples. These two modalities were not contradictory; rather they were mutually reinforcing. The first established the overall justification of the expansionist enterprise in the international context and the necessity of imperial rule in general. The second articulated an evaluation of difference that suggested particular recommendations for rule. Of course, this second cartoon did not constitute a precise policy statement, but it vaguely suggested that Cuba merited independence despite continued internal conflicts. In addition, even before the outbreak of the war between the United States and the Philippines, it foresaw a future of forced submission and imposed colonial rule for Filipinos. Further, both studious "schoolgirls" were annexed in 1898. Upon the organization of their respective civil governments in 1900, Hawai'i became an organized territory and Puerto Rico became an unincorporated territory, although the cartoon neither contemplated nor anticipated this different political trajectory. Finally, Guam, entirely absent in the second cartoon, apparently did not qualify for admission to the school of self-government and would be ruled by a military government.

In these examples, we can readily observe continuity among the legal discussions (Coudert and Fisher), the congressional debates (Beveridge), the issues raised by imperial administrators (Edwards), and the popular publications (White and the cartoons). The general underlying principle of the imperial discourse that unified these diverse texts was that there were multiple imperial subjects, each to be studied, judged, and ruled accordingly. The representations of the peoples of the insular territories formed an integral part of the discursive strategies to delineate them and to establish adequate governments.

The New-Possessions Books

The popular travelogue books were primarily vehicles of compilation and divulgation of official information, although many used original sources, including photographs. They included interviews with imperial and local officials, eyewitness accounts of journalists, photographs, and narratives by the traveling authors to create a rich description of the new possessions and foresee their future under U.S. rule. Metaphors, articulated through narratives, produced knowledge of the differences among the islands that served to devise and justify particular strategies of government. These books presented an evaluation of the advantages of the various islands for the United States, emphasizing their economic opportunities and their geopolitical importance. At first glance, the observations regarding the inhabitants of the islands might seem almost secondary and superficial, inaccurate or even extravagant. It would seem as if the publishers went out of their way to portray the peoples in the most exotic way imaginable.[18] However, these representations were not merely ideological distortions or misrepresentations of a fundamental reality. Instead, they were part of a discursive process of establishing imperial hegemony; of conceiving, creating, justifying, and governing a far-flung empire composed of an incredibly diverse group of islands. They were part of a cultural "elaboration" in the Gramscian sense: a process of working out a complex worldview that enabled politics in a particular historical context. Cultural elaboration was a necessary and practical dimension of hegemony and imperial rule.[19] In other words, these books were part of a colonial discourse that sought to define the inhabitants of Cuba, Puerto Rico, Hawai'i, the Philippines, and Guam as subject peoples and to establish new political, economic, and cultural relations with the United States.

Administrative knowledge was central to the establishment of the colonial state, which required concrete, specific information regarding the population, history, geography, and climate of the colony.[20] Published books, both popular and academic, formed an integral part of this administrative knowledge, along with the official reports and censuses. At the request of Congress, the chief bibliographer at the Library of Congress, Appleton Prentiss Clark Griffin, compiled the available published knowledge of these islands. He prepared extensive bibliographies from the holdings of the Library of Congress regarding Cuba,[21] Puerto Rico,[22] Hawai'i,[23] Guam, Samoa, and the Philippines.[24] These

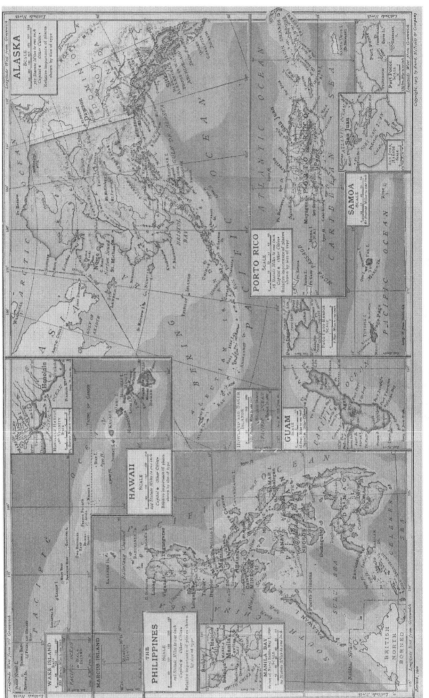

Map 1.1. U.S. Colonies and Dependencies. Boyce, *U.S. Colonies and Dependencies.*

bibliographies included a variety of texts: illustrated books for popular consumption as well as articles from the popular press, especially magazines; scholarly
books; official reports and congressional documents; maps; and books by local
authors from each site. The shifting geographical perspective of the books listed
in Griffin's bibliographies is worthy of note. Until 1898, most books focused
upon one island group, although it was not uncommon for authors to group
descriptions of places into broader regions, such as the "West Indies." Some
authors grouped together various islands and ports of call in a somewhat lin-
ear fashion according to the itinerary of their journey. Before 1898, however,
no author had grouped together the widely disparate islands of Cuba, Puerto
Rico, Hawai'i, the Philippines, and the other Pacific islands in a single work or
multivolume edition.[25] Beginning in 1898, however, numerous books began to
construct a new geography that included these widely disparate islands, scattered throughout the Pacific and the Caribbean, which had suddenly become
"our new possessions" or "our island empire."[26]

William Boyce, in what was to be the last of the new-possessions books,
published a composite map (map 1.1), originally produced in 1903, which hap-
hazardly grouped all of the islands together: it placed Puerto Rico, the Philippines, Hawai'i, Guam, Samoa, Wake Island, and Alaska all on the same map.
Boyce also inserted a few capital cities. He excluded the continental land masses
and geographic regions. Latitude and longitude were provided for each segment
of the map, but no strictly cartographic logic could provide any relationship
among the segments.[27] This was a graphic representation of the U.S. imperial
archipelago. First, the only logical association among all these areas was the
outmost political reach of U.S. overseas expansion. Second, the map presented
the islands as separate and different from the mainland United States; they were
"colonies" or "dependencies."

Among the most impressive new-possessions publications was a pair of
elaborately produced multivolume works that are still of special interest today
due to their exceptional quality, comprehensive scope, and authoritative perspective. The first of these, issued in 1901 and reprinted in 1907, was the multivolume *The New America and the Far East,* edited by George Waldo Browne, and
it included Cuba, Puerto Rico, Hawai'i, and the Philippines, as well as Japan and
China. The volumes contained around twelve hundred "photogravures, colored
plates, engravings, and maps." The authors of these volumes were among the
most influential men in overseas policy and colonial administration: Leonard
Wood (military governor of Cuba, 1899–1902); Joseph Wheeler (major general,
U.S. Army, who served in Cuba and the Philippines); Henry Cabot Lodge (U.S.
senator, 1893–1924); Charles Allen (civil governor of Puerto Rico, 1900–1902);

John D. Long (secretary of the navy, 1897–1902,); and Kogoro Takahira (Japanese ambassador to the United States, 1900–1909).[28]

The second of these was the enormously popular *Our Islands and Their People,* edited by William S. Bryan, begun in 1899 and issued in two oversized volumes in 1902.[29] The first edition sold four hundred thousand copies, and the publisher issued a reprint in 1905. It comprised more than twelve hundred black-and-white photographs, nineteen hand-colored photographs, and color maps of Cuba, Puerto Rico, Hawai'i, and the Philippines. The famous Civil War veteran General Joseph Wheeler, who had seen active service in both Cuba and the Philippines, wrote the preface. José de Olivares, a war correspondent from California, wrote the text. Both the text and the photographs attest that Olivares traveled widely with photographer Walter Townsend throughout the imperial archipelago. Although the exact itinerary of the pair is unknown, Olivares stated that he arrived in Puerto Rico with General Nelson Miles in July 1898.[30] As a result, the textual descriptions and the photographs were closely connected, and the volumes included long explanatory captions for the photographs. During his travels, Olivares interviewed journalists, soldiers and officers, colonial administrators, and local elites. In addition, he consulted and cited principal published works, official reports, and recent congressional legislation.

The discursive continuity among the representations found in the more popular publications and those deployed in official reports, congressional debates, and legal deliberations was due, in part, to a high degree of intertextuality. On the one hand, popular publications extensively utilized official publications, while, on the other hand, imperial officials contributed to the popular divulgation of the imperial project. In addition to the volumes edited by Browne and Bryan discussed above, a New York publisher issued a volume on the commercial and professional opportunities in the new possessions. The authors were Leonard Wood, William Taft (governor-general of the Philippines), Charles Allen, Perfecto LaCoste (former mayor of Havana and secretary of agriculture of Cuba), and M. E. Beall (Division of Insular Affairs, Washington).[31] In addition, the War Records Office in Washington, in collaboration with *Leslie's Weekly,* issued an official history of the Spanish-American War, including "the fullest information" regarding the new possessions. It included reproductions of photographs and illustrations.[32]

The new-possessions books used the most recent advances in photography and publishing. First, the mobility of photographic equipment had increased during the last two decades of the nineteenth century. By 1898, most photographers were using dry-plate negatives in large eight-by-ten-inch box cameras mounted on tripods. The dry-plate negative, which George Eastman had marketed in the United States since 1880, eliminated the obstacle of portable field darkrooms, which were necessary with wet-plate negatives. However, the cameras were unwieldy and did not permit action shots, so newspapers continued to rely on artists and engravers for illustrations of war scenes. The smaller Kodak box camera, equipped with roll film, had been available since 1898. It was much more manageable than the larger dry-plate box camera, but it produced lower-quality prints and its design required that the whole camera be sent in to develop the exposed film.[33]

Second, the mass reproduction of photographs in newspapers and books became possible in the 1890s with the invention of the half-tone screen, which broke up the photograph into a grid of tiny dots that allowed for a gradation of tone. This publishing technique was known as the half-tone photograph, the first of which was published in the New York *Daily Graphic* in 1890. By 1897, the New York *Tribune* was using half-tone photographs regularly, and by 1900 it was a common practice among major newspapers and magazines. These papers continued to use engravings to illustrate action scenes, while half-tone photographic reproductions were used for still views.[34]

Photographs were a distinctive characteristic of the period's books, newspapers, magazines, and official reports. Both commercial and official photographers quickly turned their attention to themes other than the exploits of war and produced a vast and multifaceted record of the new imperial possessions, their inhabitants, and the activities of colonial administrators. Photographs illustrated the most elaborate official reports concerning the new possessions. The census reports, undertaken in Puerto Rico and Cuba in 1899 and in the Philippines in 1902, were all illustrated extensively with photographs. The reports of the commissioners to Puerto Rico and the Philippines were also illustrated with photographs. Furthermore, hundreds of half-tone photographic reproductions were produced for public consumption in books, magazines, and newspapers.[35]

Photographs figured centrally in the strategies of the imperial discourse. They served principally as means of establishing the authority of the authors who claimed that their accounts were objective, realistic descriptions of the islands and their peoples. These authors based their claims to objectivity upon two interconnected discursive strategies. First, they established their narrative authority through their capacity as eyewitnesses, supplemented by their access to privileged information from interviews with insiders and/or gleaned from official documents. Sometimes the authors had practical experience as colonial administrators. More often, they stressed that they had traveled throughout the islands and had experienced firsthand the conditions and the people there. The textual accounts of what they had seen were often characterized as "pen pictures," a term not to be confused with pen-and-ink sketches. "Pen pictures" were written descriptions.[36]

Second, authors used photographs to depict "realistically" the islands and their peoples. Common knowledge of the day attributed objectivity to photography that was not a characteristic of sketches, drawings, or paintings. Photographs were supposedly more realistic and free of artistic interpretation. In his introduction to *Our Islands and Their People,* Wheeler exalted the objectivity of photography, attributing to it extraordinary capacities:

> In the exquisite photographs of actual scenes embodied in this work there is no room for the inaccuracies of chance or the uncertain fancies of the artist's imagination. The camera cannot be otherwise than candid and truthful. . . . It is real life transferred to the printed page. . . . When we view these photographs, painted by the unerring sunlight and transferred by the same process to the perfectly printed page, we know and feel that we are looking into the soul of nature and that we can see the actual counterpart of the objects portrayed.[37]

Wheeler expressed the commonsense notion that the photograph was an unerring transcription by means of a physical, causal connection between the object and the photograph. The objectivity of the photograph was based upon the instrumentality of the camera, which itself mimicked the mechanics of visual perception. From this point of view, the photograph was a perfect analogon of reality, in contrast to the subjective interpretations of graphic artists. The photographic "artist" was a grand master of realism, far surpassing anything a painting or drawing could accomplish.[38]

The authority of the written descriptions also rested upon a claim to realism, which was also doubly reinforced. First, the photographs supported the claim that the author really saw what he was describing. In many instances, the authors were accompanied by photographers or carried cameras themselves. Thus, photography reinforced the written testimony.[39] Second, the text, including the captions, explained the pictures, thus avoiding any "error" in identification or interpretation. The text "anchored" the photographs, explaining the image and its meaning.[40] Thus, the objectivity of the texts and the photographs was doubly reinforced, one complementing and bolstering the authority of the other.[41]

* * *

The wide range of texts under consideration here wrangled with the imperial problem attendant upon the acquisition of several overseas territories in 1898:

what kinds of peoples were these, and how should they be ruled? The discussions of the problem produced, in varying proportions, both descriptions of the new subjects and recommendations regarding the appropriate forms of rule, which were eventually codified as law. Throughout these texts, as we shall see in the following chapters, the metaphors of femininity, race, and childishness were used to evaluate the capacity of the various subject peoples for self-government. Colonial discourse addressed a descriptive question: what kinds of women, races, and children were these? Closely related was the political question: what was their capacity for self-government? The answers to these questions articulated descriptions of the character of the peoples within narrative accounts of the past and present while making projections or recommendations regarding their future under U.S. dominion. These narrative representations expressed comparisons and contrasts of the different colonial subjects and served to devise and justify particular strategies of rule. First, the contrast between regions (states and territories) settled by European Americans and the new possessions inhabited by "alien" peoples effectively set the limits of the republic's body politic and led to colonial rule beyond. Second, the evaluation of cultural differences among the subject peoples resulted in variations in the structures of government throughout the imperial archipelago.

It is evident from the discussion of the imperial problem above that colonial discourses constructed subject peoples as essentially, universally, and homogeneously "other," but this was quite often a rather abstract generalization. More important from a practical point of view, colonial discourses most decidedly distinguished the characteristics of subject peoples with the intent to govern them accordingly. Within the broad dichotomous field of alterity there were unmistakable, although not altogether consistent, differences and hierarchies. Given the vast field of subject peoples and, more important, given the practical considerations of imperial rule, hierarchical differences were of considerable concern in colonial discourses. For this reason, a homogeneous notion of alterity was functional only at the most general level, while the necessities of the minutia of imperial rule required an attention to particularities—that is, to differences among imperial subjects.[42] Legal scholars, Congress, colonial administrators, and the Supreme Court devised the means of governing overseas possessions based upon notions of difference not only *between* the United States and the subject peoples but also *among* the subject peoples themselves. In other words, variance in the forms of rule was a result of discursive deployments, an exploration of the imperial problem within the concrete contexts of the territories of the imperial archipelago.

Notes

1. James Fernald, *The Imperial Republic* (New York: Funk and Wagnalls, 1898); Horace Fisher, *Principles of Colonial Government Adapted to the Present Needs of Cuba and Porto Rico, and of the Philippines* (Boston: L. C. Page, 1899). See also Alpheus Snow, *The Administration of Dependencies: A Study of the Evolution of the Federal Empire, with Special Reference to American Colonial Problems* (New York: Knickerbocker Press, 1902), and William Willoughby, *Territories and Dependencies of the United States: Their Government and Administration* (New York: Century, 1905). The debates in the law journals will be discussed in detail in chapter 5.

2. The principal governmental legal study was Charles Magoon, *Report of the Legal Status of the Territory and Inhabitants of the Islands Acquired by the United States during the War with Spain, Considered with Reference to the Territorial Boundaries, the Constitution, and Laws of the United States,* 56th Cong., 1st sess., Senate, 12 February 1900, Senate Document 234; U.S. Serials 3858: 1–72. The House report on colonization appeared in "Monthly Summary of Commerce and Finance of the United States, Colonial Administration, 1800–1900," 57th Cong., 1st sess., House of Representatives, October 1901, House Document 15; U.S. Serials 4313: 1197–1631. An annotated bibliography, prepared by A. P. C. Griffin, appeared as a supplement to this report: *List of Books, with References to Periodicals, Relating to the Theory of Colonization, Government of Dependencies, Protectorates, and Related Topics,* 57th Cong., 1st sess., House of Representatives, October 1901, House Document 15, supplement; U.S. Serials 4313: 1567–1626.

3. The U.S. War Department produced two reports on Puerto Rico. Commissioner Henry Carroll submitted his report on 30 December 1898. See *Report on the Industrial and Commercial Condition of Porto Rico* (Washington: Government Printing Office, 1899). Several months later Commissioners Robert Kennedy, Charles Watkins, and Henry Curtis submitted a brief report. See U.S. War Department, Division of Insular Affairs, *Report of the United States Insular Commission to the Secretary of War, upon Investigations Made into the Civil Affairs of the Island of Porto Rico with Recommendations* (Washington: Government Printing Office, 1899). The First Philippine Commission, headed by Jacob Gould Schurman, arrived in Manila in March 1899. See Philippine Commission (Schurman), *Report of the Philippine Commission to the President,* 56th Cong., 1st sess., Senate, 31 January–20 December 1900, Senate Document 138).

4. Arrell Gibson considered the entire Pacific Basin to be "America's last frontier." His notion of frontier, adapted from Frederick Jackson Turner, was quite complex, including military, mercantile, missionary, and agrarian dimensions. In a most general sense, he viewed the frontier as a process of "Americanization." The expansion of the frontier usually included "nationalizing currents" through which a region was incorporated into the economic, social, and political life of the nation. Gibson argued that the incorporation of Hawai'i followed the same pattern as established by the Northwest

Ordinance throughout the continental United States. However, he did not consider why some regions of the Pacific Basin frontier were incorporated and others were not. See Arrell Morgan Gibson, *Yankees in Paradise: The Pacific Basin Frontier* (Albuquerque: University of New Mexico Press, 1993), 3–11.

5. Frederic Coudert, Jr., "Our New Peoples: Citizens, Subjects, Nationals or Aliens," *Columbia Law Review* 3, no. 1 (1903): 13; emphasis added. Like most authors, Coudert did not explicitly discuss Guam, although it was in a similar legal situation as Puerto Rico and the Philippines. Coudert Brothers, the law firm in which Coudert was a partner, litigated some of the Insular Cases in the Supreme Court. Bartholomew Sparrow provides a clear and informative analysis of the Insular Cases, including biographical backgrounds of the principal lawyers and judges; see *The Insular Cases and the Emergence of the American Empire* (Lawrence: University Press of Kansas, 2006).

6. Coudert, "Our New Peoples," 13–14.

7. Fisher, *Principles of Colonial Government,* 49.

8. Albert J. Beveridge, "Government for Porto Rico," *Congressional Record,* 56th Cong., 1st sess., Senate, 29 March 1900. Vol. 33, nos. 6–8, appendix, 281.

9. For a detailed study of actions of the military government and the transition to civil government in Puerto Rico, see Pedro Cabán, *Constructing a Colonial People: Puerto Rico and the United States, 1898–1932* (Boulder: Westview Press, 1999).

10. Clarence Edwards: *Annual Report of the Chief of the Division of Insular Affairs to the Secretary of War* (Washington: Government Printing Office, 1901), 34–35, and "The Work of the Bureau of Insular Affairs," *National Geographic Magazine* 15, no. 6 (1904): 239–240.

11. This library is now preserved in Record Group 350, 142.1, Library Materials, National Archives, College Park, Maryland.

12. Clarence Edwards, *Report of the Chief of the Bureau of Insular Affairs to the Secretary of War* (Washington: Government Printing Office, 1902), 3. Edwards lifted this passage verbatim from the *Report of the Secretary of War,* 27 November 1901.

13. As noted, the Division of Customs and Insular Affairs contracted the services of Charles Magoon to deal with the various legal and constitutional problems raised by imperial rule. His report was highly influential in the determination of government policy and practice. See Magoon, *Legal Status.*

14. Trumbull White, *Our New Possessions* (Boston: Adams, 1898), 584.

15. Ibid., 568.

16. Reprinted in Marshall Everett, ed., *Exciting Experiences in Our Wars with Spain and the Filipinos* (Chicago: Book Publishers Union, 1899), n.p.

17. W. A. Rogers (artist), *Harper's Weekly,* 27 August 1898, 1.

18. A few authors have dismissed these representations as inconsequential fantasies. See García, "I Am the Other." However, most have tried to describe the underlying

politics of these photographic representations and other cultural expressions. For example, Vergara has argued that the photographs in the Philippine census "harmonize with . . . jurisprudence which established the legal basis and scaffolding for the 'constitutional' legitimation of colonial sovereignty" (*Displaying Filipinos*, xiii). Rydell, *All the World's a Fair*, has also outlined the "hegemonic functions" of the "symbolic universes" of the world's fairs in terms of their political importance.

19. Edward Said discusses the concept of cultural elaboration in *The World, the Text, and the Critic* (Cambridge, Mass.: Harvard University Press, 1983), 170–172.

20. For an informative discussion of the notion of administrative knowledge in Foucault's thought, see Hubert Dreyfus and Paul Rabinow. *Michel Foucault: Beyond Structuralism and Hermeneutics* (Chicago: University of Chicago Press, 1983). Eduardo Ugarte applies the idea to the Philippines in his discussion of Filipino character; see "'Qualifications Most Necessary to Rule': The Amok in the Construction of Filipino and American Identities," *American Studies Asia* 1, no. 1 (2002): 41–73. See also Vergara's excellent study of the Philippine census, *Displaying Filipinos*.

21. A. P. C. Griffin, *List of Books Relating to Cuba: Including References to Collected Works and Periodicals*, 55th Cong., 2nd sess., Senate, 1898, Senate Document 161; U.S. Serials 3600: 1–61. The Cuban bibliography contained 195 volumes; 164 articles in U.S. periodicals; 85 congressional documents (excluding resolutions, bills, and speeches); a list of 35 Cuban periodicals received by the Smithsonian Institution; and a list of maps of Cuba, Puerto Rico, and the West Indies. The primary source of information regarding the political relations of the United States and Cuba during the nineteenth century was *Wharton's Digest of International Law,* which included multiple entries. Several other works, ranging from constitutional histories to presidential biographies and memoirs, included discussions of Cuba. In addition to these sources, Griffin's bibliography contained many volumes published in the United States throughout the nineteenth century. This bibliography was updated in 1905 and reissued in Gonzalo de Quesada, *Cuba* (Washington: International Bureau of the American Republics, 1905).

22. The Puerto Rican bibliography, published in 1901, included a list of 240 volumes; 210 articles in U.S. periodicals; and a collection of 94 documents in Spanish, consisting of various reports of local organizations and administrative bodies in Puerto Rico, as well as important works by Puerto Rican authors Salvador Brau, Cayetano Coll y Toste, and Alejandro Tapia y Rivera, among others. See A. P. C. Griffin *List of Books (with References to Periodicals) on Porto Rico,* 56th Cong., 2nd sess., Senate, 2 March 1901, Senate Document 222; U.S. Serials 4176: 1–55.

23. A. P. C. Griffin, *List of Books Relating to Hawaii* (Washington: Government Printing Office, 1898). The Hawaiian bibliography, printed in 1898, included 143 books, reports, and pamphlets, as well as 103 articles in U.S. periodicals.

24. A. P. C. Griffin, *List of Books (with References to Periodicals) on the Philippine Islands in the Library of Congress*, 56th Cong., 2nd sess., Senate, 1903, Senate Document 74, pt. 1; U.S. Serials 4423: 1–397. The Philippine bibliography consisted of two parts. The first part was a list of books, periodicals, documents, and maps and was limited to materials found in the Library of Congress. It included 1,695 volumes, 984 articles in periodicals, 152 U.S. government documents, and 94 congressional documents. The second part was the *Biblioteca filipina*, compiled by T. H. Pardo de Tavera of Manila. See Senate Document 74, pt. 2, 56th Cong., 2nd sess., Senate, 1903; U.S. Serials 4423: 1–439. Pardo claimed his bibliography to be a comprehensive list of everything published on the Philippines. In preparation for it, he had consulted the major libraries and private collections in Madrid, Berlin, Paris, London, and Leyde. He also compiled a large collection of his own. The bibliography, which included a short prologue, contained 2,850 entries, with extensive annotations in Spanish. Before 1898, the vast majority of works on the Philippines appeared in Spanish, German, or French, in that order. Griffin complained that there was "no adequate history of the Philippines in English." He noted a similar situation for ethnologies, descriptive accounts, natural histories, and so forth. Nevertheless, he listed some notable works in English, published by British authors. These included, among others, John Foreman's authoritative "historical, geographical, ethnographical, social, and commercial sketch," published in 1890, and Alfred Russel Wallace's noted works of geography and natural history. Before 1898, however, American authors were notably absent. After this date, a considerable number of books regarding the Philippines were published in the United States. Between 1898 and 1903, at least 174 publications regarding the U.S. military occupation appeared, and roughly 100 more books regarding (among other topics) ethnology, descriptive accounts, and history appeared during the same period. In 1905, Griffin updated the bibliography to include the additional literature regarding the U.S. occupation.

25. The only book that approached this geographic scope was Waldo Jiménez's volume on Cuba, Puerto Rico, and the Philippines when they were still Spanish colonies. See Waldo Jiménez de la Romera, *Cuba, Puerto-Rico y Filipinas* (Barcelona: Daniel Cortezo, 1887). Spain's exhibit at the Chicago World's Fair of 1893 also included the Spanish colonies of Cuba, Puerto Rico, and the Philippines. See Comisión General de España, *Exposición universal de Chicago de 1893, adición al catálogo de la sección española comprende las islas de Cuba, Puerto-Rico y Filipinas* (Madrid: Imprenta de Ricardo Rojas, 1894).

26. Frederick Tennyson Neely published a monthly series of photographic books from offices in London, Chicago, and New York. For example, see F. Tennyson Neely: *Neely's Panorama of Our New Possessions* (New York: Neely Publishing, 1898), and *Neely's Color Photos of America's New Possessions* (New York: F. Tennyson Neely, 1899).

Another "panoramic" series was produced in Springfield, Ohio; see A. M. Church, ed. *Picturesque Cuba, Porto Rico, Hawaii, and the Philippines: A Photographic Panorama of Our New Possessions*, no. 168 in the Farm and Fireside Library (Springfield, Ohio: Mast, Crowell, and Kirkpatrick, 1898). See also Murat Halstead, *Pictorial History of America's New Possessions* (Chicago: Dominion, 1899); Alden March, *The History and Conquest of the Philippines and Our Other Island Possessions, Embracing Our War with the Filipinos in 1899, Together with a Complete History of Those Islands from the Earliest Times to the Present* (Philadelphia: John C. Winston, 1899); Charles Morris, *Our Island Empire: A Handbook of Cuba, Puerto Rico, Hawaii, and the Philippine Islands* (Philadelphia: J. B. Lippincott, 1899); and James Baldwin, *Our New Possessions: Cuba, Puerto Rico, Hawaii, Philippines* (New York: American Book, 1899).

27. William Boyce, *U.S. Colonies and Dependencies* (Chicago: Rand McNally, 1914). Rand McNally produced and copyrighted the map in 1903. According to the table of contents, the "colonies" were Alaska, Hawai'i, the Philippines, Puerto Rico, and the Panama Canal Zone. The "dependencies" were Cuba, Dominican Republic, and the Republic of Haiti. Clearly there was not an exact correspondence between the areas on the map and the detailed contents of the book.

28. G. Waldo Browne, *The New America and the Far East: A Picturesque and Historic Description of These Lands and Peoples* (Boston: Dana Estes, 1901). R. H. Whitten also issued an edition in 1901, published in New York and Los Angeles. I have consulted the 1907 edition, published by Marshall Jones, Boston.

29. William S. Bryan, ed., *Our Islands and Their People, as Seen with Camera and Pencil* (St. Louis: Thompson Publishing, 1899). In spite of the 1899 copyright, this book was not released until two or three years later. It mentioned the capture of Emilio Aguinaldo, which occurred in 1901, and the Philippines civil government bill, submitted to the House of Representatives in 1902.

30. During the Spanish-American War, José de Olivares was a war correspondent attached to General Joseph Wheeler in Cuba and later to General Nelson Miles in Puerto Rico. He arrived in Puerto Rico with the U.S. Illinois Volunteers and took various pictures of soldiers in the field; see Bryan, *Our Islands*, 370, 372. The biography of José de Olivares appears in *Who Was Who in America, with World Notables*, vol. 5 (1969–1973) (Chicago: A. N. Marquis, 1973), 544. Additional information can be found in the *World's Fair Bulletin*, July 1901, p. 13.

31. Leonard Wood, William Taft, Charles Allen, Perfecto LaCoste, and M. E. Beall, *Opportunities in the Colonies and Cuba* (New York: Lewis, Scribner, 1902).

32. James William Buel and Harry P. Mawson, eds., *Leslie's Official History of the Spanish-American War: A Pictorial and Description Record of the Cuban Rebellion, the Causes That Involved the United States, and a Complete Narrative of Our War with Spain on Land and Sea; Supplemented with the Fullest Information Respecting Cuba, Porto Rico,*

the Philippines, and Hawaii; issued by subscription by the War Records Office, Washington, and *Leslie's Weekly,* 1899.

33. James Dewell, *Down in Porto Rico with a Kodak* (New Haven, Conn.: Record Publishing, 1898).

34. Jorge Lewinski, *The Camera at War: A History of War Photography from 1848 to the Present Day* (New York: Simon and Schuster, 1978), 46–52.

35. I have not considered the distribution of stereographic views, which made use of a different technology. Special cameras with two offset lenses produced double negatives that were used to make contact prints for stereographic cards. Customers looked at these cards with a stereo viewer, which produced a three-dimensional effect. There were four major stereographic companies, among them Keystone and Underwood and Underwood. Margarett Loke, ed. *The World as It Was, 1865–1921: A Photographic Portrait from the Keystone-Mast Collection* (New York: Summit Books, 1980). Jorge Crespo has reproduced most known stereoviews of Puerto Rico in *Puerto Rico 3D: 100 años de historia a través de la estereoscopía* (Gurabo: Centro de Estudios Humanísticos, Universidad del Turabo, 2003). For an analysis of the stereoviews of Underwood and Underwood in Puerto Rico, see Jorge Duany, *Puerto Rican Nation on the Move: Identities on the Island and in the United States* (Chapel Hill: University of North Carolina Press, 2002), ch. 4.

36. Charles H. Rector, *The Story of Beautiful Puerto Rico: A Graphic Description of the Garden Spot of the World by Pen and Camera* (Chicago: Lind and Lee, 1898). Albert Gardner Robinson, *The Porto Rico of Today: Pen Pictures of the People and the Country* (New York: Charles Scribner's Sons, 1899). Robinson's book is a compilation of reports that the author sent to the New York magazine *The Evening Post* during his stay in Puerto Rico during August, September, and October of 1898. The photographer is unknown.

37. In Bryan, *Our Islands,* 5–6.

38. For an excellent history of the notion of photographic realism, see E. Edwards, *Anthropology and Photography.* John Tagg offers a Foucauldian approach in *The Burden of Representation: Essays on Photographies and Histories* (Amherst: University of Massachusetts Press, 1988). The classic treatment of the paradox of photography is Roland Barthes, *Image, Music, Text* (New York: Hill and Wang, 1977). Barthes argued that the photograph simultaneously presents two different messages; it is at once a perfect analogon of reality and a symbolic language.

39. Each book handled this aspect a little differently. Boyce appeared in his book studying the landscape in several photographs. In Bryan's book, the photographer himself appears in several photographs, while the author narrates their journey together. In Browne's volumes, the presence of the authors was guaranteed less by the photographs than by the men's position as colonial authorities, most of whom had practical administrative experience in the islands.

40. The idea that the text anchors the interpretation of the photograph is from Roland Barthes. He argues that since the photograph is inherently polysemous, a text is needed to direct the reader's interpretation of the image. See Barthes, *Image, Music, Text*, 38–40.

41. I disagree with Vergara, who considered texts to be secondary, used only "to elaborate on the photographs." Vergara, *Displaying Filipinos*, 79–81.

42. In the congressional debates, those who argued against the annexation of Hawai'i and the possession of the Philippines and Puerto Rico frequently used images of homogeneous, undifferentiated, essentially inferior "others" as means of stressing the absolute dichotomy between the free white citizens of the United States and the colored "aliens" of the islands. Congressmen who spoke in favor of the Treaty of Paris and of the bills to establish civil governments used contrasts, as well as comparisons, to make their arguments. For a discussion of the use of racialized representations to argue against U.S. expansion, see Eric Love, *Race over Empire: Racism and U.S. Imperialism, 1865–1900* (Chapel Hill: University of North Carolina Press, 2004).

Chapter 2

Islands of Women

Gendered Politics

During the nineteenth century, hegemonic discourses of civilization circulated widely. The rhetoric of male supremacy was a common trope. White males, who embodied the fittest in the evolutionary struggle, were the agents for social progress. They were a kind of chosen people responsible for the advancement of civilization. The rest of humankind, whether women or men of the lower races, must inevitably yield to their leadership and authority, and it was "imperative to all civilization that white males assume the power that would ensure the continued advancement of white civilization."[1] Pronounced gender differentiation was an important indicator of advanced civilization. While civilized women were appropriately delicate, spiritual, and dedicated to the home, civilized men were strong-charactered, self-controlled guardians of women and children. Among the uncivilized peoples there was no clear counterpart in the differentiation of the sexes, and often roles seemed to be the inverse of civilized ways. Uncivilized women immodestly engaged in heavy, masculine labor, while uncivilized men were often emotional and unreliable; they were abusers of women and children or were themselves given to feminine characteristics. This discourse of civilization elaborated upon popular beliefs about gender, race, and evolution.

In this grand scheme, civilization denoted an advanced stage in human evolution following simple savagery and violent barbarism. Human social evolution and racial differences were conflated so that contemporary differences were attributed to the relative evolutionary advances of particular races. Just as manliness seemed to be the right mix of superior biology and cultural achievement, the popular notion of race conflated biology and culture, physical morphology and ethnology. In this scheme, only Anglo-Saxons and other white races had evolved to the stage of advanced civilization. The somewhat contradictory ideologies of social Darwinism and Protestant millennialism were resolved by a notion of civilization as the gradual perfection of the human race by means of the advancement led by the superior white race. In this way, Protestant millennialism provided a telos to the theory of human evolution. The power of this discourse derived from the link it established between male supremacy and white superiority while celebrating both as essential to human progress and perfection. Thus, the term "civilization" simultaneously denoted attributes of gender and race within a grand narrative of human evolution.[2] During the nineteenth century, this hegemonic discourse contributed to the remaking of manhood in the United States.

This chapter will focus on the extension of this discourse of civilization to the process of making an overseas empire at the turn of the century. The elements of gender, race, and evolution, which were constitutive of the general discourse of civilization, were also fundamental to the construction of the imperial archipelago. Cartoonists of the late nineteenth and early twentieth centuries frequently made use of feminine figures to represent Latin American countries and peoples. The cartoon characters usually represented one or more of three stereotypical images of women: (1) attractive and sometimes seductive; (2) virtuous but defenseless and in need of male protection; and (3) physically fragile and inviting sympathy. Johnson, in his survey of caricatures of Latin America, found no openly derogatory images of women, who often appeared as virtuous, privileged, and white—that is, "civilized."[3] Nevertheless, the portrayal of Latin American countries by means of feminine images served to underscore their inherent dependency and incapacity for reasoned political action and sustained self-government. The feminine metaphor helped create an attitude toward Latin America that was at once sympathetic and prejudiced.

Likewise, notions of chivalry, honor, and masculinity constituted key rhetorical elements in the political debates throughout the 1890s and were especially effective in producing sympathies for the cause of Cuban independence. The use of feminine figures had been widely used in the newspapers leading up to the declaration of war on Spain and the intervention in Cuba. A constant trope was that of the gentleman (read United States) who rescued the virtuous damsel (read Cuba) from abuse by an old man (read Spain). In this way the masculine ideal of chivalry played an important role in mobilizing direct intervention in Cuba. In this sense, it was a method of argument, a rhetoric, in support of war with Spain. Moreover, the masculine ideal of politics was a motivation—if not a cause—of the hawkish, expansionist impulse that led to the imperial wars.

The younger generation of politicians sought the glory and honor earned by the older generation, who had fought in the Civil War. The economic crisis of the 1890s created insecurity and doubt; the class conflicts divided the fraternity of men; the suffragists threatened the foundations of masculine political power. The "jingos" of the 1890s were literally looking for a fight to reestablish national honor and manhood. The means of masculine regeneration—war and expansion—were at hand, beginning in Cuba and then extending throughout the imperial archipelago.[4]

In this respect, of particular interest is the quintessential manly imperialist, Theodore Roosevelt, and his notion of the virtues of the "strenuous life."[5] In 1899, Roosevelt gave a speech before the Hamilton Club (Chicago) in which he used the phrase "strenuous life" to refer to a virile, aggressive manhood. Honorable men, he said, must seek the "life of toil and effort, of labor and strife," and they should shun "ignoble ease," "easy peace," and "idleness." His notion of manhood was directly linked to his expansive foreign policy: "As it is with the individual, so it is with the nation." Throughout this famous speech Roosevelt used vivid gender analogies to outline his policy with respect to the "responsibilities that confront us in Hawaii, Cuba, Porto Rico, and the Philippines." The United States had just defeated Spain and now confronted "difficult problems" in the new island possessions. It must not be "cowardly"; its leaders must not be "too weak, too selfish, or too foolish" to directly confront and solve these problems. This responsibility was incumbent upon the nation because "if we seek merely swollen, slothful ease and ignoble peace, if we shrink from the hard contests where men must win at hazard of their lives and at the risk of all they hold dear, then the bolder and stronger peoples will pass us by, and will win for themselves the domination of the world."[6] Roosevelt conceived both national responsibility and international rivalry in terms of masculinity. The boldest and strongest nation could win over its rivals and dominate the world. It would have been a sign of effeminate weakness to avoid action in the world arena.

Thus, according to Roosevelt it was the manly duty of the United States to directly and energetically confront the problems of the new possessions. Other authors have analyzed this mobilization of masculinity in support of overseas expansion in general; however, they have ignored Roosevelt's analysis of the problems attendant upon the cultural differences that the United States confronted throughout the imperial archipelago.[7] The nation should be manly, indeed, but how should this masculinity translate into specific practices in each site? What, exactly, was a man to do? Roosevelt outlined the different problems and his proposed solutions in the following way:

The problems are different for the different islands. Porto Rico is not large enough to stand alone. We must govern it wisely and well, primarily in the interest of its own people. Cuba is, in my judgment, entitled ultimately to settle for itself whether it shall be an independent state or an integral portion of the mightiest of republics. But until order and stable liberty are secured, we must remain in the island to insure them, and infinite tact, judgment, moderation, and courage must be shown by our military and civil representatives in keeping the island pacified, in relentlessly stamping out brigandage, in protecting all alike, and yet showing proper recognition to the men who have fought for Cuban liberty. The Philippines offer a yet graver problem. Their population includes half-caste and native Christians, warlike Moslems, and wild pagans. Many of their people are utterly unfit for self-government and show no signs of becoming fit. Others may in time become fit but at the present can only take part in self-government under a wise supervision, at once firm and beneficent. We have driven Spanish tyranny from the islands. If we now let it be replaced by savage anarchy, our work has been for harm and not for good. I have scant patience with those who fear to undertake the task of governing the Philippines, and who openly avow that they do fear to undertake it, or that they shrink from it because of expense and trouble; but I have even scanter patience with those who make a pretense of humanitarianism to hide and cover their timidity, and who cant about "liberty" and the "consent of the governed," in order to excuse themselves for their unwillingness to play the part of men. Their doctrines, if carried out, would make it incumbent upon us to leave the Apaches of Arizona to work out their own salvation, and to decline to interfere in a single reservation. Their doctrines condemn your forefathers and mine for ever having settled in these United States.[8]

This passage expressed the fundamentals of the discourse of rule in the imperial archipelago. First, each site possessed different capacities for self-government in the international area. Second, since the islands were so different, no single form of rule would suffice throughout all of the new possessions. This was Roosevelt's particular articulation of the imperial problem: on the one hand, a description of difference and, on the other hand, a prescription for government. It is evident in this passage that both gendered and racialized representations served to define differences and to outline the specific strategies of rule. According to Roosevelt, Puerto Rico was but a small island—weak, passive, and without political will or capacity. As we shall see below, popular representations of Puerto Rican women and children supported Roosevelt's succinct characterization. The policy implications were clear: Puerto Rico was unable to govern itself locally and "stand alone" internationally. In contrast, Cuba was "entitled" to its independence since its men had "fought for Cuban liberty." The popular feminine representations of Cuba, so prevalent in the call to arms that led to declaration of war with Spain, were now matched with the "proper recognition" of the masculine qualities of its brave and capable leaders. The United States should help establish order in Cuba, but its men had earned the right to self-destiny and self-government. This was the rhetoric of masculine right and honor. Roosevelt accepted that Cuba could be granted at least a limited degree of political manhood, although the United States would have to protect the same in the international arena. Cuban independence was, then, a kind of man-to-man agreement, although one of the parties was decidedly weaker and would require support and supervision.

Gendered representations were clearly in the foreground in these brief descriptions of both Puerto Rico and Cuba. In contrast, racialized descriptions established the diagnosis of the problem in the Philippines. Roosevelt argued that it was an aggregate of widely different races, ranging from those who were "utterly unfit" to those who "in time may become fit" for self-government. In sharp contrast to the Cubans, the Filipinos had no right to liberty or to the "consent of the governed," and only "savage anarchy" could prevail in the absence of U.S. rule. In the face of armed resistance, the first priority was to establish the "supremacy of our flag," and only then could "the great work of uplifting mankind" be undertaken. Specifically feminine representations would add a unique and unsympathetic dimension to the evaluation of the Philippines, as we shall see below, but racial and religious dimensions occupied the foreground here. Regarding the Philippines, Roosevelt used gendered notions chiefly to launch an attack against his opponents in the United States. He accused his critics at home of being unwilling to "play the part of men" and called their words treasonable. In this complex formulation, the duty of the white man was to give order to anarchy and civilize the savage. Only then would any talk of self-government be considered. Here Roosevelt appealed principally to an analogy of tribes: just as Apaches were completely incapable of self-government, so were the "tribes" of the Philippines. This analogy proved to be one of the most persistent tropes in the descriptions of the Philippines, as we shall see in the following chapter. In addition, Roosevelt appealed implicitly to the doctrine of Manifest Destiny, which had played such an important role in the continental expansion. Although this doctrine provided a facile justification for overseas expansion, it could not attend directly to the problems of rule in areas in which there was no previous or anticipated Euro-American settlement.

Thus, Roosevelt's speech showed a complex use of gender and racial meta-phors to both outline the duty of the United States and to describe the particular situations in Puerto Rico, Cuba, and the Philippines. These brief descriptions provided the rationale for policy in each area. In this chapter, I will further explore the use of diverse gendered representations in the construction and legitimation of an imperial archipelago under U.S. political dominion. This chapter will place gendered representations in the foreground but will also integrate the related processes of racialization and class formation.

Pretty Puerto Rico

José de Olivares, who wrote the text of *Our Islands and Their People,* saw the white, aristocratic women of Puerto Rico as "Spanish" and distinct from the "Porto Rican" women, whom he saw as black and mulatto and from the working classes. Several photographs of these aristocratic women were included in the book, including that shown in figure 2.1. The caption of the photograph identi-fied the person as a "pretty Spanish girl" from Mayagüez, an important city on the west coast of Puerto Rico. The signs of civilization are clear: the studio por-trait, the Roman column, the book, the elegant dress. This photograph, as well as others like it, reinforced the argument in the text regarding the beauty and civilized charms of the Spanish women.

The aristocratic women of Puerto Rico, according to Olivares, represented the best of Spanish civilization as it was a century ago: "The women of the aristo-cratic class of Porto Rico represent the higher and better civilization of Spain as it existed a hundred years ago. Born and reared in their secluded isle, they have neither receded nor advanced, but remain today just what their mothers were three generations ago. We can imagine the unique sensation that these beautiful exotics will produce when they visit their practical and matter-of-fact sisters of the great modern Republic."[9]

In these few sentences, the author contrasted two competing civilizations, both represented by women. On the one hand, Spanish civilization, in its island seclusion, had not progressed, but neither had it degenerated. It was an aris-tocratic civilization; its symbol was the beautiful, elegant, and refined woman. Note, however, that Olivares identified this woman as "Spanish" (peninsular) rather than Puerto Rican and thus implied that a uniquely national culture was inconsequential. On the other hand, the American women represented the civi-lization of a great industrial republic. They were practical, straightforward, and modern. For Olivares, these "sisters," the Spanish and the American, could not have been much more different.

Figure 2.1. Pretty Spanish Girl of Mayaguez, Porto Rico. Bryan, *Our Islands.*

One of the modern American sisters, Margherita Hamm, also wrote an account of Puerto Rico.[10] Her book was unique in its focus upon women, domestic life, and social activities. Like Olivares, she concluded that the modernization of Puerto Rico must include the transformation of feminine roles in accordance with the ideas of equality and progress. Puerto Rican women, she wrote, were not equal to men and were limited by their poor education, lack of professions, and exclusion from public life. Unlike Olivares, she did not describe upper-class women as "Spanish." Instead, she described the women according to daily activities, class, and color. Her descriptions betrayed a fascination with the beauty of the complex palette of skin color among the women. She described upper-class women as slightly darker than the Spanish, but extremely beautiful:

> Owing partly to nationality and partly to the climate the complexion of the Porto Ricans is a trifle darker than that of the Spaniard, Portuguese or Italian. Probably the admixture of red and black blood has something to do with it; but the fact remains that they show greater varieties of brunette skin than any other people in the New World. Beside the orange-yellow of the mulatto there is a curious red-orange which is very striking. When this is combined with the reddish hair of Spain it makes a color scheme which is picturesque and novel if not beautiful. Young girls of this red-orange tint present a startling appearance when attired in low-cut evening dress of white silk or of black silk and velvet. The coloring is so intense that an ordinary brunette seems a sallow gray by contrast, and a northern blonde to be suffering from anemia. Another type which is very beautiful has an oval face and Spanish features in the outline, but Carib in the delicacy; soft brown eyes, a warm olive skin, and Spanish red hair. The natives claim that this was the complexion of the celebrated beauty, Queen Isabella, and judging from the portraits which have come down of that great sovereign the comparison is borne out by the fact. The Moorish type is quite common, especially where there is a dash of African blood. This serves to make the eye darker, to give the corner a bluish tinge, and to change the pearly Spanish teeth into the whiter ivories of the Ethiop. To an outsider this Moorish type is lovelier than the so-called Spanish blonde, but the natives themselves seem to prefer the latter.[11]

In this section, Hamm elaborated four types of women according to color. First, the *mulata* was "orange-yellow." The second color was "red-orange" and was so intense that the "ordinary brunette" seemed "sallow gray" and the "northern blonde" appeared anemic. Third, the Spanish blonde had brown eyes, olive skin, and red hair. Finally, the "Moorish" type was darker, and the coloring contrasted with her ivory white teeth. Hamm's somewhat shorter description of the popular classes in the market was similar in its detailed attention to color, although she identified different colors: "The market people are almost as varied in color as the goods they sell. It makes a weird combination when three or four young peasant women with flashing eyes, erect carriage, and well-rounded figures form a group and begin to chat. The yellow arm resting upon the bronze shoulder, the black hand patting the olive back, the copper fingers arranging the ruddy red hair around the white face, compose an odd study in the variations of color."[12]

In these two sections, Hamm both stressed the attractiveness of the women and linked it precisely to the mixing of the races. Her deployment of color was fundamental to these descriptions of variety, which also implied miscegenation. Indeed, she was quick to point out that although many Puerto Ricans might "pass muster as whites," if "all the mulattoes, quadroons, octoroons, quinteros and other mestizos were included with the blacks instead of the whites, the proportions would be changed and the blacks would have a handsome majority upon the island." Despite her attention to the variety of colors she had witnessed, here Hamm implied a normative black/white dichotomy, compromised by the varied proportions of black/white mixtures, indicated by a series of terms in English and Spanish.[13]

Despite their divergent opinions regarding minor issues, Olivares and Hamm agreed that Puerto Rican women were of mixed race and very attractive. Other authors also signaled the beauty of the mixed-race Puerto Rican women. In 1898, White published a photograph of a "coloured [sic] belle of Puerto Rico" (figure 2.2). She posed in the street, a sign that she was not from the elite, yet her dress and demeanor were strikingly elegant. The caption stressed the limits of race mixing and suggested social segregation by color, but only within the upper class. However, the photographer focused upon this "higher type" of colored, rather than white, woman as the object of desire: "The mixture of African with Spanish blood is not found in all people of this island. The higher classes of white people hold themselves as strictly in their own society as in any other country. This attractive colored girl is of the higher type of that race."[14]

As we have seen so far, the darkish color of the women of Puerto Rico did not diminish in any way their attractiveness. Indeed, Charles Allen, the first civil governor of Puerto Rico, recounting his travels throughout the island, found the Puerto Rican woman to be a "sable Aphrodite." She was a comely racial blend of her African ancestors and "the haughty sons of old Castile." He cited an unnamed poet to the effect that there was no difference, except color, between the "dusky tropical belle" of Puerto Rico and the white European beauty:

Figure 2.2. A Coloured Belle of Puerto Rico. White, *Our New Possessions.*

"The loveliest limbs her form composed,
Such as her sister Venus chose
In Florence, where she's seen,
But just alike, except the white,
No difference, no—none at night,
The beauteous dames between."[15]

Figure 2.3. A Porto Rican Cigarette Girl. Bryan, *Our Islands.*

Puerto Rican women of the working classes frequently caught the attention of the authors, who emphasized both their mixed race and their industriousness. In the photograph in figure 2.3, published in *Our Islands and Their People,* the "cigarette girl" was dark skinned and a wage worker. She was photographed on a common sidewalk, not in a studio or even the town square. The street scene and her occupation in the tobacco industry signaled her working-class background.

Other pictures in the same volume also focused on the occupations of women. A common theme was the washerwomen who did washing on the riverbank and dried their clothes on nearby fences, bushes, or grass. Figure 2.4 shows women coffee sorters in a small establishment in Yauco, a town of the interior mountain range. The author went into considerable detail regarding the women's attitude and appearance, the labor process, wages, and the cost of living:

> The sorting is done by women and girls, who receive less than 25 cents a day, but they appear to be satisfied with their lot and are happy and light-hearted. Bananas are cheap, and the cost of women's clothing in this mild climate is a small matter. In fact, many of them are satisfied with a wardrobe but little more elaborate than the traditional costume worn by Eve. In every large Porto Rican factory you find women picking over the coffee grains and separating the good from the bad. In the smaller factories the picking is done sitting on the floor before a long box covered with cloth. In the larger ones, there are long tables cut up into little boxes by many partitions, and before each box a Porto Rican girl sits with a pile of green coffee from sunrise until sunset. Some of these brown-skinned maidens are quite pretty, with large, languishing black eyes and teeth of pearly whiteness. They laugh and sing as they work, and no doubt get as much enjoyment out of life as many of their fashionable and more fortunate sisters.[16]

In spite of the alleged happiness and lightheartedness of these women workers, their facial expressions were serious and pensive. Given the somber tone of the photograph, it would have required considerable effort to imagine these women laughing and singing as they worked.[17] The text offered a brief description of the process of coffee sorting that the photograph corroborates. It should be noted, however, that the book included the photograph of the "smaller factory" rather than one of the larger workshops. In the smaller factories, as shown, the women sat on the floor, while in the larger ones they stood or sat before long tables. Sitting or squatting on the ground gave the impression of inefficient, pre-industrial procedures and suggested backward culture in general. The text also assured the reader that the sorters were quite diligent in their labor and accepted very low remuneration for a full day's work. The interaction between the text and the photograph had a promising if somewhat unstable affect: these women were happy, attractive, and sensual; had few needs; and yet were accustomed to the rigors of wage labor!

These authors were captivated by the Puerto Rican women; however, they were not favorably impressed by Puerto Rican men. In striking contrast to the photographic and textual presence of women, men—even those of property, commerce, and government—were noticeably absent. It is impossible to find

Figure 2.4. Girls Assorting Coffee at Yauco, Porto Rico. Bryan, *Our Islands.*

an individual or group portrait of the men of the elite in any of the popular books. This absence symbolically evoked the necessity of a masculine presence, that of the U.S. government and its functionaries. The dominant class, in the guise of aristocratic women, was cultured but not fit to lead or govern. In an era when women neither voted nor held public office, the profusion of feminine representations, along with the absence of masculine ones, supported the more general conclusions that the people of Puerto Rico were entirely unfit for self-government.

When the popular books did describe the men of Puerto Rico, it was only in unfavorable terms.[18] Olivares found the aristocracy of San Juan to live in a state of continuous indolence:

The average denizen of San Juan is a silent, but most eloquent, exponent of habitual somnambulism. He appears to be perpetually wrapped in slumber. I have sometimes thought his ambulatory hours, if anything, the more restful, because therein he need never so much as dream of having to work. In the course of my visit I took occasion to inquire of a certain scion of this insouciant aristocracy what he considered the most violent tax on his exertions, where-upon, with a touch of genuine pathos in his tones, he replied: *Acostarme en la noche y levantarme en la mañana*—climbing into bed at night and crawling out in the morning.[19]

If Olivares found the men to be without vigor, Hamm did not find them very manly: "Muscular types of either manhood or womanhood are extremely rare; the arm of the average man being no better than of an American girl's of four-teen, and the leg being no larger or stronger than the arm of an average New York man. In social gatherings a Porto Rican gentleman seems a slender youth alongside of his colleague from England or America."[20]

In spite of the considerable energy expended in the disparagement and symbolic exclusion of Puerto Rican men, it was necessary to deal with the local leaders, even if only as subordinates. Accordingly, their presence was more readily apparent in documents of a more practical, administrative nature. The census of 1899, for example, included several group photographs of the local census takers, whom the military government had recruited from the cities and towns of Puerto Rico. Figure 2.5, which was the frontispiece to the census volume, showed the supervisors from the island's seven census districts. The photograph displayed all the signs of civilization. It was taken in a studio with a backdrop and a rug. The composition was a standard, symmetrical arrangement of four men standing and three seated in chairs. The men were all dressed in tai-lored, three-piece suits with ties. Three have visible watch chains and one wears spectacles. All are of light complexion and have well-groomed hair and beards or moustaches. Finally, and perhaps most important, the caption afforded them the status of a first and last name: "Supervisors of the Puerto Rican Census: Luis Muñoz Morales, Enrique Colóm, Manuel Baldrena, Guillermo Riefkohl [back], Luis Torregrosa, Ricardo Hernández, Félix Seijo [front]." By all appearances, they might be the prominent men of any American, European, or Latin Ameri-can city.[21] However, the underlying message was one of limited leadership and subordination. The report made clear that the War Department had undertaken the census with the cooperation of the prominent men and women of the prin-cipal towns. According to the census instructions, each of these supervisors and enumerators was required to be sworn "to the faithful performance of duties"

Figure 2.5. Supervisors of the Porto Rican Census. U.S. War Department, *Report on the Census of Porto Rico, 1899.*

according to the "form and manner prescribed by the Secretary of War."[22] As the experience in the Philippines more explicitly demonstrated, the census was an indicator of the peaceful state of affairs and civil order throughout the country.[23] It showed that the educated population was willing and able to work under the supervision of colonial administrators and that this collaboration worked. In addition, the ability to carry out a complete and accurate census of the island was an important prerequisite for the transition to civil government. The participation of the leading citizens and the educated men and women legitimized the work of the census and, in general, the War Department.[24] While the travelogues omitted men of the elite altogether, the official reports included photographs of them in clearly subservient positions within the administration of the military, and later civil, government. Special Commissioner Henry Carroll also mentioned the leading men of Puerto Rico, sometimes as a group, sometimes by name, and his conclusions supported the policy of imperial rule based upon collaboration and limited self-government.[25]

Nevertheless, the elite shared considerable values with the officials of the new regime. Indeed, one could argue that the elite were not even perceived as "others" and that there was, in fact, a meeting of the minds regarding autonomous

government and economic development.[26] The elite, however, expected that
"autonomy" would be politics as usual on the island and their exercise of patronage, at least at the municipal level, would be held intact or even expanded.
Recently granted an autonomous government by the Spanish, they hoped for a
U.S.-style territorial government with even more political power. Instead, they
were disappointed when colonial administrators established firm central control
over the government and regularly admonished or removed municipal leaders
for corruption, inefficiency, and party politics. It was as if the elites and colonial
administrators were speaking a common political language but with different
meanings. Conflicts and resistance to the new regime arose primarily over the
meanings, practices, and extent of autonomy and democratic participation.[27]

Cuban Virtues

Before the war with Spain, the adventure of Evangelina Cisneros garnered
headline after headline in the U.S. press.[28] Her plight became a call to arms.
According to reports in the New York Journal, Evangelina had been imprisoned
for refusing the advances of a Spanish official and for her revolutionary sympathies. She was taken into custody in her hometown and then imprisoned in
Havana, where she was sentenced to serve time in a Spanish penal colony. William Randolph Hearst, the editor of the New York Journal, vowed to free Evangelina. He mobilized a campaign of letters and petitions sent by U.S. women to the
New York Journal, U.S. officials, the queen of Spain, and the pope. When these
efforts produced no results, he sent a young reporter, Carl Decker, to plan and
execute Evangelina's escape from jail. This rescue was successful, and Evangelina was soon in the care of women in New York. In the popular press, the cause
of Evangelina was understood as a symbol of the cause of Cuban liberty. The les-
son for foreign policy was clear: men must take action and intervene militarily
in Cuba. Mere diplomacy would not suffice. The daring and chivalrous actions
in the aid of Evangelina implied that military intervention of the United States
against the Spanish to aid Cuba was both manly and effective.

Olivares recounted the story and provided photographs of the principal
locations: the girlhood home of Evangelina in Nueva Gerona, Isle of Pines; the
residence of the former Spanish mayor (alcalde) in Nueva Gerona who first
imprisoned Evangelina; the jail at Nueva Gerona, interior and exterior views; the
jail in Havana (Recojidas); the street in Havana by which she made her escape.
Two of these photographs showed the new mayor of Nueva Gerona, a Cuban
revolutionary who had tried unsuccessfully to protect Evangelina from the Spanish official.[29] Olivares also included a sketch (not a photograph) of Evangelina
(figure 2.6).

Figure 2.6. Evangelina Betancourt Cisneros (sketch). Bryan, *Our Islands.*

The story, as Olivares recounted it after the war, was more complex than previous historical analyses had granted, especially with regard to the ending. It was indeed a compelling romance: the rescue of a beautiful young woman from the clutches of her abuser by a chivalrous gentleman. In this story Evangelina represented Cuba, and the old mayor, Spain. The American reporter, Decker, represented the United States. However, in Olivares's account, several Cuban men were important, especially Carlos Carbonel, who, working with Decker, arranged Evangelina's escape from jail and transit to the United States. Indeed, it is doubtful that Decker could have accomplished very much without the participation of Carbonel, who maintained communication with the imprisoned Evangelina, drove the getaway coach, and provided a safe house. Evangelina, disguised as a sailor, left Havana for New York by ship a few days later in the company of Decker.

The story did not end, however, with Evangelina's escape to New York. According to Olivares, Carbonel had fallen in love with Evangelina during the few days they had spent together after her escape from jail. After the war, Carbonel arranged to travel to New York on official business (he was by then a lieutenant under the command of Fitzhugh Lee) and took the opportunity to meet with Evangelina. He declared his love for her, and she reciprocated his affections. They were married soon after and made their home in the suburbs of Havana.[30]

What, then, of Cuban men? Hoganson concluded that the newspapers tended to write Cuban men out of the story.[31] However, she also noted that the more ardent supporters of Cuban independence recognized Cuban men as brothers in the struggle for liberty. The geologist Robert Hill published a description of Cuba in the May 1898 issue of *National Geographic Magazine*. In his discussion of Cubans, he wrote the following: "Under the influence of their surroundings, they have developed into a gentle, industrious, and normally peaceable race, not to be judged by the combativeness which they have developed under a tyranny such as had never been imposed upon any other people. The better class . . . are certainly the finest, the most valiant, and most independent men of the island, while the women have the highest type of beauty. It is their boast that no Cuban woman has ever become a prostitute, and crime is certainly unknown to them."[32]

Hill was emphatic in his criticism of "Spanish misrule" and sympathetic in his support for the struggle for "self-government" and "Cuba Libre." His description of Cubans emphasized that although they were of "Spanish blood," they were an entirely "different class" of people, possessing "strong traits of civilized character." They were learned professionals, both in Cuba and in the various countries to which they had been forced to migrate, including the United States. The women were both beautiful and virtuous. They had supported their men in the cause for Cuban independence and were consequently imprisoned and abused by the Spanish. Hill's short piece articulated the basic elements of the narrative: the men, especially those of the "better class," were heroic in their struggle against Spanish misrule and oppression; the women were their virtuous companions. These "Cubans" were white. He discussed the black and colored population in another section with the rubric "Negroes." He stated that the "black and colored people of the island as a class are more independent and manly in their bearing than their brethren of the United States." The mixture of "Negroes" with "Spanish stock" produced a "superior class of free mulattoes of the Antonio Maceo type."[33]

White also included these common elements. According to him, the Spanish regime had abused both women and children, who were still (in 1898) wracked by poverty and starvation in the countryside. Urban women were beautiful but rarely ventured from the privacy of their homes unaccompanied by men. The open window casements permitted him glimpses of domestic life, but the feminine inhabitants were ensconced behind "light iron railings." Regarding Cuban men, White considered the insurgents to be decidedly inferior as soldiers when compared to the U.S. Army. Nevertheless, he defended their valor and heroism in the face of insurmountable odds and cautioned against "shallow judgments" that did not take into due consideration "centuries of life under the Spanish yoke and the demoralizing tutelage of Spanish methods." Indeed, he defended their claim to have "fought so heroically and tirelessly for the priceless boon of liberty."[34]

Even Murat Halstead, one of the most vocal expansionists and supporters of the military adventures in Cuba, Puerto Rico, and the Philippines, granted the role of protagonist to the Cuban leadership. He included in his book, *A History of American Expansion* (1898), a composite portrait of the "Last Revolutionists of Spanish-America": Antonio Maceo, José Martí, Máximo Gómez, and Calixto García (figure 2.7). This portrait was adorned with the Cuban flag, machetes, and palm fronds, which symbolized the nation, its poorly equipped armed revolt, and its tropical geography respectively. The composite portrait was of the same style and size used to portray other protagonists of the imperial wars: "Men of Spain"; "Our Young Naval Heroes"; "Men of the Army"; "Military Governors and Leaders."[35] In contrast, the author included only a small inset photograph of Emilio Aguinaldo in this volume and completely excluded any photographs of Puerto Rican political leaders or the Hawaiian royalty. For Halstead, the important protagonists in this overseas expansion were the Cubans, who needed help in their valiant struggle; the Spanish, who were oppressing them; the victorious armed forces (army and navy) of the United States; and the dedicated colonial administrators who subsequently followed.

Olivares also emphasized the courageous men and virtuous women who had fought for the Cuban cause. A very popular image (both textual and photographic) was the Cuban woman ensconced in her home, often standing in a window covered by bars.[36] Townsend, the photographer for *Our Islands and Their People,* elaborated upon this idea and produced the unique composition in figure 2.8. In his photograph, a Cuban patriot who lost an arm in battle with the Spanish on the outskirts of Cardenas protects the honor of his sister, secluded behind the casement bars of her window. The caption reads: "The young Cuban leaning against the barred casement of his sister's apartment was formerly a Lieutenant in the patriot army, and lost his arm in one of the battles in the outskirts of his native town." This caption signaled various elements of fundamental discursive

Figure 2.7. Last Revolutionists of Spanish-America. Halstead, *The History of American Expansion.*

Figure 2.8. A Pretty Cardenas Senorita and Her Battle-Scarred Brother. Bryan, *Our Islands.*

importance. The young man was an officer (which suggested his elite status) in a patriot army—that is, a legitimate army of national liberation. He had made sacrifices for the cause of Cuban liberty. Finally, he was no longer in the army, so he was ready to serve, perhaps, in civilian capacity in the provisional government. He had earned the right to govern.

In sum, the representations of Cuban men stressed their patriotism and heroism, while the images of Cuban women stressed their beauty and virtue.

Metaphorically, Cuba was attractive and under the watchful eye of jealous, patriotic menfolk. The acknowledgment of Cuban men as manly patriots and women as their virtuous companions provided a symbolic justification for Cuban independence. It was a symbolic recognition of their armed resistance to Spanish colonial rule and their status as a nation of free people. Still, there was a lingering question. These men had shown the will and the capacity to fight, but were they able to govern? The answer would turn on the issue of race, as we shall see in the following chapter.

Hawaiian Eve

The textual descriptions of Hawaiian women all agreed that they were beautiful, passionate, uninhibited, happy, hospitable, and kind. The authors usually focused upon the exotic characteristics of the women, especially the customs of *hula-hula*, luau, and their sexual hospitality. Regarding their beauty, one of the most elaborate descriptions came from Senator Henry Cabot Lodge, writing in *The New America and the Far East*. The following is his description of the single Hawaiian woman: "The young *waihine*, woman, a dazzling vision of sparkling eyes, pearly teeth, bright flowers, and bare legs, is never more happy than when, astride of her flying pony, she startles the timid stranger with her boldness of address, her voluptuous bust rounding in graceful curves, her undaunted head bound with a brilliant bandeau, a riding-robe of orange or crimson encircling her waist, hips, and limbs, and thence suspended waving on each side like triumphal banners in token of confident victory, as she dashes past as free and fleet as the trade-wind fanning her brow." Likewise, he described the married Hawaiian woman in unequivocal terms: "With her profusion of raven hair, tied with a gay bandelet of feathers and ohia blossoms, softly expressive dark eyes, pleasant countenance, erect figure, graceful and steady carriage, she commands the admiration of the beholder."[37]

The hula dancer appeared as the most common representation of the exotic nature of the Hawaiian women. In his volume in *The New America and the Far East* series Lodge included a full-page color photograph (figure 2.9). The dancer was dressed in a ti-leaf skirt and was adorned with a lei of flowers and leaves. She was barefoot with anklets. Her torso was covered with a camisole, suggesting a modicum of modesty only barely containing an excess of sensuality. Rather than dancing, however, she struck a rather defiant pose, suggesting the boldness and directness described by Lodge. Olivares included photographs of dancers in similar dress—a grass skirt with a camisole—in *Our Islands and Their People*. He noted, however, that "The Hula is the national dance, but it is not so much indulged in now as formerly; it has also been modified in many respects, both as

Figure 2.9. A Hawaiian Hula Dancer. Browne, *The New America,* vol. 1.

to the dress of the participants and the character of the dance. [One] photograph represents the Hula girls in their native costume, which is not now worn except on very rare occasions."[38]

In other words, the exotic hula dancer in her ti-leaf skirt was a thing of the past, even though authors focused upon her as the principal representation of Hawaiian women. Indeed, one of the photographs supplied by Lodge showed some of the recent changes in the costume of the hula dancer (figure 2.10). In it, the dancers were dressed in mid-length, full cloth skirts with long-sleeved, high-necked blouses. They were barefoot with anklets. Lodge included another photograph of dancers wearing stockings and shoes.

Other photographs showed the custom of the luau, a "native feast." Figure 2.11 appeared originally in *Our Islands,* but it also appeared in several later books, an indicator of its popularity.[39] The photograph showed a group of women and children outdoors. The group is seated on the ground at a banquet in a lush tropical setting. They are eating with their hands from traditional gourd bowls. The women are naked to the waist and are partially covered by leis or palm fronds. Two women hold guitars. Their nudity suggests their sensuality and sexuality, even though the leaves and ferns connote a certain modesty and the

Figure 2.10. Hula Girls. Browne, *The New America,* vol. 1.

Figure 2.11. Luau or Native Feast. Bryan, *Our Islands.*

tropical naturalness of the setting suggests innocence. Olivares penned the following caption: "While nominally Christian, the natives still adhere to many of their old pagan superstitions, some of which resemble the ancient Druidical worship of the early Britons. The feast represented in this photograph partakes of that character, and is at the same time a social picnic enlivened by music and singing."[40] Olivares thus suggested that although they were Christians, the natives were never far removed from their ancient customs. Still, their pagan ways were almost European. Their love of nature was almost religious. Their hospitality was legendary: "It was their custom while in a state of paganism to surrender their grass huts, and even their wives and daughters, to the full and free gratification of strangers who visited them." The Hawaiians were portrayed as natural, sensual beings, "gentle in heart and pure in life," only once removed from the state of nature. Of course, the pagan and promiscuous customs of old had been modified under the influence of Christianity, but they still expressed themselves in the pleasant sociability and hospitality of the inhabitants. The current manifestations of the old customs, especially the luau, were a throwback but not a drawback.[41] Indeed, the luau was adapted by haoles as well, who turned it into a luxurious picnic.[42]

Figure 2.12. Natives Preparing Poi. Browne, *The New America*, vol. 1.

The descriptions of the Hawaiians did not distinguish much between the activities of men and women. Both were equally fond of "idle pleasures" and "entertainments" such as the luau, swimming, surfing on longboards, fishing, gathering flowers, and tending their taro patches. Photographs of these pastimes were frequent. On the first page of his *New America* volume, Lodge showed a full-page color photograph of a man and woman working together pounding taro to make poi (figure 2.12).[43] They are sitting on low benches and using simple instruments. Lodge also included a full-page color photograph of a shrimp fisherman using a simple net as he sits on a rock along the shore (figure 2.13).[44] Olivares explained that Hawaiians scarcely regarded these activities as work; rather they were part of their simple subsistence lifestyle:

> The Kanaka [native Hawaiians] despise labor. Indeed, it is not usual to see a native work even around his own home except to care for his taro patch, and in this he is as affectionate to his lily plants as he is with wife and children. The taro furnishes the starchy poe [*sic*], as necessary to him as water to drink or the sea in which to bathe. The Hawaiian women will wade waist deep in the water and mud banks for clams and shrimps, or scramble among the rocks at low tide to gather the sea weeds and mollusks and the cuttlefish, and seine the small fry that remain in the little wells and lakelets left among the rocks when the tide goes out. They will gather the leaves and the succulent roots and the

Figure 2.13. Shrimp Fisherman, Hawaii. Browne, *The New America,* vol. 1.

tubers of the artichokes and *ti,* and wild potato ferns and other native vegetation, for food; and they will gather the tube roses and the myriads of wild flowers and string them upon the fibers of the plantain, thus creating the famous leis and wreaths with which to bedeck their lovers or friends, or to sell. Of all this, however, the Hawaiian makes light, declaring it a diversion most enjoyable. If it were demanded of them, they would likely refuse.[45]

Olivares's description, amply documented by photographs, portrayed the Hawaiians as natives very close to a state of nature with a veneer of civilization. They lived close to the land and the shore and were not inclined to labor except to meet their simple needs, so they would not meet the demand for labor on the plantations. Many of the photographs portrayed customs that by the end of the nineteenth century had been modified under the influence of the Euro-American settlers and missionaries. They represented a style of life that scarcely survived but that still defined their character. Figure 2.14 shows the adoption of Western clothing: the women appear in dresses with long sleeves and high collars. Their hair is carefully arranged, pulled up and back rather than long and flowing. They adorn themselves with traditional leis of flowers and leaves both in their hair and around their necks. This was a studio photograph with a symmetrical arrangement in front of a tropical tapestry. Three women in the back were seated, yet the chairs were not visible. In front, two women recline on the floor. The photograph presented a juxtaposition of Victorian style—the style of dress and the studio portrait—with the exotic charms of Hawai'i—reclining women adorned with leis. Such descriptions and photographs suggested that the Hawaiian woman, most beautiful and desirable, could be educated and civilized without losing her enchanting and exotic charms. She was a native of paradise who could be possessed by the civilized man. Furthermore, the rather passive, childlike Hawaiian men were hospitable and had welcomed their foreign visitors, who in turn had taken over the island. Hawaiian women frequently married Euro-American settlers, who, by teaching them Christian norms, had eliminated little by little their nudity and sexual customs, which were understood as promiscuous. Yet as these descriptions suggest, they were never far from their exotic ways.[46]

Disillusion in the Philippines

"Civilized women," wrote Olivares, "are very much alike the world over, in their refining and elevating influence. They are poetic by instinct and are always looking for the beautiful and the good."[47] Accordingly, observers found the upper-class women of Manila—usually described as either Spanish or mestiza—to be quite attractive. The most attractive were of mixed Spanish and Tagalog blood. Olivares wrote, "Among the Mestizo [sic] girls of Spanish fathers there are many who possess a wonderful beauty. They are lithe and graceful in form and figure, with soft olive complexions, scarlet lips and teeth white as pearls; long, waving, jet-black hair, and dark, languishing eyes that glow with the subdued passions of the tropics. Many of these girls have been highly educated in the convents, and possess a culture and refinement of manner equal to that of the best American and European Society."[48]

Figure 2.14. Hawaiian Girls' Style of Dressing. Browne, *The New America*, vol. 1.

Notwithstanding this favorable description of the educated mestizas, Olivares found a profound difference between these refined upper-class women and those of the lower classes. He attributed a very low level of civilization to the latter: "There are many grades and classes of women in the Philippine Islands. Some are as highly cultivated and perhaps almost as beautiful as the divine creatures who impart so great a charm to American society; but a majority of the women of this archipelago belong to a low grade of civilization, and some are but little above the condition of beast of field and forest."[49] On one extreme, he found "divine creatures," while on the other, most women were only barely civilized "beasts." In this context, low civilization translated as ugliness. Other authors also found the "Malay girls," in contrast to the "Spanish" women, to be dark skinned, homely, poorly dressed, and possessing of revolting habits.

White offered up a striking comparison: "Pretty [Spanish] women, bare-headed, and dressed in cool, refreshing white, look enchanting to one who has seen nothing but yellow and brown Malay girls all summer and whose experiences in society have been confined to young, barefooted Philippine ladies who

Figure 2.15. Type of High-Class Woman of Manila. White, *Our New Possessions,* 1898.

smoke cigars and wear gauze waists with rags reefed around them."[50] Moreover, his text directed the reader away from the possible conclusion, based upon these popular photographs of women in native costumes, that the Filipinas were attractive. His own book included a high-class woman of Manila with an "admixture of Chinese blood" (figure 2.15). In the caption, he described Malay women like her as "delicate in form and feature." Nevertheless, in order to avoid any misreading, he was compelled to refute published photographs of attractive women by means of a rather surprising tactic. The photographs, he argued, were deceiving and did not correspond to his everyday experience in the Philippines: "The women in their costumes may look very pretty in the selected costumes we see printed [in photographs], but as we saw them every day about Manila they are, as a rule, the most unattractive women to be found anywhere. It is true that their novel dress and appearance may make them interesting for a time, but their filthy tobacco and other repulsive habits make them anything but attractive."[51]

Like many other writers, White incorporated the themes of misreading and disillusion into the discussion of the Filipinas. The narrative structure was fairly simple. At first sight, as the story went, the women seemed attractive due to their "novel dress and appearance." Studio photographs served only to further mislead. This first impression, however, was a gross misrepresentation since upon closer contact, the women were found to be "anything but attractive." The initial misreading, followed by a rude awakening, led to a singular deprecation and disgust.[52]

Likewise, Olivares refuted previous descriptions and elicited the correct interpretation: "A native author declares that, as a rule, 'the Mestizo girls are often of wonderful beauty,' but his imagination appears to be more vivid than the facts warrant."[53] Here Olivares quoted Ramon Reyes Lala, the Manila-born author of *The Philippines Islands,* which was published in 1899.[54] Lala and Olivares printed many of the exact same photographs, but their respective descriptions varied considerably. Lala described these native women in the most favorable terms (figure 2.16). Of the upper-class women, he wrote the following: "Many of the women are pretty, and all are good-natured and smiling. Their complexion, of light brown, is usually clear and smooth; their eyes are large and lustrous, full of the sleeping passion of the Orient. The figures of the women are usually erect and stately, and many are models of grace and beauty."[55]

Olivares had mixed feelings regarding the high-class women. He published the same photograph as that shown in figure 2.16 with a caption that emphasized their elegant dress and their ability to "converse as fluently as the women of civilized countries."[56] However, in another caption he stated that the "cast of countenance" of the Malay women (in contrast to the Spanish-influenced mestizas) "shows plainly in the rather unpleasant scowl of their faces."[57] Olivares also incorporated various versions of the above-mentioned trope of expectation, misreading, disillusion, and deprecation. One of the most elaborate accounts came from Will Levington Comfort, a correspondent from St. Louis who provided Olivares with the following narrative. Comfort's story began with great expectations upon his arrival in Manila after very favorable impressions of the

Figure 2.16. Native Women. Lala, *The Philippine Islands.*

women in both Puerto Rico and Cuba. In the following section, he related his disappointment with the Filipinas, explained his inability to understand or communicate with them, and finally described their characteristics in the most unflattering terms:

> After seeing Porto Rican and Cuban maidens, a man entering Manila will expect to be thrilled again by great, lustrous, dark eyes; but the glance of the Filipino woman will never thrill you. Her eyes are not large, but they are black

and beady and unreadable. Very often hunger looks out at you; often hatred, but it is not passionate hatred. It is a stare which neither revolts nor appeals. It seems to be the result of instinct, rather than an action of the brain. Vaguely the thought sinks into your mind as you peer into her dull, unsmiling face—the thought that her gaze has been fixed so long upon the tragedy of living that she regards it stolidly now. Her nose is flat and thick-skinned. The cavities are haplessly visible, and a play of the nostrils is wholly impossible. Hence the fine charm of sensitiveness is denied her. The nose of the Filipino woman is for breathing purposes only, and it is the most ugly of her uncomely features. Her brow is insignificant and hair grows low upon it. Her lips and teeth are of a hue best expressed by bronze-vermillion, such is the combined stain of tobacco and the betel nut. Her hair is dead black. The lack-luster effect is probably caused by continued exposure to the sun. Frequently it falls down to her waist and is never braided. When freshly combed it presents a drippy appearance, because it is soaked [with cocoanut oil] to make it shine.[58]

Comfort's unflattering details of the features of the Filipina seem excessive, if not obsessive. He was not satisfied to say simply that she was unattractive, but rather took the time to thoroughly consider her particular features: the nose and nostrils, the eyes, the brow, the lips and teeth, the facial expressions, the color and texture of the hair, the color and complexion of the skin. He also considered her habits of smoking tobacco, chewing betel nut, and combing her hair with cocoanut oil. Finally, he speculated on her mental state, which for him was unreadable and incomprehensible, "as hard to fathom as a sheet of Chinese correspondence." There was little doubt, however, of her dislike for the "white man." Finally, the correspondent concluded: "From the white man's standpoint she is least like a woman of any feminine creature."[59]

Central to this trope was the shift from descriptions of women of the upper class to those of the lower. Lower-class women were not only unattractive, but also they were neither hospitable nor sociable. Olivares pictured a native fruit seller (figure 2.17) and wrote in the caption that the women of the "lower orders have an unpleasant cast of countenance, which indicates a surly disposition." He found that none of the women who sold fruits and flowers on the street were good looking, and their "dispositions are not, as a rule, of the most loveable character." The final degradation of the Filipinas was the following simile: "Her presence is needful, like that of the *carabao* [water buffalo]." Despite any virtues they might have—loyalty to the family, love of children, hard work—the authors reduced these women to a beast of burden, the water buffalo. The *carabao* would also appear as a metaphor for men; we shall take up that issue

Figure 2.17. Native Fruit Seller. Bryan, *Our Islands.*

in the following chapter concerning the "Filipino character." It should suffice at this point to say that these hateful, scowling, ugly women were the counterparts of their rebellious menfolk, who were portrayed as unruly children who dared rise up in armed resistance when their claim to an independent country was denied. Indeed, Will Comfort suggested the underlying cause of the animosity and discordance of the Filipina was the war that the United States was waging against the Filipino revolutionaries: "[The Filipina] cannot understand why these white men with guns intrude upon her ancient customs. She doesn't like the white man anyway. Her eyes tell him so, and she wishes he were back in his own land."[60]

The narrative of disillusion suggested the initial goodwill and high expectations of the United States, as well as the unjustified and ungrateful reaction of the Filipinas and, by extension, their menfolk. This negative image, similar in tone and substance to the pejorative racial stereotypes of savagery, was largely a product of the war. It articulated both the depths of Filipino resistance to the colonial regime and the lack of sympathy and understanding toward them on the part of U.S. observers. It also suggested that although pacification had been achieved and civil government established, eventual independence, not assimilation, would be the long-term goal. In the meantime, colonial rule would provide the necessary political control over a population that was not, at least at first, cooperative. Collaboration would require new strategies, both practical and discursive.[61]

* * *

The texts of the period used the feminine metaphor to paint a sympathetic picture of the Puerto Rico, Cuba, and Hawai'i under U.S. dominion.[62] The use of feminine representations provided an important justification for U.S. political and cultural hegemony. More than a simple justification, however, the descriptions of women would suggest certain paradigms that paralleled the particular strategies of rule in each site. In general, the native woman became an important rhetorical figure to elicit sympathy and desire.[63] Yet each island—"woman"— had her own charms, her own story. The narrative that justified the intervention of the United States in the Cuban revolution against Spain had been the "damsel in distress." Immediately following the end of the war, Cuban women were found to be not only beautiful, but also virtuous and patriotic. They stood alongside their brave, protective menfolk, who had fought for their independence against the Spanish and earned the right to rule. The United States had promised to help the cause of liberty in Cuba but later decided that Cubans should not be left entirely to their own devices. The United States would help

set up a formally independent government but would establish the legal right
of direct intervention in Cuban affairs. For all practical purposes, it treated the
country as a protectorate. It recognized the legitimacy of the nationalist elite but
had only limited confidence in its capacity.

The refined, educated women of Puerto Rico represented the grand contribution of Spanish civilization to the island. This appraisal symbolically cleared
the way for the bold, aggressive entrance of the United States. First, it defined
the existing accomplishments of civilization as a result of "Spanish" influence
upon the local populations. Second, it characterized Spanish civilization as
effeminate, antiquated, and unproductive; even the male elite was portrayed as
effeminate and passive. These gender representations managed to both displace
the Spanish influence and suggest the necessity of a masculine presence, symbolized by the United States, which would introduce a modern, dynamic civilization in Puerto Rico. In this narrative of backwardness yielding to progress,
the Puerto Rican woman offered a very special interest: she was pretty, hard
working, and of mixed race. This image provoked sympathy, even desire, but
also established fundamental inequalities. Practically speaking, it suggested the
possibilities of cultural and economic assimilation but circumvented any discussion of independence; it was right to assist these women (and children, as
we shall see in chapter 4), but they were not proper political subjects. The male
elite were recognized as subordinate collaborators, especially in the documents
of a more administrative nature, such as the census. This paradox of uplift and
assimilation without political equality would result in the creation of a new kind
of governance: a colonial tutorial state in a territory that belonged to, but was not
a part of, the United States.

The rhetoric of desire reached its culmination in the descriptions of
Hawai'i. The Hawaiian woman was incomparable: an Eve in paradise under
the missionary influence. While many photographs presented partially nude
Hawaiian women in outdoor scenes, other photographs showed their adoption of European dress together with the traditional adornments of flowers and
leaves. The Hawaiian woman, beautiful and desirable, could be educated and
civilized without losing her exotic charms. When located within a narrative of
white settlement and democratic evolution (chapter 4), this representation suggested a close, intimate political relationship with the United States: complete
assimilation and full annexation.

In striking contrast, the new-possessions books used a negative portrayal
of women to paint the local peoples of the Philippines in the most unfavorable
light. In this case, the feminine metaphor served to express just the opposite
of sympathy and desire. In contrast to the women of other islands, the Filipina

turned out to be a great disillusion: somewhat attractive at first glance, she was, upon closer inspection, most undesirable under the imperial gaze. The authors narrated their disillusion and deception in considerable detail, analyzing each physical aspect of her ugliness. They were shocked at her hatred for the white man. Thus, the figure of the Filipina became but an object of rhetorical deprecation—but not the only one, as we shall see in the following chapter regarding the analogy of tribes. It is no coincidence that it was precisely in the Philippines that the United States found the most tenacious armed resistance to the colonial regime. These hateful women, along with their unruly and uncivilized men, could not presently govern themselves, could not survive in the international context, and so must be controlled absolutely and ruled directly. These gendered representations suggested that the period of tutelage might be indefinite, but the Philippines would never be assimilated. Consequently, the United States projected, first, pacification, and then civil government firmly under the control of colonial administrators. The most civilized and cooperative of the elite were both necessary and proved to be open to cooptation. Again, political tutelage would become the order of the new regime.

Notes

1. Bederman, *Manliness and Civilization,* 42.

2. Ibid., 25–28. Bederman does not explicitly consider class differences as a particular feature of civilization.

3. Johnson, *Latin America in Caricature.*

4. Hoganson, *Fighting for American Manhood.* Hoganson's book is a contribution to the project defined by Joan Scott in her book, *Gender and the Politics of History* (New York: Columbia University Press, 1988). Scott showed how symbolic representations of gender, which were embedded in social institutions, evoked normative interpretations, produced subjective identities, and expressed—even produced—relations of power. In her empirical studies of the French working classes and her reflections on the working-class historiography of France, England, and the United States, she argued that gender was a "primary field within which or by means of which power is articulated" (45). By this she meant that gender, composed of its symbolic, normative, institutional, and subjective elements, both legitimized and constructed social relationships, including, of course, relations of power. Scott's definition, however, ignored the importance of race or ethnicity in both gender and politics and was limited to an analysis of the circumscribed field of working-class politics in the national arena. Both Hoganson and Bederman extended Scott's analysis and showed the complex interconnections between gender and race in the process of U.S. continental and overseas expansion.

5. Bederman, *Manliness and Civilization,* 184–186, 196. The process of civilizing inferior races, of racial competition, could overcome the problem of overcivilized racial decadence. Constant expansion of the white race became a racial imperative, the only remedy to the danger of the effeminate tendencies of the most advanced civilization. "This concept of overcivilized decadence let Roosevelt construct American imperialism as a conservative way to retain the race's frontier-forged manhood, instead of what it really was—a belligerent grab for a radically new type of nationalistic power. As Roosevelt described it, asserting the white man's racial power abroad was necessary to avoid losing the masculine strength Americans had already established through race war on the frontier. . . . If they retained their manhood, they could continue to look forward to an ever higher civilization, as they worked ever harder for racial improvement and expansion. But if American men ever lost their virile zest for Darwinistic racial contests, their civilization would soon decay. If they ignored the ongoing racial imperative of constant expansion and instead grew effeminate and luxury-loving, a manlier race would inherit their mantle of the highest civilization" (186). However, this imperialist manliness was not completely self-serving since it aimed at the uplift of the primitive peoples and sought the general advancement of civilization.

6. Roosevelt, "The Strenuous Life."

7. Hoganson, *Fighting for American Manhood;* Bederman, *Manliness and Civilization.*

8. Roosevelt, "The Strenuous Life," 5–6.

9. In Bryan, *Our Islands,* p. 384.

10. Margherita Arlina Hamm, *Porto Rico and the West Indies* (London: F. Tennyson Neely, 1899). For more on Hamm, see *Who Was Who in America,* vol. 1 (1897–1942) (Chicago: A. N. Marquis, 1943), 512. According to *Neely's Panorama of Our New Possessions,* she was the "inspector of supplies" in Puerto Rico. She is listed as photographer, along with Gilson Willets and Burr McIntosh, in *Photographic Views of Our New Possessions* (Chicago: Waverly Publishing, n.d.). The same thirty photos that appear in her volume on Puerto Rico also appear in *Neely's Panorama.* I assume Hamm was the photographer.

11. Hamm, *Porto Rico,* 66–67. Silvia Álvarez has recognized the uniqueness of this book and provides an interesting analysis of it. She refers to the introduction of the U.S. symbols in Puerto Rico as a "battle of the signs." Nevertheless, instead of a battle, her article details the rapid acceptance and widespread use of these same symbols locally. See Silvia Álvarez Curbelo, "La batalla de los signos: La invasión norteamericana de 1898 y la vida cotidiana en Puerto Rico," *Revista Mexicana del Caribe* 1, no. 2 (1996): 202–215.

12. Hamm, *Porto Rico,* 117.

13. Ibid., 65–66.

14. White, *Our New Possessions,* 357.

15. In Browne, *The New America,* vol. 8, 1418. Allen wrote the section on Puerto

Rico in this volume. This poem apparently referred to the women of Cuba, although Allen quoted it here as an apt description of Puerto Rican women as well.

16. Bryan, *Our Islands*, 325.

17. It should be noted, however, that smiling for a photograph was not the norm in this period.

18. In her study of English literature, Krishnaswamy argues that "effeminism" was a discourse that discredited colonized men by stressing their lack of masculinity. See Revathi Krishnaswamy, *Effeminism: The Economy of Colonial Desire* (Ann Arbor: University of Michigan Press, 1998). I would suggest that "effeminism" was strongest in Puerto Rico and Hawai'i and weakest in Cuba. For a discussion of the deployment of gender metaphors in a citizenship case in the Supreme Court, see Sam Erman, "Meanings of Citizenship in the U.S. Empire: Puerto Rico, Isabel González, and the Supreme Court, 1898–1905," *Journal of American Ethnic History* 27, no. 4 (2008): 5–33.

19. In Bryan, *Our Islands*, 257.

20. Hamm, *Porto Rico*, 68.

21. Virginia Dominguez has published a detailed comparative study of the censuses of Cuba, the Philippines, and Puerto Rico. She argues persuasively that the inclusion of photographs of local census supervisors and enumerators was novel; it was not the norm for the U.S. censuses of the time. The censuses of Cuba and Puerto Rico followed a similar pattern: they included studio photographs of groups of supervisors and enumerators, both men and women. According to Dominguez's analysis, they appeared to be educated, well-dressed citizens who bore no resemblance to the stereotypical portrayals in the travel books. In contrast, the census of the Philippines emphasized the categorization and description of the "tribes" and bore all of the trappings of the construction of the colonial subject as "other." See Virginia Dominguez, "When the Enemy Is Unclear: U.S. Censuses and Photographs of Cuba, Puerto Rico, and the Philippines from the Beginning of the 20th Century," *Comparative American Studies* 5, no. 2 (2007): 173–203.

22. *Census of Porto Rico, 1899*, 361.

23. Section 6 of the organic act of 1902 ordered a census to be taken after the pacification of the Filipinos: "That whenever the existing insurrection in the Philippine Islands shall have ceased and a condition of general and complete peace shall have been established therein and the fact shall be certified to the President by the Philippine Commission, the President, upon being satisfied thereof, shall order a census of the Philippine Islands to be taken by the Philippine Commission." "An Act Temporarily to Provide for the Administration of the Affairs of Civil Government in the Philippine Islands," *U.S. Statutes at Large*, vol. 32 (1902), 693.

24. For example, General Davis, in his report as outgoing military governor, included a photograph of the Puerto Rican Supreme Court in the new civil government.

George Davis, *Report of the Military Governor of Porto Rico on Civil Affairs*, in *Annual Reports of the War Department for the Fiscal Year Ended June 30, 1900*, 56th Cong., 2nd sess., House of Representatives, House Document 2, part 13 (Washington: Government Printing Office, 1902).

25. Carroll, *Report*, passim.

26. García, "I Am the Other"; Dominguez, "When the Enemy Is Unclear." Both García and Dominguez argue that Puerto Ricans were not characterized as "others" in a radical and unambiguous fashion in the documents they examine. This point is well taken, and this may account for the high degree of integration of Puerto Rico to the United States as provided by the organic act. In addition, García argues that the elite shared core values with the U.S. officials and in this sense were not "others." An interesting twist to this argument is provided by Go. He argues that, for example, the shared values and vocabulary of "autonomy" masked a fundamental divergence in the actual meaning and practice of local self-government; see Go, *American Empire*. However, I do not believe that U.S. authorities ever considered the Puerto Rican elite to be equals and not "others" or foreigners. If the U.S. observers had recognized the Puerto Ricans as fully "kith and kin," as equals in every sense, they would not have excluded them from the body politic of the republic under the guise of an unincorporated territory.

27. Go, *American Empire*.

28. I have used summaries of newspaper accounts by Hoganson, *Fighting for American Manhood*, 56–62. Louis Pérez, Jr., analyzes this event in a similar fashion in *Cuba in the American Imagination: Metaphor and the Imperial Ethos* (Chapel Hill: University of North Carolina Press, 2008).

29. The photographs appear in Bryan, *Our Islands*, 55–58.

30. In Bryan, *Our Islands*, 155. In addition to the story of Evangelina and the photograph of the lieutenant and his sister, Olivares also recounted briefly the story of Ampara [sic] Obra, the girlfriend of a Cuban revolutionary, Antonio López de Colona. Ampara was from a "good family" of Matanzas, the "birthplace of Cuban liberty." While Antonio was in hiding, Ampara joined her "sweetheart," and both were captured by Spanish troops and imprisoned in the fortress of San Severino. She was released, but Antonio was transferred to El Morro prison in Havana. Escaping the vigilance of her parents, who had "locked her up" to keep her out of danger, Ampara took a horse, rode to Havana, gained admittance to the prison, and was married to Antonio by the prison chaplain. She stayed with Antonio in prison until they escaped later and joined up with the Cuban revolutionaries. According to Olivares, this "dauntless little woman" stayed by her husband, "nursing the wounded, riding a horse like a man, and armed with machete and revolver, which she could use on occasion" (134). Once again, Cuban women were presented as virtuous and brave patriots.

31. Hoganson, *Fighting for American Manhood*. See also L. Pérez, *The War of 1898*.

32. Robert Hill, "Cuba," *National Geographic Magazine* 9, no. 5 (1898): 229.

33. Ibid., 230.

34. White, *Our New Possessions,* 545, 555, 557, 585. White did not personify Spanish abuse in the figure of a Spanish gentleman or autocrat as most authors did. In another example of the personification of Spanish misrule and abuse, Leonard Wood recounted a story, set in the early nineteenth century, of Miralda Estales, who was almost forced to marry a Spanish gentleman until her Cuban suitor persuaded Governor Tacon to intervene. Furthermore, Wood described the "prison-like effect" of the horizontal bars in the windows of urban dwellings. In contrast to other authors, he described Cuban men as "light and graceful" since "their indolent lives have robbed them of those manly qualities we look for in men, to offset the gentler graces of their sisters." Wood's text appears in Browne, *The New America,* vol. 8, 1321, 1330–1336, 1351–1352.

35. Murat Halstead, *The History of American Expansion* (United Subscription Book Publishers of America, 1898). The titles indicated in the text were the captions to the composite portraits. The photographs appear on pages 362, 469, 487, and 703. The author also included composite portraits of the U.S. and Spanish peace commissions.

36. F. Tennyson Neely, *Neely's Photographs: Panoramic Views of Cuba, Porto Rico, Manila and the Philippines* (New York: F. Tennyson Neely, 1899); Neely's Educational Library, No. 10. Neely included several similar photographs.

37. In Browne, *The New America,* vol. 1, 163. Lodge included a photograph of the young women mounted on horseback, but it was of rather poor quality (see p. 117). Cf. Bryan, *Our Islands,* 471.

38. In Bryan, *Our Islands,* caption 455.

39. Among the other books, Boyce's *U.S. Colonies and Dependencies.*

40. In Bryan, *Our Islands,* 427.

41. The love of nature and sexual hospitality were linked conceptually in this discourse. See ibid., 425 and 454.

42. Browne, *The New America,* vol. 1, 154. The author included a photograph of a "Hawaiian Feast" on this page. It showed a large group sitting on mats before a very long, low table appointed with china and crystal.

43. Cf. White, *Our New Possessions,* 648.

44. Cf. Bryan, *Our Islands,* 508.

45. In ibid., 454–455. Olivares attributes this description to the Hon. John W. Stailey, designated as the author of chapter 21 in the Bryan volume. Regarding their childlike nature, he wrote the following: "The native Hawaiian—Kanaka, as he loves to designate himself—is constitutionally opposed to laboring in any manner. His wants, beyond his simple food and scant clothing, are so few; his ambitions so limited, and his cares so insignificant, as he views life, that there is really no need for exertion. Inordinately fond of idle pleasures, he is childish in his entertainments. Hospitable to a fault,

good natured, and honestly kind to a degree that is exceptional; tractable as a child, and honest in the highest sense, the kanaka is truly *sui generis* of the *genus homo*. The parent adores his children—all children, indeed—and the child worships the parent and holds old age sacred" (453).

46. For a detailed analysis of these representations in the context of late-nineteenth-century anthropology and the marketing of Hawai'i as a tourist destination, see Jane Desmond, "Picturing Hawai'i: The 'Ideal' Native and the Origins of Tourism, 1880–1915," *Positions: East Asia Cultures Critique* 7, no. 2 (1999): 459–501. Desmond reaches similar conclusions.

47. In Bryan, *Our Islands*, 589. Olivares made this generalization in the section on high-class Filipinas.

48. Ibid., 570.

49. Ibid., 589.

50. White, *Our New Possessions*, 167–168. Cf. Boyce: "The Tagalog women are not pretty, but many of the Mestizas are" (*U.S. Colonies and Dependencies*, 235).

51. White, *Our New Possessions*, 177–178.

52. Somewhat later, Brigadier General William Aumen provided one of the shortest versions of this trope: "Going along the streets one would notice a woman of good figure and apparently very fine looking, but when one came alongside of her, and looked into her face, he would see she was smoking a cigar and was marked with smallpox." In Lilian Powers and H. C. Phillips, eds., *Report of the Lake Mohonk Conference of Friends of the Indians and Other Dependent Peoples* (Lake Mohonk, N.Y., 1909), 106.

53. Bryan, *Our Islands*, caption to the photograph "Mestizo Boy and Girl," 550. Note that Olivares is not entirely consistent. Previously, he spoke favorably of the beautiful mestizas. Here, however, he questions that characterization.

54. Ramon Reyes Lala, *The Philippine Islands* (New York: Continental Publishing, 1899). Biographical information on Lala is provided in the preface.

55. Ibid., 93. The description of the mestizas, as cited by Olivares, was on the following page. The description read as follows: "The mestiza girls are, as a rule, often of wonderful beauty. They are lithe and graceful and of a soft olive complexion, with red lips, pearly teeth, and ravishing black eyes, whose long lashes droop coquettishly in response to the admiring glance of a stranger."

56. In Bryan, *Our Islands*, caption 645.

57. Ibid., caption 551.

58. The correspondent distinguished the Filipinas from the "Chinese, Japanese, Eurasians, Mestizos, or halfcastes, and pure Castilians" in Luzon. His description applied only to "the native Filipino [sic] female, who is in the villages, cities, highways, swamps, markets and rivers." He sought to describe the common women, not those of the elite (i.e., Castilian or Mestizo) "races." In Bryan, *Our Islands*, 590–591.

59. Ibid., 590.

60. Ibid., 591.

61. For an analysis of these shifts in politics and discourses, see Kramer, *The Blood of Government.*

62. I use the term "metaphor" in a most general sense as any rhetorical figure based upon a comparison or resemblance: the islands were like women. However, in a more technical sense, the feminine representations were synecdoches, which take a part (women) to represent the whole (each island group). See Tzvetan Todorov, *Symbolism and Interpretation* (Ithaca, N.Y.: Cornell University Press, 1982), 72–76.

63. Cf. Spurr, *The Rhetoric of Empire,* 170–183. Spurr identified twelve different rhetorical figures—tropes—of the European colonial discourse.

Chapter 3

Narratives of Evolution

The Control of the Tropics

The theory of social evolution informed much of the thinking about the peoples of the imperial archipelago. An English author, Benjamin Kidd, was widely read in the United States; his book, *Social Evolution,* published in 1894, was very popular, and a second edition followed the year after. In 1898, he published *The Control of the Tropics,* in which he applied his evolutionary ideas to the "foremost question occupying the attention of the American people": what would be the future government of the tropical regions? He argued that tropical products were extremely important for world trade, but tropical peoples had not shown themselves to be capable of either sustained economic development or good government. This situation provoked the problem of the "control of the tropics": how should the United States (as well as the European powers) rule in the tropics? Kidd spoke out against several historical alternatives. First, outright possession of the tropical lands, based upon the agricultural estate and forced labor, gave no regard to the well-being or progress of the local inhabitants. Second, tropical peoples had shown themselves incapable of free and independent government. Third, the self-governing "white" populations of the temperate climes were not suited to settle in the tropics, principally because they became isolated from their political and cultural traditions. The combination of factors two and three—the political incapacity of tropical peoples and the absence of extensive white settlement in the tropics—justified imperial rule. It meant that the "white man" must find ways to govern from afar. The countries of temperate climates must directly supervise the government of the tropics, but only for the benefit of the local inhabitants. Trade with the tropics must not be exploitative, but rather mutually beneficial to all participants.

Kidd argued that imperialism was a moral duty, a benevolent enterprise that would both expand world trade and civilize the tropics, which must be governed as a "trust undertaken in the name of civilization."[1] His emphasis on the benevolent mission of imperialism was a recurrent theme in U.S. imperial discourse. Indeed this notion was central to the argument that U.S. imperialism was fundamentally different from European, especially Spanish, imperialism. This idea provided a foundation of what later was known as "American exceptionalism."[2]

Kidd's formulation of the imperial problem was based upon a simple dichotomy: the relationship of the white man to the tropics. This formulation of the problem did not stress differences among the imperial subjects, but rather the stark contrast between the "white man" and the tropical "other." Nevertheless, Kidd's theory of social evolution implied both differences among the world's peoples and the possibility of improvement under the guidance of the "white man," a theme we will take up in the next chapter. Kidd's argument concerning the white race in the tropics provided a general justification for imperial rule, and it highlighted a similar concern among U.S. expansionists: the issue of white settlement. However, Kidd's argument was imprecise and inaccurate, even according to his own criteria. First, he overlooked the colonization of Cuba and Puerto Rico by Spanish and other European immigrants. Second, he completely ignored the settlement of Hawai'i by immigrants from the United States. For Kidd, the frontiers of white settlement established the limits of the imperial problem, but he inaccurately ruled out the efficacy of white settlement in the tropics and failed to consider its political implications. In contrast, U.S. expansionists were concerned specifically about the possibility of self-government among the white settler colonies in the tropics. First, Hawai'i was widely recognized as an *American* colony—that is, a white settler colony. It was the only site to be incorporated within the territorial scheme of the United States. Second, Cuba was recognized as to be under the control of a white *Cuban* elite and was thus accorded an independent government, albeit one limited by the right of intervention by the United States. Thus, Kidd's general argument regarding white settlement in the tropics was modified according to U.S. practice: where white Americans were hegemonic, territorial self-government applied (Hawai'i); other areas were more or less equipped for self-government depending upon the presence of an elite, preferably white, that had demonstrated its capacity to rule (Cuba).

As noted, Kidd's formulation of the problem of the control of the tropics did not stress differences among the subject peoples. Nevertheless, in his previous work on social evolution, Kidd had articulated a doctrine that emphasized cultural variation as a result of unequal and varied evolutionary progress. Differences with respect to race and culture were explained as the result of different stages of evolution. Progress was possible precisely because peoples might, with the guidance of the most advanced, become increasingly civilized. Thus, the notion of "race" was not entirely biological since it also stressed cultural aspects and the effects of climate. During this period, "race" and "culture" were not clearly distinguished, and the leading theories of social evolution adopted a Lamarckian perspective. The leading anthropologists of the nineteenth century—Lewis Henry Morgan, Edward Burnett Tylor, James George Frazer—were social evolutionists who stressed the comparative study of religion, kinship, and politics. Tylor, perhaps the first to develop an anthropological definition of "culture," argued that the three basic levels of civilization were related to the three basic types of religion: savages were animists, barbarians were polytheists, and civilized men were monotheists.[3] In the United States, leading sociologists—Albion Small, Franklin Giddings, and William I. Thomas—were also Lamarckian evolutionists who believed that although racial characteristics were inherited, they were ultimately the product of social and environmental factors. "Race temperaments," "customs," or "habits" were acquired, selected according to their adaptability, and passed on or "inherited."[4]

In general, then, the theory of social evolution deployed both a trope of classification and a narrative of progress.[5] On the one hand, peoples were classified, ranging on a scale from the most backward to the most advanced. On the other hand, the narrative of progress held out the hope that backward peoples could advance, especially under the tutelage of superior civilizations. This chapter will deal with the attempts to classify the various human groups in the imperial archipelago and the determination of their aptness for self-government. In the next chapter, I will deal more specifically with plans for their progress. The trope of classification as a means of description, in combination with a narrative of the past that projected a probable future, would set the stage for the development of strategies of rule and the justification of a better tomorrow.

Cuba in Black and White

After the completion of the Cuban census, the editors of *National Geographic Magazine* announced "unexpected" and "gratifying" results: the white population was larger than anticipated. This, they argued, would guarantee that the "native-born whites" would remain in control of the government after the withdrawal of the United States and the replacement of the military administration. Cuba, they reassured their readers, would not become a "second

Haiti."[6] This conclusion expressed, on the one hand, uneasiness about the "colored" population and, on the other, optimism based upon the large proportion of "native-born whites." The Cuban census, as well as the Puerto Rican census, traced the shifting proportions of "white" and "colored" populations through the nineteenth century. Unlike the Puerto Rican census, however, the Cuban census noted a rise in the colored population during the first decades of the century, after which the proportion of whites gradually attained a majority: "The reason for the great increase in number and proportion of the colored up to 1841 is doubtless the continued importation of blacks from Africa, which persisted, in the form of smuggling, long after its official prohibition. Their diminution relative to the whites, during the last half century, is doubtless but another illustration of the inability of an inferior race to hold its own in competition with a superior one, a truth which is being demonstrated on a much larger scale in the United States."[7]

In contrast to the constant whitening described in Puerto Rico, the Cuban census noted an increase in the slave population followed by its reversal at mid-century. This persistent African element was a cause for concern, even though the white, native-born population outweighed it demographically and the white elite prevailed politically. Robert Hill considered the "whites" to be distinct from the "Negroes"; he discussed the white elite under the rubric "the Cubans" and then proceeded to describe "the Negroes." He adopted the same argument as the editors of the *National Geographic Magazine:* Cuba should not be compared with Haiti. He argued that "miscegenation" was common in Cuba and had a positive effect: the mixture of blacks with "Spanish stock produced a superior class of free mulattoes of the Antonio Maceo type" (for a photograph of Maceo, see figure 2.7). For these two reasons—the presence of the white elite and the superior characteristics of the mulattoes—there was little possibility of the "Africanization" of Cuba.[8]

Furthermore, the census concluded, in the section on "Nativity and Race," that the "superior race" would prevail eventually in Cuba and white domination was practically assured. The section entitled "Citizenship" was dedicated to the proportions of native and foreign-born inhabitants. It concluded that the native-born whites constituted a majority of the "citizens," although about half were illiterate. This terminology—"citizens" and "citizenship"—implicitly recognized Cuban nationhood. (In contrast, this terminology was not used in the Puerto Rican census.) In the popular books, optimism regarding the presence of an educated, professional, white elite prevailed. According to White, the educated Cuban elite had avidly supported the "insurgent cause" and continued to animate intellectual life. The Cuban elite was made up of a highly regarded

Figure 3.1. Courtyard of a Cuban House. White, *Our New Possessions.*

"professional class," mostly lawyers and doctors, in contrast to the "Spanish," who were primarily merchants.[9] Photographs of Cuban homes with their columned facades and pleasant interior patios were symbols of a social class that was capable of governing the country. White published a photograph of an elite Cuban family in its interior courtyard (figure 3.1).

Likewise, according to Olivares, the "creole population," of Spanish heritage, made up the "aristocrats of the island," a "distinct caste." Olivares wrote that they were "as pure of blood as any race on earth"; they did not "intermarry with the mixed races," nor did they "associate with them on terms of equality." He presented a photograph of Dr. Meodore Fernández Lombard, a "hero in the war with Spain" and a "graduate of Princeton College," in his backyard (figure 3.2).

Figure 3.2. Dr. Meodore Fernández Lombard. Bryan, *Our Islands*.

The doctor was awarded a prominent place in the Bryan volume because he had extended unspecified courtesies to Olivares and the photographer. In addition, as a well-to-do doctor, educated in the United States, impeccably dressed in a dark, three-piece suit, with a stylish straw hat, he represented the professional class that was to lead Cuba.

The rest of the Cuban population was of "mixed race," but it was largely partaking of and exhibiting "Spanish" ways and customs. This was Olivares's way of suggesting national unity in the face of racial hybridity: "It can hardly be said that the masses of Cuba people belong to any particular race. Spanish blood and features, of course, predominate, and Spanish customs prevail every-where; but the people are a mixed race, as any one can see by a glance at our illustrations."[10]

In the section on the "Race Question in Cuba," Olivares stated that class dif-ferences—that is, between the "aristocracy" and those who worked—were more substantial than race differences. However, he defined the upper class precisely in racial terms: it was white and did not mix with blacks. In contrast, most of the middle and lower classes were "hybrid."[11] In a photograph of "votaries of the cockpit," Olivares showed black and white practitioners of cockfighting (figure 3.3). The photograph illustrated two black men and one white man "mixing" in a social setting. They appeared as social equals: they wore the same style of dress and were side by side in public. In the caption, the author developed even further the theme of hybridity. The man in the center held a *patogallo*, which was described as "partaking both the nature of a chicken and a goose [*sic*]." According to Olivares, this species of game bird was "one of the most formidable known," stressing the superior qualities of the "hybrid."[12] As we shall see below, it was hoped that the hybridity of the Cuban population would also produce a superior character of citizens among the middle and lower classes.

Despite the frequent mention of the "mixed race," the presence of "blacks" or "Negroes" signaled negative elements that still inhibited progress among Cubans. Olivares expressed his concern by narrating various legends dealing with fetishism and sorcery. He concluded as follows: "Not least of the tasks yet to be accomplished in Cuba, through the medium of advanced civilization, is the elimination of the fanatical tendencies and customs from among the black population of the island. While superstition is an accepted characteristic of the African race, it seldom exists to a more inordinate degree than among the Cuban negroes, where fetishism [*sic*] is as prevalent as among the most barbarous tribes of the Congo region."[13] Olivares also expressed his great concern regarding the "Ñañigo fraternities" organized by the "black element": "The members of this society were originally pledged to protect their fanatical customs [i.c., fetishism],

Figure 3.3. Votaries of the Cockpit. Bryan, *Our Islands*.

and to kill their enemies at every opportunity. In time this order developed the fiercest lot of criminals ever known to the island. By the direction of its Obi men, murders were committed on every hand, and, although the offenders were from time to time apprehended, the Spanish officials were powerless to suppress the element."[14]

In 1898, Frederick Tennyson Neely produced a number of photographs illustrating the backwardness of the "Negroes" and their way of life in Cuba.[15] The first of these was of an old man tweaking the nose of a girl who was kneeling

Figure 3.4. Relics of the Plantation. Neely, *Panorama.*

obediently before him as he sat, sideways, on a chair (figure 3.4). The old man was dressed as a cane cutter; he wore an apron and a bandana and held a broad-brimmed hat. Beside him was a basket of bananas and two other children, who were looking rather glum, presumably because they were being punished also. The caption stated that the "oldest negroes guard the children and discipline them." The "sign of office" was the key that was hanging around the old man's neck. The caption stated that he had "locked disobedient children in the house." The old man and the community practices of child care were referred to as the "relics of plantation life," yet they were somehow appropriate for unruly black children who lacked more appropriate parental control and family structure.

Neely's second photograph was of two bachelors and their servants on the steps of a house in the suburbs of Havana (figure 3.5). The details of the photograph are fascinating but not entirely decipherable. We see the two well-dressed bachelors in stylish straw hats. According to the caption, a "retinue of servants [was] jumbled around them." Seated between them was a black woman in a simple cotton blouse and striped skirt, presumably the maid. One of the children, a young girl, showed affection to one of the bachelors by placing a hand on his shoulder and leaning close. The other bachelor held a naked baby on his lap. One of the older children stuck out his tongue in a playful manner. One of the boys did not appear to be a servant; he was well dressed in a dark suit, with

Figure 3.5. Two Bachelors. Neely, *Panorama*.

short pants, a tie, shoes, socks, and a hat. His style of dress was the same as the bachelors but markedly different from that of the rest of the children. The caption stated, "Clearly a strong, supreme, female ruling hand is lacking." Here the author disapproved of this domestic group because it did not include a proper white woman to establish a decent family and an ordered domestic sphere; there appeared to be neither wife nor legitimate children. Furthermore, the arrangement of the group did not suggest a clear distinction between the servants and their employers. Indeed, the white bachelors, incapable of establishing domestic order, seem to have been overrun by their servants.[16]

Neely's third photograph was of the "senior class" of a public school in Havana (figure 3.6). The caption states that "at the age of eight they graduate," and "no further schooling is provided for by the Spanish government." These "negro children" are all dressed and wearing shoes. They are playing, without a teacher in sight, "in front of the schoolhouse." The lack of education was a major concern, and here it was associated with both the negligence of the former Spanish government and the black population in Cuba. In addition, it reproduced the stereotype, expressed in the caption of a different photograph of a "negro dance," that "negroes are children of fun and sun." Although the caption did not mention them, the photograph showed two huge *timba* drums, used for dancing and religious rituals. Stereotypically, the boys seemed quite happy and content in playing them.

This series of photographs suggested that the black population of Cuba was uneducated and backward. Although generally content, it could be disobedient and required strong discipline. Finally, it lacked the strong family structure and the clearly defined domestic life of the elite. In general, then, the distinction between the white elite, on the one hand, and mulattoes and blacks, on the other, was an important detail in these depictions. The authors placed considerable faith in the capacity of the white elite to rule Cuba but also expressed some concern over the presence of blacks, who were deemed culturally backward. The hope for Cuba was predicated on the white elite, which had the capacity to rule the mulattoes and blacks and maintain order in the country. At the same time, these authors regarded racial mixing in a somewhat positive light since it diluted the "African" element in both racial and cultural terms, thus making the black population less segregated and more assimilated. The resultant mulattoes, it was hoped, would be of a superior "Antonio Maceo type." More important, these authors concluded that political leadership in Cuba would have to come from the white elite.

The Whitening of Puerto Rico

The first census of Puerto Rico under U.S. supervision (1899) used two basic racial categories: "white" (sometimes "pure white" or "Caucasian") and

Figure 3.6. Senior Class. Neely, *Panorama*.

"colored." The latter category was further divided into "mulatto" (sometimes "mestizo") and "black."[17] The statistics showed that the majority (62 percent) of the population was white while 38 percent was colored. Furthermore, the census placed these figures in the context of a historical trajectory using the various Spanish censuses of the nineteenth century. In this way, the census told an optimistic story regarding the changing racial composition of the population: a continuous whitening of the population. The report concluded that the population statistics "point to a secular change whereby the pure negro blood has lost ground before the mixed, as the two together have apparently lost ground before the whites."[18] A full-page graph illustrated this whitening of the population. The illustrated narrative created by the census, then, was optimistic in its ambiguity: the Puerto Ricans were a racially mixed population tending toward whiteness. However, unlike in the Cuban census, the terms "nationality" and "citizenship" were entirely absent. Instead, the vocabulary of the Puerto Rican census, as expressed in the subtitles, referred only to "race," "nativity," and "males of voting age." "Race," as we have seen, referred to color. "Nativity" referred to either the native-born—that is, Puerto Ricans—or the foreign-born—that is, Spanish (although other nationalities were present in very small proportions). The implication was clear yet never explicitly stated: Puerto Ricans were defined by their place of birth and their race, but they were not citizens of a nation. Male suffrage, then, was a concession to occur strictly within a context of imperial rule, not as a right or exercise of sovereignty.

Nevertheless, there were some detractors from this census characterization. In his memoirs of the military campaign, Karl Hermann refuted this racial representation in no uncertain terms: "Almost one sixth of the population in this island—the educated class, and chiefly of Spanish blood—can be set down as valuable acquisitions to our citizenship and the peer, if not the superior, of most Americans in chivalry, domesticity, fidelity, and culture. Of the rest, perhaps one-half can be molded by a firm hand into something approaching decency; but the remainder are going to give us a great deal of trouble. They are ignorant, filthy, untruthful, lazy, treacherous, murderous, brutal, and black."[19]

Hermann's text included an observation that was common among the popular illustrated books: he considered the "educated class" to be "Spanish."[20] This class made up roughly 16 percent of the population, according to the author's estimate, and was worthy of U.S. citizenship. He was not so optimistic about the rest of the population. He believed that one-half of the population might be shaped into "something approaching decency," but only with great effort on the part of his compatriots. However, his evaluation of the "black" population (34 percent, corresponding roughly to the census distribution of "colored") was quite deprecating. This hostility toward the black inhabitants was quite unusual, and his pessimistic description was a rare instance of the classification of the Puerto Rican population according to distinct racial categories, each with its own characteristics.

In general, the writers of the popular illustrated books considered Puerto Ricans to be racially mixed without any overt distinct racial divisions except between the pure-blood "Spanish" and mixed-blood "Porto Ricans." Although Olivares mentioned the "pure-blooded African," he did not attribute any specific characteristics to that category. Like the authors of the census, he believed that the "African race is declining, and will either eventually disappear or be amalgamated with the white race."[21] Olivares described the "peons" as "white or light mulatto in color, and showing their African origins more or less plainly." In the same vein, he wrote that the "majority of the peons are whites, although there are many mulattos, and not a few negroes." Like most writers, he described these Puerto Rican agricultural laborers in the most favorable terms:

> They have good faces and are naturally intelligent. They are very quiet and peaceable. They are kind to their families, and are on the whole, good citizens. Americans who have employed them say that they are excellent workers, and that they are glad to do all they can to earn their money. They work from sunrise until sunset, and are as reliable as the average American workmen. Some trouble is had as to the numerous holidays and feast days which have been

customary, but the most of the men will do their work irrespective of these, asking for Sunday only.[22]

The census of 1899 presented a photograph with the title "Type of Mestizos" (figure 3.7). These agricultural laborers—one with a heavy ax and the other with a machete—were standing in front of two oxcarts on what appeared to

Figure 3.7. Type of Mestizos. U.S. War Department, *Report on the Census of Porto Rico, 1899.*

be a sugar plantation.[23] The photograph gave the overall impression that the population was "colored," humble, and working class in origin, either from the countryside or small villages and towns.

In contrast to the Puerto Rican working class, Olivares identified the local elites as "Spanish" or "Castillian," whether or not they were actually born in Spain. Indeed, he believed the majority to be native-born. He identified the "landholding, dominating and wealthy class" as "Spanish," although he noted that there was very little sympathy between the "two classes of Spanish," those born in Spain and those born in Puerto Rico of Spanish heritage.[24] This identification of the local elite as "Spanish" resulted in the symbolic displacement of Puerto Ricans as political leaders. It was uncommon to find either photographs or descriptions of educated and propertied Puerto Ricans, except for women, as we have seen in chapter 2. This symbolic displacement reinforced the argument that Puerto Ricans were incapable of governing themselves. After all, "Puerto Ricans" were supposedly of humble origin—artisans, workers, and peasants— and were a "mixed race." The "Spanish" had dominated them for roughly four centuries, and as a result they were poor, uneducated, and entirely unfamiliar with the principles and practices of self-government. Likewise, the "Spanish" elite could not be expected to institute democratic rule on their own.

Curiously, most of the popular books emphasized the indigenous past. Long sections or entire chapters were devoted to idyllic descriptions of the Taíno Indians and to the cruelty of the Spanish conquerors of the sixteenth century. In addition, the texts occasionally described the present-day inhabitants as "natives" or "aborigines." This textual emphasis on the indigenous past resulted in a discursive instability between the texts and the photographs. The photographs showed black and mulatto people, while the texts talked about "natives" and "aborigines." Olivares's caption for photograph shown in figure 3.8 was particularly contradictory: "These people are direct descendants of the original Indian inhabitants of Porto Rico, and although some of them have African blood in their veins, they are interesting as the last remnants of an extinct race."[25] Accordingly, the population was indigenous, yet African. The Spanish had exterminated the original inhabitants, yet they remained alive and well. It would seem that this was the author's rather awkward attempt to divert attention away from the "colored" population, with all of its negative connotations, and stress the simple nobility of the local population that had endured Spanish imperialism.

In addition, the speculations concerning the whitening of the population introduced a cautiously optimistic tone. The various authors suggested that it was not an impossible task to civilize and whiten the Puerto Ricans under U.S. tutelage and hegemony. The rhetoric of racial deprecation, although not

Figure 3.8. Descendants of the Aborigines. Bryan, *Our Islands*.

entirely absent, was quite subdued. The use of strong racial epithets among the military personnel was not common, as it was in the Philippines. Indeed, only Dinwiddie mentioned, disapprovingly, the use of the term "dago" by U.S. rank-and-file soldiers to describe Puerto Ricans. In contrast, he claimed that U.S. officers always maintained excellent relations with the local populations, especially the elite.[26]

According to the texts and photographs, the main fissure within Puerto Rican society was between the Puerto Ricans, who were mostly poor workers and peasants, and the Spanish, who held political and economic power. Puerto Ricans were seen as poor and oppressed but neither as savages nor barbarians. If they were backward, it was due to the Spanish domination. Finally, the contrast between the "Spanish" elite and the humble "Puerto Rican" justified the control of the United States over the government of the island. The presence of the local elite was displaced, although ambiguously, by their characterization as "Spanish." Underlying the texts ran an assumption of homogenous culture. There were many colors of people, given their various origins and subsequent mixtures. There was, however, but one people: Puerto Rican. There was no discussion of striking regional, racial, cultural, or linguistic differences among them.

Despite the textual emphasis on whitening, the photographs consistently showed blacks and mulattoes, often raggedly dressed or naked children. Virtually every publication of the epoch contained at least one photograph that emphasized the nakedness of the children. Figure 3.9 appeared in the report of General Davis with the title "Porto Rican Peones" and in the census with the caption "Native Negroes." Although almost all of the children were dressed, the obligatory naked child could be found front and center. The other children were dressed raggedly but in modern clothing made of manufactured cloth. There is one adult woman in the back, but no adult men are pictured. The captions of the photographs suggested that these children were either typical Puerto Ricans or agricultural laborers; Davis's report stressed occupation or social class (peones), while the census caption signaled race (Negroes). The dwelling in the background was constructed of palm fronds *(yagua)*, a common building material among the agricultural laborers throughout the countryside and villages of Puerto Rico (and Cuba). Most striking, however, is that the children appeared

Figure 3.9. Porto Rican Peones. Davis, *Civil Affairs*, 1899. [Native Negroes. U.S. War Department, *Report on the Census of Porto Rico, 1899.*]

to be "pickaninnies": stereotypical black children who served as a symbol of an inferior people.

With these representational elements, the principal narrative was of Spanish domination and future progress under U.S. control. The indigenous population, the Taínos, played a more symbolic than denotative role in the narrative: they represented the oppressed Puerto Ricans under centuries of Spanish misrule. No author actually described Puerto Ricans as Taínos, yet every author discussed the sad history of this noble and simple people. In this context, the ubiquitous descriptions of sixteenth-century indigenous life served as an allegory of Spanish domination of the humble Puerto Ricans. The texts completely ignored the history of slavery, although it was implied by the "African" origin of some of the inhabitants. Instead, the textual descriptions emphasized the whitening of the population during the nineteenth century. The whiteness of the population and its possible further whitening was a metaphor for the potential cultural and economic improvements that the United States would oversee. In general, as noted, Puerto Ricans were described as a mixed race—white, mulatto, black—of peasant and working-class origin. Furthermore, the term "mixed race" implied that there were no clearly defined racial or ethnic groups. Instead, the depictions of Puerto Ricans suggested that they were rather homogeneous from a cultural point of view, although this was never stated explicitly. The only exception was the description of the local elite, whether "white" or "Spanish," as both different from and exploitative of the common Puerto Ricans. The texts were sympathetic to the lower-class Puerto Ricans and discussed the elite indirectly, obliquely, if at all. They suggested that poor Puerto Ricans would respond positively to both educational and material improvement. Nevertheless, the authorities would target the elites for political tutelage. As the census photographs suggested (see chapter 2), the elite was capable of some political participation and administrative responsibilities, but they were not the leaders of an independent country, nor did they want anything more than autonomy.

Hawai'i: From Native Monarchy to Republic

Since the mid-nineteenth century, Hawaiian monarchs had produced and circulated photographic portraits of themselves in an effort to convince the European powers and the United States of the legitimacy of their independent nation in the international arena. Elegant photographs, at first daguerreotypes and later *cartes-de-visite,* diffused images of a monarchy that was not only civilized but also modern and sophisticated. King Kamehameha IV (Alexander Liholiho) and Queen Emma were the first monarchs to publicly distribute photographs of themselves. They sent daguerreotype portraits to a London exhibition in 1862 and impressed Queen Victoria and the English public with their stylish European grooming, dress, and adornments. When David Kalākaua ascended the throne in 1874, he expanded this representational strategy. He minted silver coins and printed stamps with his image and that of Queen Kapiʻolani. He also produced popular *cartes-de-visite* and authorized their sale in Hawaiʻi and North America. These images were usually photographic prints mounted on cardboard about the size of a playing card. They were widely circulated and collected, especially by the middle classes. Kalākaua also commissioned a local engraver in 1875 to produce an elaborate foldout book of photographs and paintings of the royal family. It was printed by a company in Frankfurt and distributed worldwide. Kalākaua was a tireless promoter of Hawaiian sovereignty and traveled widely throughout Asia, Europe, and the United States. His portrait in full regalia was well known, appearing in many popular books (figure 3.10). His successor, Queen Liliʻuokalani, and the next heir to the throne, Princess Kaʻiulani, also attempted to project an air of elegance and civility by means of photographs. Maxwell has argued that these photographs were "an instance of subversive mimicry"—that is, they were part of a strategy to adopt modern European styles of presentation in order to convince the most powerful nations that Hawaiʻi was a civilized country led by a modern monarchy.[27]

The new-possessions books, however, turned the tables on this strategy. They reproduced several of the royal photographs but placed them within a different narrative, one of political evolution. Lodge published portraits of Queen Emma (but not King Kamehameha IV), Prince Leleiokoki, and the late King Kalākaua and his queen, Kapiʻolani. He also included portraits of the recently deposed queen, Liliʻuokalani, and the immensely popular Princess Kaʻiulani. According to this political narrative, the monarchy had evolved from a feudal system at the beginning of the century to a constitutional monarchy. According to Lodge, this progress had occurred with the guidance and influence of New England missionaries, who had first arrived in the 1820s. These missionaries "proved to be more than the advisers and promulgators of the spiritual welfare of the natives, but became their temporal counsellors, as well as preachers, and helped to establish a civil government capable of protecting the acquired rights of the inhabitants." Lodge described in detail the how the feudal monarchs acceded to a declaration of rights in 1839, which he called the "Magna Carta of Hawaii," and to a written constitution in 1840. After some political intrigues and much international diplomacy, France and England recognized the political sovereignty of the Kingdom of Hawaiʻi in 1843. During the 1840s, the local government was reorganized, and land reform made possible the individual ownership of landed property. The political evolution of the kingdom was marked by constitutional reforms in 1852,

Figure 3.10. King Kalākaua. Browne, *The New America*, vol. 1.

1864, and 1887. The "bayonet" constitution of 1887 severely limited the powers of the monarchy. It created, in the words of Lodge, a "peculiar combination of republican and monarchical ideals, engrafted on a kingly power."[28] It concentrated the power in the legislature and the cabinet, both controlled by haoles. As a result of this power shift, the United States was able to gain exclusive control over Pearl Harbor in exchange for a renewal of the Reciprocity Treaty, which allowed Hawaiian sugar duty-free entry into the U.S. market.[29]

This narrative of political evolution sounded progressive, liberal, and democratic. Yet underlying it was an uneasy feeling about the backsliding of the royalty at several junctures. Some rulers, like Kamehameha IV, had attempted to restore "paganism," old customs like the hula dance, and kingly rule. King

Kalākaua showed his "race prejudice" when he "seemed to consider only the interests of the native Hawaiians, and to look on foreign residents as alien invaders." Kalākaua also often tended toward "personal despotism." The royalist threat headed by his successor, Queen Lili'uokalani, eventually led in 1893 to the abrogation of the monarchy, followed by the establishment of a republic the next year. Lodge placed full blame upon Queen Lili'uokalani, whose "despotism" and "race prejudice" led her to advocate a new constitution that would extend her monarchical powers: "That the policy of the queen was short-sighted and reactionary was evident; that she was stubborn in her determination to restore certain monarchical rights is beyond question; the constitution she would have promulgated in its full intentions, as offered, would have disenfranchised every white man on the islands unless the husband of a Hawaiian woman, and would have made the property of the whites alone subject to taxation."[30]

The overthrow of a monarchy in order to form a republic was a justification easily understood by nineteenth-century Americans. In addition to this simple narrative of natural, albeit conflictive, political evolution was the justification of race and gender: the particular monarchy in question was represented by a native woman who sought to dominate white men and limit their rights. The implication was that the native monarchy was not a legitimate form of rule: at best it was mere imitation of European traditions; at worst it suppressed the democratic and republican desires of its white male citizens. In this story of political evolution, the monarchy had naturally given way to a small fledgling republic and, finally, to annexation by the greatest of all modern republics.[31]

Similarly, Olivares published photographs of statues of Kamehameha I, Kalākaua, Lili'uokalani, and Ka'iulani. His narrative, like Lodge's, began with Kamehameha I and followed the succession of rulers until the overthrow of Lili'uokalani. Like Lodge, he emphasized how "pagan" religion and the "feudal system" slowly gave way under the influence of missionaries. Some of the rulers were "enlightened," but many, such as Kalākaua, were "autocratic and arbitrary" and reintroduced the *hula-hula* and "superstitious rites." Conflict broke out in 1893 when Lili'uokalani sought "the extension of royal prerogatives and [the] abridgement of popular rights." According to Olivares, the overthrow of the monarchy was the only way to "secure the permanent maintenance of law and order, liberty and property."[32] White presented a similar narrative but with more emphasis on the 1890s. His story emphasized the overthrow of the monarchy, the establishment of the provisional government with annexationist aspirations, the foundation of the republic, the counterrevolution of the monarchists, and the final annexation to the United States. White, ever wary of alternate interpretations, did not publish any photographs of the Hawaiian monarchy.[33]

This story of political evolution actually appeared much earlier in Richard Dana's travelogue *Two Years before the Mast*, published in 1840.[34] Dana's story stressed the efforts of the missionaries to teach the populace to read and write, in both English and Hawaiian, and to "cipher and to sew." The population was exposed to great literature in the English language: "works of devotion," including the Bible, and works of "science and entertainment." According to Dana, the transformation that ensued was remarkable:

> Whereas, they [the missionaries] found these islanders a nation of half-naked savages, living in the surf and on the sand, eating raw fish, fighting among themselves, tyrannized over by feudal chiefs and abandoned to sensuality, they now see them decently clothed, recognizing the law of marriage, knowing something of accounts, going to school and public worship more regularly than the people do at home, and the more elevated of them taking part in conducting the affairs of the constitutional monarchy under which they live, holding seats on the judicial bench and in the legislative chamber, and filling posts in the local magistracies.[35]

Dana's political narrative began with feudal chiefs and ended with a constitutional monarchy. Years later, Halstead quoted Dana and updated the story to include the establishment of the republic. Underlying this political narrative was a profound cultural transformation: from savagery to civilization. In this way, the political history of Hawai'i was joined to the narrative of Americanization through settlement and civilization of local peoples. Thus, the evolution of the capacity for self-government was fundamentally a result of Americanization. Halstead agreed that Hawai'i was thoroughly "Americanized" in terms of "its material interest and customs and principles."[36] The "material interest" was principally that of commerce, especially access to the U.S. market for sugar. With respect to the local "customs," Halstead explained that English was the language of education, commerce, law, and government and that Protestantism was the dominant religion. Finally, the "principles" were those of republican self-government, modeled explicitly upon U.S. traditions. According to Halstead, the process of Americanization began with the arrival of the missionaries and culminated in the annexation of Hawai'i by the United States.

The trope of political evolution in Hawai'i was a part of the grander narrative regarding the process of Americanization through settlement. This narrative was unique to Hawai'i since it was the only location in the imperial archipelago to have a significant immigration of European Americans during the nineteenth century. This colonization commenced in the 1820s with the arrival of Protestant missionaries. By the end of the century, these Euro-American immigrants and their descendants exercised hegemony in Hawai'i on all fronts: economic, political, and cultural. The Hawaiian Islands were the last frontier of a vast geographic expansion, predominantly continental, of the United States. Lodge wrote that the history of Hawai'i was "one of the most interesting chapters in the westward march of the United States." It was the "story of the natives and of our own people who went among them." In the words of Lodge, the islands were an "American colony."[37] In other words, this expansion was undertaken through colonization—that is, through the migration and settlement of European Americans, who displaced indigenous populations, dispossessed them of their land, and dominated them politically. These Euro-American immigrants and their descendants were known locally as haoles, literally foreigners or outsiders.[38]

White also emphasized the colonization of Hawai'i by U.S. immigrants. His description of Honolulu was a study of contrasts: Hawai'i was at once tropical yet decidedly New England in character:

> Every traveler who visits Honolulu admits his first impression to be as surprising familiarity in the scene. In spite of volcanic mountains for a background, and the foliage of tropic vegetation in riotous profusion everywhere, there is a never-failing suggestion of the New England country village, in this island metropolis. There are the same white picket fences, white frame houses with green blinds, and the same gables and gateways that characterize the New England homestead. When one looks at these through a vista of royal palm trees and bananas, the effect is quite startling.
>
> It was not only in the visible forms of household life that the people from Plymouth Rock made their impression in the Pacific. They found a people who, though mild of manner and disposition, generous and hospitable, had absolutely no synonym or conception of the word decency. Their personal habits and conversation were gross beyond description. The history of missionary labors offers no other instance so notable of a remarkable alteration in conditions. To-day the Hawaiian islands in every part are as orderly and well defined in their organized society as our own American communities.[39]

In his description, White began with the contrast between geography—volcanoes, bananas, palm trees, and abundant tropical vegetation—and architecture—picket fences and white frame houses with gables and green shutters. This architecture evoked both the household life and villages of New England, curiously placed in the tropics. But the presence of the "people from Plymouth Rock" went much farther than a superficial visual evocation of New England.

Their moral efforts had spread Protestant "decency" throughout the islands. They had established homesteads. Their presence resulted in an "organized society" every bit as "orderly and well defined" as "our own American communities." These people were pilgrims, missionaries, and settlers who transplanted their own moral and political community in that most unlikely of places, the tropics. The Hawaiian natives themselves were transformed from a "primitive people" by this direct contact with "modern civilization."[40]

Olivares and his photographer were also struck by this contrast and published a large, hand-colored photograph of a Victorian frame house and its owner, identified as a "citizen of Hawaii" (figure 3.11). The owner, sporting a long, white beard and accompanied by a large dog, stood on the grounds of his expansive property. The proper ladies of the house observed from the large veranda. This European American man represented symbolically those citizens that deserved and demanded full political rights; he bore a certain resemblance to Sanford Dole, the president of the Hawaiian republic and later first territorial governor.

According to Olivares, "the ruling and influential class in Hawaii is of course American and will remain so." This "American-European element, consisting of white men, chiefly of American origin," was numerically the smallest group, less than 10 percent of the total population, but it was the "most important by

Figure 3.11. A Citizen of Hawaii and His Home. Bryan, *Our Islands.*

intelligence, energy, and wealth." Notwithstanding their small numbers, these "Americans" were hegemonic in both politics and economics. They had also imposed English as the language of government, business, and public instruction. This elite had had the "management of the islands in its hands for many years, since it guided and furnished ministers for the latest native sovereigns" of the previous constitutional monarchy.[41]

This narrative of political evolution inevitably culminated with the annexation of the small republic, Hawai'i, to the great one, the United States. Trumbull White was an ardent expansionist, yet he sympathized with the situation of the native Hawaiians. He wrote that as a minority in their own land, they had just been deprived of their political leadership. His description of the annexation ceremony in 1898 was particularly melancholy: "It was a solemn rather than a festive ceremony, which marked the final transfer of the sovereignty over the Hawaiian islands. There were more tears than cheers" (figure 3.12). The ceremony included a twenty-one-gun salute from the battleship *Philadelphia* in the harbor: "When the sound of the last gun died away the Hawaiian band began 'Hawaii Ponoi,' the Hawaiian national anthem. But there were tears in the bandmaster's eyes. There were quavers in the notes of the familiar air which the composer never put there, and it was but a remnant of the band which went through what was to every one of them an ordeal. Of the twenty-six members, fifteen are native Hawaiians, and these at their own earnest request were excused from playing for the last time their country's national anthem." After the playing of "The Star-Spangled Banner," the U.S. flag was raised amid light enthusiasm and weak cheers: "The transfer of sovereignty was complete. The flag of a gentle, hospitable and generous but dark-skinned people had been given away by aliens in blood to aliens in blood. . . . There was not one active participant who had in his veins a single drop of blood of that people who gave their name to the flag that was obliterated or the sovereignty of which was surrendered."[42]

White restricted his description of the native Hawaiians to a single phrase: "gentle, hospitable, and generous but dark-skinned people." He did not speak of the aristocracy. White, like other authors, described the monarchy as a succession of individuals—kings and queens, princes and princesses—but not as a class or status group. Olivares elaborated upon the idea. According to him, the character of the *kanakas,* or native Hawaiians, had changed very little over the centuries, except for their conversion to Christianity. Ever since the days of the first European contact, their peacefulness and hospitality had been renowned. He wrote with a certain admiration and sympathy, but it was little more than nostalgia. No author questioned the right of the haoles to own property, impose their language, preach their religion, or rule.[43]

Figure 3.12. The Annexation of Hawaii–"Old Glory" Hoisted at Honolulu. White, *Our New Possessions.*

Henry Cabot Lodge, in his contribution to the first volume of Browne's *The New America and the Far East,* wrote that Hawaiians were not "savages" but rather "barbarians of a milder and more progressive type." They had a complexion of "olive and sometimes reddish brown," but they were neither "yellow like the Malay nor red like the American Indian." Furthermore, they often had features "resembling the Europeans." His remarkable conclusion was that the Hawaiian belonged "to a branch of the Polynesian race, which was undoubtedly of Aryan stock, migrating at a remote period from Asia Minor through India, Sumatra, and Java, to the Southern Pacific Islands, from thence advancing slowly northward to New Zealand, Samoa, Tahiti, and Hawaii."[44] As we saw in chapter 2, according to the textual accounts, Hawaiians lived from fishing, gathering, and subsistence agriculture. They lived in simple huts next to their taro patches and adorned themselves with flowers. These descriptions of the "native Hawaiians" and their customs were sympathetic and nostalgic. These noble savages stood in contrast to the corrupt monarchy. The descriptions focused upon a past that was fast disappearing along with the declining numbers of native population. Indeed, both the photographs and the descriptions often evoked a way of life that was mostly a memory.

Whether for economic, demographic, or cultural reasons, native Hawaiians did not supply the necessary labor required by the large plantations. To meet the demand for agricultural labor in the extensive plantations of sugar, pineapple, coffee, and other tropical products, plantation owners employed thousands of immigrants from the Madeira Islands (off the coast of Portugal), China, and Japan.[45] All of the authors agreed that the Hawaiians were far superior—according to their hierarchical racial scheme—to the Filipinos, the Chinese, the Japanese, and even the North American Indians. Notwithstanding this supposed superiority, the Hawaiians were a minority in their own land, having a smaller population than either the Chinese or the Japanese. The haoles sought to limit the Asian influence in Hawai'i but at the same time needed immigrants from China and Japan to work on the plantations. However, most of the authors of the illustrated books ignored these populations, even though the Chinese were roughly 40 percent of the total population and the Japanese were about 30 percent. Halstead and March barely mentioned these populations, and White failed even to imply their existence.[46] These authors simply ignored the racial diversity occasioned by labor immigration. However, important authors such as Lodge and especially Olivares published photographs and fairly extensive textual descriptions of the Portuguese, Chinese, and Japanese.[47] They emphasized the fragmentation and segregation of the ethnic groups and their consequent lack of political power or aspiration. Olivares was particularly interested in the diverse, exotic aspects of all his destinations, and he was attuned to the political implications of this diversity. Regarding Hawai'i, he concluded the following:

All these four elements, Portuguese, as well as native Hawaiian, Japanese and Chinese, are quite unfit for free government. The Portuguese, though a good sort of people, have had practically no experience in it, and have no taste for it. The other three races are, of course, in a still lower stage. All these four race groups have, moreover, no national organization among themselves. Three of them have come lately to the islands, while among the natives the ancient system of rule by chiefs has completely vanished. Nor has any of these four groups anything in common with any of the others except local contiguity. The two Asiatic races hate one another. No group can speak the language of any other, and it will take a good while before they learn to use English as their common medium of communication. This is an advantage for the ruling Americans, because it prevents a hostile combination against their authority. But it increases the difficulty of establishing representative institutions, or of impressing American ideas upon the mass of the inhabitants. The Japanese are the only foreigners who will in any substantial degree compete with the Americans for supremacy.[48]

In this way, Olivares claimed that no racial group, except for the "Americans," was capable of, or even sought, self-government. The only justification, the only secure foundation, of the republic was European American hegemony, which was guaranteed precisely by the lack of unity and common cause among the other groups. The two largest groups, the Japanese and the Chinese, were "hereditary enemies." Olivares wrote that there was an "'irrepressible conflict' between the two races, and they do not mix in their social relations, and have as little to do with each other as possible in their business transactions."[49] As a result, the Japanese and the Chinese could not constitute a unity that might have threatened haole hegemony. In addition, neither group enjoyed political rights, not in the later years of the kingdom, not in the republic, and not in the Territory of Hawai'i.

Olivares's analysis was entirely consistent with the report of the Hawaiian Commission. The commissioners wrote that the entire population was "dominated politically, financially, and commercially, by the American element," even though it was a minority. The Chinese and the Japanese had no "important relation to the body politic, except as laborers." Most of the Chinese were contract laborers who would return to their country of origin. The Japanese were more inclined to stay in Hawai'i but busied themselves with business concerns, not politics.[50] Lodge also ruled out the possibility of Chinese political participation, although he recognized that many Chinese were prominent businessmen and professionals. However, the vast majority were not citizens but rather aliens. In contrast, the Japanese were inclined to "meddle in politics."[51]

The popular books described both the Japanese and Chinese as "alien races" but considered the former to be superior to the latter. Olivares compared the two "races" in the following manner:

The Japanese are much superior, as a race, to the Chinese. They possess the same industrious and frugal habits, but they are more conscientious in the performance of their contracts, cleaner in their persons and houses, and far more intelligent. . . . The Japanese of Hawaii are a cheerful and industrious people, very much inclined toward clannishness, but close imitators of good ideas. Aggressive and ambitious, they never lose a vantage ground that has once been gained. Quick to pick up the customs, manners and habits of thought of the better class of those among whom they sojourn, they must needs soon be recognized as part of the sinew of the land. They have come to the islands to stay, and, with their intelligent emulation of the white man's standard of living, are destined to be his more severe competitors in the evolution of the new Hawaii. They are not only imitative, like the Chinese, but they also originate, and are progressive in all their tendencies. A Japanese will adopt any contrivance that he fancies, and improve upon it, while the Chinaman will slavishly copy whatever he sees; even the imperfections. These are marked distinctions of character between the two races.[52]

In spite of their supposed inferiority, Olivares presented this very positive description of the Japanese character. Nevertheless, he worried that they might some day compete with Americans for supremacy in Hawai'i since they were "aggressive and ambitious." The author presented a photograph of a Japanese laborer, his wife, and his newborn child (figure 3.13). The friendly countenance

Figure 3.13. Japanese Laborer and His Wife. Bryan, *Our Islands.*

Figure 3.14. Chinese Laborer on Sugar Plantation, Island of Kauai. Bryan, *Our Islands.*

of the wife, the peaceful slumber of the child, and the hand-holding husband created a sympathetic image. In addition, the man was properly attired for cutting sugar cane: his long-sleeved shirt was buttoned up and tucked in; he wore shoes with leggings. The photograph left no doubt that this was a proper, hardworking family that had "come to stay."

Despite his deprecating remarks regarding the Chinese, Olivares appreciated their work habits and their industriousness. He included a photograph of a Chinese laborer in a cane field (figure 3.14). Other photographs show that he had paused for the photographer in the field, where he was using his shovel to direct water into shallow irrigation channels. He was dressed in the customary garb of Chinese contract laborers who came to work but usually returned when the contract was fulfilled. Although they were a great contribution to the plantation economy, they were considered "unwanted" and an "alien race." Many Chinese who originally came as contract laborers stayed on and managed to buy small farms and shops, go in business for themselves, and establish families in Hawai'i. Nevertheless, the presence of Chinese laborers was an obstacle to the annexation of Hawai'i since many in the United States alleged that they threatened the standard of living of the white working class. In 1882, Congress had passed the first Chinese Exclusion Act, which prohibited Chinese immigration to the United States for ten years. In 1892, a new exclusion act was passed that extended the immigration prohibition for another ten years. Upon the acquisition of Hawai'i, the prohibition of Chinese immigration applied to the new territory. In addition, the annexation act prohibited Chinese immigration from Hawai'i to any other state or territory of the United States.[53]

In sum, the narratives regarding Hawai'i emphasized the political evolution from a feudal system to the creation of a constitutional monarchy, its overthrow, and the subsequent establishment of a republic, which was finally annexed to the United States. The principal actors in this drama were the European American settlers, who had gained hegemony by the end of the nineteenth century by gradually displacing the Hawaiian monarchical rulers. The Euro-Americans exercised control on all major fronts: economic, political, and cultural. The racial complexity of the islands was sometimes ignored in the narratives, but most important sources emphasized the social aggregate of Hawaiians, Portuguese, Japanese, and Chinese. This complexity did not, however, mean that Hawai'i was unfit for annexation; the reader could rest assured that it was completely under the control of loyal American settlers. Quite a different situation was portrayed in the Philippines.

Races, Tribes, and Religions in the Philippines

Many were fond of the adjective "incomprehensible" to describe the character of the people of the Philippines. Even the Filipino author Ramón Reyes Lala found the character of his people puzzling: "Incomprehensible inconsistencies obtain in nearly every native. Students of character may, therefore, study the Filipinos for years and yet, at last, have no definite impression of the mental or moral status."[54]

Trumbull White published the same description as Lala's, word for word, in his travel book on the new possessions.[55] Government officials also used the adjective "incomprehensible" to describe the peoples of the Philippines. It found its way into reports such as *The People of the Philippines*, produced by the U.S. War Department's Division of Insular Affairs, and the 1903 census of the Philippines.[56]

Similarly, Leonard Sargent stated that the Filipino was "all three [in] one": "courteous gentleman," "respectful servant," and "stubborn and intractable brute." This description of a volatile and unpredictable combination of positive and negative characteristics was common. Sargent summarized the basic strategy that derived from this description: "If the brute must be broken, let us hope that the respectful servant and the gentleman will be encouraged."[57] Symbolically, this pointed to a strategy of roundly defeating the military challenge and coopting the elites.

Margherita Hamm also described the Filipino character as a mixture of inconstant and incongruous elements. As mentioned in chapter 2, she used the water buffalo, the *carabao,* as a symbol of the Filipino character: "The Philippine buffalo bears a striking resemblance to the Philippine islander. In his wild state he is fierce, intractable and cruel. Once broken in and domesticated he becomes docile, patient, and long-suffering. When tamed he is intelligent, affectionate and grateful, and yet when imposed upon too far the old savage nature is apt to break out and the terrible wild beast reassert itself."[58] According to Hamm, the Filipino was unpredictable and unstable due to the closeness to primitive ways; even the civilized Filipino was never far from the state of savagery. Civilization was but a veneer, a thin covering. This description and diagnosis was consonant with the idea that Filipinos had a propensity to "run amok." While this term was most specifically associated with Muslims, it was soon applied to all Filipinos.[59] Lala also attributed the inconsistencies in the Filipino character to the closeness to the savage state, especially in those more isolated rural areas not under the positive influence of the city. This description favored the educated, urban elites without ever actually naming them. Lala also blamed three centuries of Spanish domination and "generations of tropical ancestors" for the negative traits. Nevertheless, he defended the many positive traits of his compatriots and argued that improvements in character would accompany better political conditions and economic opportunities.[60]

The problem of the determination of national character went hand in hand with attempts to produce and use a detailed system of "tribal" classifications. The Schurman Philippine Commission produced a highly influential report regarding conditions in the Philippines. The report attempted to address the problem of inadequate knowledge: "The most diverse and contradictory statements are frequently met with concerning the inhabitants of the Philippine Islands, at present collectively known as 'Filipinos.'"[61] However, these "Filipinos" did not form a homogeneous group, but rather were a collection of diverse peoples. The report described what was known about this heterogeneity according to three broad criteria. From part 2 of the table of contents, we find the following summary: "The native peoples of the Philippines. 'Filipinos'—three distinct races, Negrito, Indonesian, Malayan—Divided into numerous tribes, Christian, Mohammedan, and pagan; collectively do not form a nation or people—Table of tribes, giving name, number, habitat."[62]

Although the report acknowledged considerable debate regarding the proper racial classifications, it decided upon a rather simple tripartite division of the population: Negrito, Indonesian, and Malay. The Negritos were not important demographically, although they were objects of curiosity, and many speculated about them as an evolutionary "missing link." The Indonesians were impor- tant primarily in the south and were also considered to be a small minority. In general, then, the population of the Philippines was understood as sharing a predominant racial foundation: Malay. However, this racial substratum did not produce a national unity. Major General Wesley Merritt, who helped subdue the revolution in the Philippines, wrote, "There never was a Philippine nation— only a collection of many tribes, speaking different languages, and having little in common except that they all belong to the Malayan race."[63]

While these descriptions (with minor exceptions) acknowledged a common racial stock—Malay—they discounted its importance for national unity. Instead, the descriptions deployed a "trope of plurality": an elaboration of cultural hetero- geneity that was a sign of general inferiority because it indicated both the lack of nationhood and the incapacity for self-government.[64] The Schurman Philip- pine Commission divided the three basic races into eighty-two different tribes, identified by their particular linguistic and cultural characteristics and listed in a table. A few years later, the census would use a classification system of twenty- four tribes. In addition to the criteria listed above, the tribes were ranked accord- ing to their level of civilization, ranging from "wild" to "civilized." They were also distinguished by their religion. The religious categories were "Christian," "Mohammedan" or "Moro" (Muslim), and "pagan" (animist). The latter two were often grouped together, and the tribes that adhered to them were known as the "non-Christian tribes." In general, the report described the "Filipinos" as an aggregate of three races, divided into many tribes (distinguished by language and level of civilization) and forming three fundamental religious groups. Many times, however, the term "Filipino" designated specifically the peoples of the civilized Christian tribes.[65]

In his study of the Philippine census, Benito Vergara argued that the census failed as a "means to knowledge" because its classifications were so imprecise and inconsistent. Nevertheless, I would argue that the census, and all texts that reproduced its logic, were very successful because their descriptions suggested concrete conclusions with respect to the strategy and necessity of imperial rule. The three dimensions of race, tribe, and religion worked differently in the rhetoric of empire. First, the notion of race served as a marker of absolute difference between the Philippines and the United States; it was a sign of fundamental otherness. Except for the insignificant numbers of Negritos and Indonesians, the population was principally Malay. However, a basic racial unity was not matched by a corresponding cultural or national unity. This description established clearly that the population could neither be culturally assimilated into the United States nor displaced through American settlement. It is important to note that "race" was deployed during the Philippine-American War in order to justify the "pacification" of the population through violence.[66]

Second, the notion of tribes marked the peoples as an aggregate, not a nation. The use of the term "tribe" to describe the peoples of the Philippines, placed with the narrative of social evolution, was a powerful argument against their nationhood and consequently their right to a sovereign government. The narrative of evolution was of great importance in the representation of the peoples of the Philippines; it appeared to group representatives of all phases of human evolution, with emphasis on the earlier stages. The lack of a coherent national character signaled the absence of a compact nation capable of self-government. Indeed, during the fighting in the Philippines, the supporters of the war regularly used the argument that the rebellion of a "single tribe" could not be compared with a legitimate national revolution for independence since none of the multiple "tribes" within the Philippines was capable of governing the whole country in all its diversity. Even though particular classifications might be questionable, the overall project of ethnological study and hierarchical classification of tribes remained intact and was a strong justification of imperial rule. The imprecision or inconsistency of the census or the official reports in no way undermined their usefulness in defining and justifying an overall strategy of rule; on the contrary, the analogy of tribes was the principal strategy. The difficulty of a precise determination of the various peoples that inhabited the islands simply reinforced the fundamental idea that they were but a geographical aggregate of tribes in various stages of social evolution. As such, however, they did not constitute a nation.

Third, religion further distinguished the peoples of the Philippines according to their general level of civilization and consequently their capacity for local self-government and participation in representative democracy at the national level. Depending upon the level of civilization, local self-government, guided by an overarching imperial rule, could be gradually institutionalized under American tutelage. The Christian tribes were more or less "civilized," but the non-Christian tribes—whether "Moro" or "pagan"—were definitely not.[67] As we shall see in chapter 5, religion was the fundamental criterion that served to divide the Philippines into provinces with different forms of government.

Thus, the general appraisal articulated a complex trope of plurality, making abundant use of an analogy of tribes articulated within a more general narrative of social evolution.[68] The great diversity of peoples appeared to represent all phases of human evolution, and of particular interest were the earliest or lowest types. The narrative of evolution required a classificatory and hierarchical scheme. Although there was indeed much confusion and speculation regarding the exact number of tribes and how to distinguish them, this paradigm served as the main support for the demographic reports and ethnographic research in the Philippines.[69] Like the official publications, the popular publications uniformly used an analogy of tribes and the narrative of evolution, although they dispensed with scientific pretensions. The popular illustrated books emphasized the basic racial foundations (Malay, with some Negrito and Indonesian), the immense diversity of language and culture (the "tribes"), and the fundamental divisions of religion. They grouped the peoples of the Philippines into three convenient categories: the "wild," "pagan" hill tribes (either Negrito or Malay); the Muslim tribes ("Moros," of either Malay or Indonesian stock); and the Christian tribes (Malay, often called "Filipino," or, when of mixed Spanish or Chinese ancestry, "mestizo").

Clearly the popular texts followed the same paradigm as found in the official reports and ethnographic studies, although they were sometimes wildly inaccurate in their descriptions. For example, Olivares consulted many authoritative sources for his book, among them John Foreman, Ramón Lala, Dean Worcester, and Alfred Russel Wallace, all of whom had published important and influential books.[70] He also suggested in his book that he had visited the Philippines, where he interviewed officials and journalists. However, he mistakenly included extensive quotations about New Guinea from *Malay Archipelago,* by Alfred Russel Wallace. He treated much of Wallace's discussion of Oceania as if it were a part of the Philippines. This confusion is evident in Olivares's inclusion of several photographs of Papuans (of British New Guinea) as one of the tribes of the Philippines. He apparently thought that the Malay archipelago was coextensive with the Philippine archipelago. This factual error of including tribes beyond the political boundaries of the Philippines merely amplified the trope of plurality; it was entirely consistent with the analogy of tribes and did not diminish its discursive truth.

Although they constituted only a demographic minority, the hill tribes were of great interest to the public and experts alike.[71] In 1898, one such expert, Dean Worcester, published an article in *National Geographic Magazine* devoted entirely to the most primitive tribes. According to Worcester, the "wild peoples" throughout the Philippines were "harmless and inoffensive so long as they are well treated." He stated that, rather than being a threat, they "afford an interesting problem in civilization" and "a most interesting study to the anthropologist."[72]

Some years later, after considerable experience in the hill country of Luzon, Worcester published, also in *National Geographic Magazine,* three lengthy and profusely illustrated articles on the "wild men," the "head hunters," and the "non-Christian tribes."[73] Photographs of the "savages" and their primitive ways were treated extensively in the popular books as well, even though they lacked the ethnographic authority of Worcester. The Aetas, also known as Negritos, were of particular interest. Considered to be the original inhabitants of the Philippines, they supposedly represented the earliest phase of human evolution, sometimes disparagingly called the "missing link." According to Olivares, "These pygmy peoples are . . . descended directly from the original stock of the so-called missing link."[74] They were racially similar to the "black race" but distinct from the Malays. Their physical smallness; their use of bows and arrows; their economy of hunting and gathering; their nomadic existence; their poorly constructed, temporary houses were all signs of a profound and troublesome inferiority. They were deemed beyond improvement and so destined to disappear. According to Worcester, *"They are a link which is not missing, but soon will be!"* In his opinion, they were "absolutely incapable of civilization."[75]

In his book, White placed a photograph of "Negritos" alongside a studio portrait of a native harpist (figure 3.15). The latter, an elegantly dressed woman,

Figure 3.15. Native Harpist of the Philippines and Negritos in the Island of Luzon. White, *Our New Possessions.*

was shown seated before a studio backdrop while playing a full-sized European concert harp. The caption stated that Filipinos had "intensely musical tastes" and that the harp was "one of their favorite instruments." In contrast, the caption described the Negritos as "aboriginal savages [who] are now becoming extinct." The photograph showed two half-clad men with a fully dressed woman with a scarf covering her head; she is squatting on the ground in front of a fence. There are at least two contradictions in the photograph. For one thing, White (and other authors) described the Negritos as inhabitants of the most remote mountainous areas, while the photograph showed them in what appears to be an urban or village locale. For another, the Negritos were described as "pagan" tribes that scarcely wore clothing, yet the woman in the photograph was fully clothed in the attire adopted by many Muslim women. Despite the contradictions between the text and the photographs, the central message of this photographic arrangement was clear: there was a marked difference between the civilized and the wild tribes. Some of the Christian tribes had evolved under the influence of the Spanish and had attained a high degree of culture. In contrast, the hill tribes were of the most primitive peoples in the world. If they could not be civilized soon, then they were doomed to extinction. The many views of brown people in their curious dress and exotic houses, their labor-intensive agricultural techniques, and their pre-industrial manufacturing technologies were all exterior signs of the absence of civilization. The Filipino elite was at pains to establish the difference between its high level of civilization and the "primitive tribes" and the racially based idea that Filipinos as a whole must evolve from the most primitive conditions. The former narrative suggested a prominent place for the elite in the colonial, and eventually the sovereign, state, while the latter justified the indefinite, direct control of colonial administrators.[76]

In the southern regions there were various Muslim tribes, also known collectively as "Moros," after the Spanish designation. The photograph in figure 3.16, taken circa 1901, was from the collection of the Bureau of Insular Affairs. It is another example of the ethnographic photograph: a careful composition of a young man of the Bagobo tribe (from Mindanao) in traditional dress and accoutrements. The caption, however, warned against a benign reading of the photograph and stressed the warlike nature of the Muslims: "The appearance of this Bagobo man is really misleading. To judge from his wistful expression and cupid lips, one would get the impression that he was effeminate. To be truthful, he is a valiant fighter and cruel to the extreme. When armed he carries a strongly tempered steel barong and kris dagger or merely the kris. The barong is a heavy weapon, razor-edged, and the fighter can, with a single blow, halve his opponent at the waistline. To cleave the enemy to the neck is child's play for this meek appearing pagan."

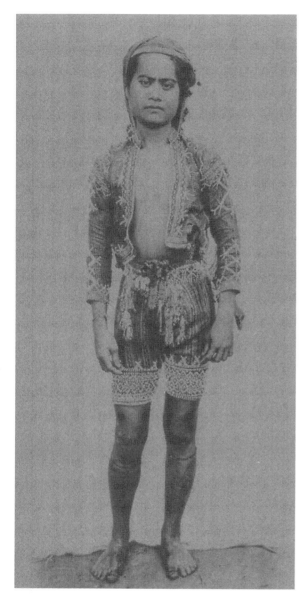

Figure 3.16. Young Bagobo Man. National Archives, Record Group 350-P Box 9 Bab-1-5-1.

This particular young man also appeared in another photograph as a musician with his instrument. It was not at all clear that the young man was armed in this photograph, although he may have been wearing a kris at the waist just above the pouch. However, other photographs from this same series clearly showed that blades in sheaves were a part of the traditional costume.[77] The popular publications sometimes published photographs in the ethnographic style but usually preferred more sensational compositions. In contrast to the studied style of the photograph in figure 3.16, the one in figure 3.17 showed a "group of Moros" posing aggressively with their knives and rifles and having a grand time. Although lacking any ethnographic pretensions, this photograph better expressed the official view of the Muslim tribes and needed little textual clarification to prevent a misreading of the image. The caption indicated that the photograph showed the "style of dress and equipment" of the "Moros," without specifying any particular tribe. In addition, the caption identified the man with the rifle and the raised barong as the "Sultan's younger brother." Although the sultan's brother put on a fearsome face, the rest of the group was joking around. To the left of the photograph we see evidence that it was taken on the gun deck of a battleship, and to the right we see the outstretched arm of a taller man in a long-sleeved coat, presumably a naval officer who seemed to be arranging the group for the photographer. The author did not indicate the occasion, but we know that until the abrogation of the Bates Agreement in

Figure 3.17. A Group of Moros. Bryan, *Our Islands*.

1903, the United States recognized the authority of the sultanate in Mindanao. This photograph showed part of the entourage of a *datu* or sultan on an official visit.[78]

Without exception, all authors had a dim view of the Muslims, in part because they practiced polygamy and allegedly possessed and sold slaves. The emblem of their character was the *juramentado,* often conflated with the notion of "running amok." First described by the Spanish colonizers, the *juramentado* was a sworn oath made by individuals or small groups to assault invasive Christian outposts or communities and to fight to the death in hand-to-hand combat. According to Ugarte, it was a Malay variant of *jihad,* with deep religious and political connotations. The notion of "running amok," in contrast, referred to the supposed general "Malay" trait of going into a violent frenzy that implied the incapacity of the Malay for reason, judgment, and self-control. The conflation of the two terms by writers suggested that a racial propensity of the Malay was to simply lose control and go on a rampage. The conflation also diminished the symbolic, religious importance of the *juramentado* and reduced it to a frightening exhibit of violent madness.[79]

In general, writers considered the "Moros" to be anti-Christian and fanatical. Wheeler worried that "With this fanatical people it would seem the American government is likely to have its most serious trouble, when brought into direct contact with them. At present an armistice or compromise [Bates Agreement] has been arranged by which they are to remain under their local authority, but acknowledging fealty to the republic. How long this will last or how creditable it is to republican ideas of government remains to be seen."[80] As we shall see in chapter 5, the Bates Agreement did not last long. It was abrogated immediately after the Christian nationalists were overcome by U.S. armed forces. At this point, the United States began its violent campaign to subdue and rule the Muslim areas.

The "Christian tribes," also often known as "Filipinos," were considered to be the most civilized. These included, among others, the Tagalogs and the Visayans. The Christian Malay also constituted the rural peasantry. The photograph in figure 3.18, from the countryside of Luzon, showed men and a boy with agricultural implements and accompanied by two women. The caption suggests that they are a "hybrid race, manifesting no definitive racial characteristics." The author also explained that as members of the "peasantry," they were little more than "slaves to the ruling class." The elements of the composition suggest a lack of civilization: the men were barely clad and did not use shoes; their tools were rudimentary; some squatted on the ground.[81] Most important, the caption suggested that they lacked both freedom and national identity and as such could not

Figure 3.18. Natives of the Island of Luzon. Bryan, *Our Islands.*

be self-governing citizens. Indeed, Elihu Root made precisely this argument. He described the Tagalogs as "in political condition practically in the state of peonage, totally devoid of the most rudimentary idea of liberty or personal independence, and accustomed for centuries to accept and blindly follow whatever local political superior has happened to be put over them."[82] This rhetoric of absence inscribed the inferiority of the diverse peoples, prescribed the necessity of economic development, and justified the political tutelage of the United States.

Opinions regarding the Christian tribes, especially the Tagalog, were often polarized. Olivares called them the "Anglo-Saxons of the archipelago" and regarded them capable of self-government.[83] On the other extreme, Halstead was not at all interested in the variety of cultures in the Philippines. Instead, he reduced all Filipinos (and mestizos) to the lowest level of civilization and referred to them in general as an "inferior race[who] eat with their hands, go barefooted, and sit on the ground." They behaved both as "Indians" and "monkeys." He concluded that there was an "enormous difference between them and a white man," and so they were totally unfit for any kind of self-government.[84] Those that compared the Filipinos to the Cubans argued in favor of their rapid independence. Those that reduced them all to savages found no basis for any forms of self-government whatsoever. Between these two extremes, authors, officials, administrators, and legislators tried to distinguish and govern accordingly.

Wheeler represented the dominant position. He included a photograph of "leaders of the insurrection" in his volume on the Philippines (figure 3.19). The photograph portrayed a group of men in military garb (except for one man in a white civilian suit), armed with pistols and swords, in an outdoor setting. It resembled many of the photographs of the Cuban revolutionaries, but the title revealed subtle distinctions. These officers were described as leaders of an "insurrection," not of a national struggle for independence. This "insurrection" had begun only recently, in 1899, although Wheeler ignored the revolution of 1896, which had resulted in the exile of Aguinaldo and other officers to Hong Kong. Indeed, Wheeler discounted the participation of Aguinaldo and the Philippine forces in the defeat of the Spanish ground forces in Luzon. He argued that the Filipino army had never been an autonomous entity, but rather the result of a temporary agreement between the U.S. forces and Aguinaldo. In contrast, in the Cuban case most descriptions recognized the long struggle of the Cuban people that had begun with a ten-year war in 1868 against Spanish rule. The renewed struggle against the Spanish broke out again in 1895 and gained the sympathy of the U.S. public, as well as the legislative and executive branches. According to this narrative, the United States had stepped in only to help Cuban independence, whereas Aguinaldo had stepped in only to assist the

Figure 3.19. Group of Officers. Leaders of the Insurrection, 1899. Browne, *The New America*, vol. 2.

U.S. expedition in the Philippines. Wheeler did not find the provisional government of Aguinaldo acceptable: "The provisional government which, under the dictation [sic] of Aguinaldo, assumed control of affairs in the Philippines, upon the overthrow of the Spanish domination, was a military despotism." He argued that military officials filled all posts in the provisional government. In addition, he appealed to the analogy of tribes to discredit Aguinaldo and the provisional government: his government represented only a minority of the population and would not be able to control the entire archipelago in the face of internal dissension and foreign intervention.[85]

The analogy of tribes was highly offensive to educated Filipinos.[86] They objected to the use of the term "tribe," the suggestion that there was no national unity among Filipinos, and the argument that the "insurrection" was led by a "single tribe." In 1900, Sixto Lopez, in his anti-imperialist tract, *The "Tribes" in the Philippines*, summarized the pervasive misunderstanding of the situation in his homeland: "Statements have been made to the effect that we are divided into eighty-four tribes, speaking different languages, and of all degrees of barbarism and civilization; that these 'tribes' are at enmity with each other; that they would never agree to form a united, strong government; and that one warlike 'tribe' is seeking to dominate all the others, and to rule with an iron hand the weaker and peaceable citizens of our country."[87]

Lopez identified the primary source for these statements as the Schurman Philippine Commission. However, this general characterization circulated widely, both in official documents and popular literature, and, as noted, was based upon the analogy of tribes. A single recalcitrant tribe, the Tagalog, had rebelled against U.S. rule because it wanted to dominate the country. This idea was known among anti-imperialists as the "single tribe fiction."[88] Lopez considered such characterizations to be so widespread and pernicious that he devoted his entire tract to their refutation. He concluded as follows:

> With the exception of the few uncivilized tribes in Central Mindanao and the Sulus, and the semi-civilized Igorrotes and Negritos of Luzon to which I have referred, the Filipinos are a homogeneous people belonging to the Malayan race. They speak different dialects, but they are *one* people. They constitute an overwhelming majority of the inhabitants of the Philippines. They are opposed not solely to American but to any foreign rule; and they are united in the desire for independence and for the purpose of maintaining a stable, independent government. In conclusion, I again assert without fear of contradiction, that the alleged antagonisms between the inhabitants of the provincial districts, or between the so-called "tribes," have arisen not in the minds of the Filipinos

themselves, but in the minds of those who do not understand our peoples and who have reached conclusions in no way warranted by the facts.[89]

Against the argument of diversity (expressed in the analogy of tribes), Lopez asserted the racial and linguistic homogeneity of the Filipinos, who constituted the overwhelming majority of the population. They formed a unified people seeking national sovereignty. In addition, Lopez described the Filipinos as a "Christian people practicing the morals and arts of civilization." The political implications of this debate were clear. A Christian, civilized, and unified people were worthy of self-government. An aggregate of widely diverse and wildly uncivilized tribes could never join the community of nations. Filipino leaders asserted their status as a "civilized nation" against the prevalent image of a "collection of tribes." In this way they claimed their right to political sovereignty.[90] Ironically, the nationalists ultimately won their independence in battle, but it would be postponed for decades because they lost the symbolic war; Congress was not convinced that they constituted a viable nation just yet.

* * *

A close examination of U.S. imperial texts of the period reveals that culture— understood as differences in customs and civilization—was just as important as race—understood as the biological substratum of human differences—in the discursive strategies of imperial rule. In general, "race" and "culture" were basic elements for the descriptions of the local peoples and functioned in two ways with respect to recommendations for rule. On the one hand, authors, whether official or popular, frequently invoked race in their representations. However vague the notion, it had an important function in imperial discourse. It justified and naturalized inequalities between the United States and its subject peoples; it was a sign of fundamental otherness. On the other hand, imperial rule was based specifically and concretely on an idea of potential cultural change and progress toward civilization: "social evolution." Indeed, the main justification for imperial rule was the conviction that through material improvement and education, the subject peoples could learn how to prosper economically and eventually to govern themselves. This image of the subject peoples established the strategy of tutelage in governmental matters, especially in the Philippines and Puerto Rico. In Cuba, the portrayal of nationhood led to a formally independent country, although concern over the capacity of the elite and the character of the general population resulted in a protectorate. In addition, the idea of "Americanizing" the subject peoples, in various ways and to different degrees, was thoroughly cultural in content, although it was never completely independent, either analytically or practically, from the notion of race, which postulated an inherent inferiority.

Despite the concern over the strong presence of blacks and mulattoes in Cuba, most authors placed considerable faith in the capacity of the white, educated elite to rule the country without direct intervention by the United States. The authors regarded racial mixing among the lower and middle classes in a somewhat positive light since it diluted the "African" element in both racial and cultural terms. Thus, the hope for Cuba was predicated upon the notion that the white elite had the capacity to govern the mulattos and blacks and that the black population would become less segregated and more assimilated among the general population. These resultant mulattoes, it was hoped, would be whiter and superior to either Afro-Americans or Haitians. This combined image of a militant national cultural led by a white elite provided a justification of Cuban independence. The Cuban elites took advantage of this situation to accommodate themselves favorably, thus gaining political power, social status, and economic advantage. They sacrificed full national sovereignty.

Puerto Ricans were described as a mixed race—white, mulatto, and black—of humble, working-class origin. The "whiteness" of the population and its possible further "whitening" was a metaphor for the potential cultural and economic improvements that the United States would oversee. "Mixed race" implied there were no clearly defined racial groups among the Puerto Ricans. Instead, a rather homogeneous culture was everywhere suggested although never stated explicitly. The only exception was the description of the local elite as either white or Spanish, as both different from and exploitative of the common Puerto Ricans. The texts were sympathetic to the poor, working-class Puerto Ricans and discussed the elite indirectly, obliquely, if at all. It was both educational and material improvement of the common people that defined and justified the imperial project. The symbolic displacement of the Puerto Rican elite and the image of a needy, passive, working-class populace formed the basis for the establishment of a colonial state in Puerto Rico with the promise of incremental integration to the United States. The elites sought only autonomy and believed the new regime would expand their power and privilege. They welcomed the projects of public education and capital expansion.

The principal narrative of Hawai'i emphasized the political evolution from a feudal system to the creation of a constitutional monarchy, its overthrow, and the subsequent establishment of a republic, which was finally annexed to the United States. The principal actors in this drama were the Hawaiian monarchical rulers, who were gradually displaced by European American settlers, who had gained hegemony by the end of the nineteenth century. The latter exercised control on all major fronts: economic, political, and cultural. The racial complexity of the islands was sometimes ignored in the narratives, but most important sources emphasized the aggregate of Hawaiians, Portuguese, Japanese, and Chinese by means of both text and photographs. This complexity did not, however, mean that Hawai'i was unfit for annexation; it was completely under the control of loyal American settlers. This narrative expressed the perspectives and interests of the annexationists and established the rationale for the establishment of a territorial government in Hawai'i.

In the Philippines, the rhetoric of social evolution predominated as a means of describing the considerable diversity of the islands and justifying the domination of the United States—no single native group was capable of governing itself, much less all the others. The notion of both cultural inferiority (incapacity to rule) and diversity (absence of a compact nation) justified the imperial project of the United States. The analogy of tribes was widely invoked. Religious differences were key categories with immediate and practical consequences for imperial rule, as we shall see in chapter 5. In addition, the notion of "cultural area" was frequently used. The dimensions of race, tribe, and religion functioned differently. The notion of race served as a marker of fundamental difference between the Philippines and the United States. The notion of tribe marked the peoples as an aggregate, not a nation, and therefore incapable of self-government or sovereignty. Religion further distinguished the peoples according to their general level of civilization and consequently their capacity for government at the municipal and provincial levels. In accordance with this general narrative of the evolution of diversity, the United States would establish a colonial state with the purpose of tutoring the elite and building a new nation. The imperial authorities actively sought out collaboration with the educated, Christian (read "civilized") elite, who were willing to negotiate privilege and power in exchange for the promise of independence in an indefinite future. The elite had struggled on both military and symbolic battlefields and had lost on both in the short term. However, their willingness to fight and to prove their high level of civilization led eventually to their independence several decades later.

Notes

1. Benjamin Kidd, *The Control of the Tropics* (New York: MacMillan, 1898), 1, 45, 56. See also the introduction by Jim Zwick in his Boondocksnet edition of Kidd's book at http://www.boondocksnet.com/editions/kidd/. Retrieved 28 January 2002.

2. Julian Go, "Introduction," in Go and Foster, *The American Colonial State in the Philippines*.

3. See M. D. Murphy, "Nineteenth Century Social Evolutionism," Department of Anthropology, University of Alabama; http://www.as.ua.edu/ant/Faculty/murphy/evol.htm. Retrieved 1 June 2006.

4. George Stocking, *Race, Culture, and Evolution: Essays in the History of Anthropology* (Chicago: University of Chicago Press, 1962), ch. 7, passim. Stocking notes that the "racist potential" of Lamarckian theory depended upon the specific application of its principles. The racist variant stressed the difficulty of changing centuries of racial inheritance. The "liberal" variant stressed the malleability of the social environment. Fabian argues that this hierarchy expressed a temporal dimension: the most primitive were examples of the earliest stages of human evolution. See Johannes Fabian, *Time and the Other* (New York: Columbia University Press, 1983). Julian Go argues that the Lamarckian scheme (of the "liberal" variant) was a fundamental premise in the process of racialization in the Philippines but not in Guam or Samoa. See Go, "Racism and Colonialism."

5. On the former, see Spurr, *The Rhetoric of Empire*, 69.

6. "The Cuban Census," *National Geographic Magazine* 11, no. 5 (1900): 205. On the metaphor of a "second Haiti," see L. Pérez, *Cuba in the American Imagination*, ch. 3.

7. U.S. War Department, Office Director Census of Cuba, *Report on the Census of Cuba, 1899* (Washington: Government Printing Office, 1900), 97. Lt. Col. J. P. Sanger was the director of the census. Henry Gannett and Walter Wilcox were the "statistical experts."

8. Hill, "Cuba," 230–232.

9. White, *Our New Possessions*, 584–585.

10. In Bryan, *Our Islands*, 255–256.

11. Ibid.

12. *Patogallo*, translated literally, means drake rooster. Upon seeing this photograph, Pedro Pérez Sarduy, author of several books on Afro-Cuban culture, confirmed that this was a fighting bird known as a *guineo*. For its speed and aggressiveness, it was once a popular fighting bird in Cuba but has almost disappeared from the countryside in recent times. Contrary to Olivares's definition, the bird is not a hybrid but rather a distinct species.

13. In Bryan, *Our Islands*, 103–104.

14. Ibid., 106–107.

15. Neely, *Panoramic Views*. Neely's book series contained photographs with captions but without any additional text.

16. This photograph stands in contrast to those of the elite—for example, White's photograph of a Cuban courtyard in figure 3.1. See also several views of the elite in their homes with their families, sometimes with servants, in Neely, *Panoramic Views*.

17. U.S. War Department, Office Director Census of Porto Rico, *Report on the Census of Porto Rico, 1899* (Washington: Government Printing Office, 1900).

18. Ibid., 58.

19. Karl Stephen Hermann, *From Yauco to Las Marias, Being a Story of the Recent Campaign in Western Puerto Rico by the Independent Regular Brigade, under the Command of Brigadier-General Schwan* (Boston: R. G. Dadger, 1900), 34–35.

20. According to Picó, military officials often referred to the elite Puerto Ricans as "Spanish" to distinguish them from the "Puerto Rican" colored masses. In part, this distinction arose from the mandate of the army to protect private property from the *tiznados*, workers who rose up against the rural estate owners and destroyed property and account books. See Fernando Picó, "Las construcciones de lo español entre los militares norteamericanos en Puerto Rico, 1898–99," *Revista de Indias* 57, no. 211 (September–December 1997): 625–635.

21. In Bryan, *Our Islands*, 287.

22. Ibid., 297, 299.

23. The photograph appeared on page 33 of U.S. War Department, *Report on the Census of Porto Rico*. It was originally part of a series of three photographs. The census omitted the other two, which were titled "Type of Negro, Not So Black" and "Type of Negro, Very Black." Thus, the author of the census picked the "mestizos" rather than the "Negroes" to represent the Puerto Ricans. Javier Morillo Alicea analyzed this series of photographs, today located in the National Archives, in "Looking for Empire."

24. In Bryan, *Our Islands*, 297.

25. In ibid., 288.

26. William Dinwiddie, *Puerto Rico: Conditions and Possibilities* (New York and London: Harper and Brothers, 1899), 149–150.

27. Maxwell, *Colonial Photography*, ch. 7. Maxwell does not, however, consider the deployment of many of these same photographs in the narratives of the expansionist illustrated books. The notion of mimicry is from Homi Bhabha, "Of Mimicry and Man: The Ambivalence of Colonial Discourse," in Bhabha, *The Location of Culture*, 85–92. The members of the Hawaiian monarchy also used their membership in local Masonic lodges and their international contacts with fellow Masons as a means of legitimating their rule during the nineteenth century. See Frank Karpiel, Jr., "Mystic Ties of Brotherhood: Freemasonry, Ritual, and Hawaiian Royalty in the Nineteenth Century," *Pacific Historical Review* 69 (2000): 357–397.

28. Browne, *The New America*, vol. 1, *Hawaii*, by Henry Cabot Lodge, 84–85, 104.

29. Osorio, *Dismembering Lāhui;* Elizabeth Buck, *Paradise Remade: The Politics of Culture and History in Hawai'i* (Philadelphia: Temple University Press, 1993), 73–77.

30. Lodge in Browne, *The New America*, 84–85, 103–104, 113.

31. For recent scholarship that refutes this narrative, see Osorio, *Dismembering Lāhui;* Silva, *Aloha Betrayed;* and Juri Mykkänen, *Inventing Politics: A New Political Anthropology of the Hawaiian Kingdom* (Honolulu: University of Hawai'i Press, 2003).

32. In Bryan, *Our Islands*, 460–467 (concerning political events), 513–523 (concerning land tenure).

33. White, *Our New Possessions*, 632–662. A very similar, but much shorter, narrative is found in March, *The History and Conquest of the Philippines*, ch. 15. March also omitted any photographs of the Hawaiian royalty.

34. Richard Dana, *Two Years before the Mast: A Personal Narrative of Life at Sea* (New York: Harper and Brothers, 1840). Surprisingly, Dana never visited Hawai'i; instead he interviewed Americans who had come to California from the islands. Castle Freeman, Jr., *Harvard Magazine*, May 1998. Downloaded 20 May 2004 from harvard-magazine.com.

35. Dana, *Two Years before the Mast*; cited by Halstead, *Pictorial History*, 209.

36. Halstead, *Pictorial History*, 203.

37. Lodge in Browne, *The New America*, vol. 1, xxiii, 155.

38. Silva, *Aloha Betrayed*. See also Buck, *Paradise Remade*, glossary.

39. White, *Our New Possessions*, 667–668.

40. Ibid.

41. In Bryan, *Our Islands*, 431–432.

42. White, *Our New Possessions*, 652–656.

43. In Bryan, *Our Islands*, 425.

44. Lodge in Browne, *The New America*, vol. 1, 21–22.

45. The classic study of plantation life is Ronald Takaki, *Pau Hana: Plantation Life and Labor in Hawai'i, 1835–1920* (Honolulu: University of Hawai'i Press, 1984). Regarding prejudice against Japanese, see Gary Okihiro, *Cane Fires: The Anti-Japanese Movement in Hawaii, 1865–1945* (Philadelphia: Temple University Press, 1992).

46. Love argues that depictions of racial diversity undercut the annexationist movement and supporters were keen to avoid them. Opponents usually drew attention to the racial composition, emphasizing that Euro-Americans were but a minority. Love, *Race over Empire*.

47. See Bryan, *Our Islands*, 431–432.

48. Ibid., 432.

49. Ibid., 457.

50. Hawaiian Commission, *Report of the Hawaiian Commission*, 55th Cong., 3rd sess., Senate, 1898, Senate Document 16; U.S. Serials 3727: 3.

51. Lodge in Browne, *The New America*, vol. 1, 144.

52. In Bryan, *Our Islands*, 457–459.

53. The chronology of the exclusion acts can be found in Rosalie Jones, *The American Standard of Living and World Cooperation* (Boston: Cornhill Publishing, 1923), 89–108.

54. Lala, *The Philippine Islands*, 83. John Foreman published a similar comment in 1890. He quoted a Franciscan friar from Batangas: "The native is an incompre-

hensible phenomenon" (*The Philippine Islands*, 181). Wheeler quoted Foreman in his contribution to Browne, *The New America*, vol. 2, 212.

55. White, *Our New Possessions*, 239. White probably copied from Lala, who, according to his preface, began research for his book in the 1880s.

56. U.S. War Department, Division of Insular Affairs, *The People of the Philippines*, 56th Cong., 2nd sess., Senate, 26 February 1901, Senate Document 218; U.S. Serials 4043: 16. This report quoted extensively from Lala, *The Philippine Islands*, among others. See also U.S. Bureau of the Census, *Census of the Philippine Islands. Taken under the Direction of the Philippine Commission in the Year 1903*, 4 vols. (Washington: Bureau of the Census, 1905), vol. 1, 492, 518.

57. Leonard Sargent, "In Aguinaldo's Realm," *The Independent*, 14 September 1899, 23. In October and November 1898, Sargent, along with W. B. Wilcox, both naval cadets, made an extensive tour of Luzon, as authorized by Admiral Dewey. They prepared a report for Dewey, who forwarded it to the secretary of the navy. Subsequently it was read in full in the Senate. Senator Hoare collected this report, along with several of their articles, which had appeared in the magazines *Outlook* and *The Independent*, and published them as a Senate Document; see W. B. Wilcox and Leonard Sargent, *Affairs in the Philippine Islands*, 56th Cong., 1st sess., Senate, 9 January 1900, Senate Document 66; U.S. Serials 3850: 1–44. Olivares quoted this same description and prescription in Bryan, *Our Islands*, 656–658.

58. Margherita Arlina Hamm, *Manila and the Philippines* (London: F. Tennyson Neely, 1898), 153.

59. Eduardo Ugarte has argued that the notion of "running amok" was understood as the principal attribute of the Malay character, especially evident among Muslims because they were less civilized, pure Malay. See Ugarte, "'Qualifications Most Necessary to Rule.'"

60. Lala, *The Philippine Islands*, 83–88.

61. Philippine Commission (Schurman), *Report*, vol. 1, U.S. Serials 3885: 11. The census of 1903 counted twenty-four tribes; other reports have different numbers of tribes. See Vergara, *Displaying Filipinos*, 49–58.

62. Philippine Commission (Schurman), *Report*, vol. 1, table of contents.

63. In *Youth's Companion*, *Greater America: The Latest Possessions* (Boston: Perry Mason, 1902), 98. Wesley Merritt, Charles B. Howard, George Howe, and C. A. Stephens contributed to the chapter on the Philippines. *The Youth's Companion* was an illustrated family paper published weekly. This book is apparently a collection of articles from that paper, which also published several books on the United States and other countries.

64. Vergara, *Displaying Filipinos*, 50–68. I agree with Vergara's general idea of the "trope of plurality." However, I have broken the trope into its specific components:

race, tribe, and religion. In addition, I argue that the analogy of tribes (including the separation of tribes by religion) was the most important component of this trope.

65. The Spanish used the term "Filipino" to refer to those of Spanish heritage born in the Philippines. They called indigenous peoples *indios*.

66. Paul Kramer has shown that the Philippine-American War was understood and justified as a "race war." That is, the U.S. military established both the ends (direct control over the Philippines) and the means (military force) in racial terms. Specifically, the Filipinos were understood in general as a savage, uncivilized race that could be pacified only by violence. During this period, dehumanizing terms, such as "nigger," and derogatory neologisms, such as "gu-gu," came into use. According to Kramer, the war constituted a period (1899–1903) of "racial exterminism." Kramer, *The Blood of Government*, ch. 2. I should add, however, that the war was also justified as the revolt of a "single tribe" (Tagalog), and some hill tribes were recruited to fight under the direction of the U.S. military command. In addition, the southern provinces, inhabited by Muslims, were not pacified until after the so-called end of the Philippine-American War. Therefore, the "trope of plurality" was active simultaneously with "racial exterminism" even during the war.

67. Vergara, *Displaying Filipinos*, 48.

68. The use of the term "tribe" suggested an analogy: the peoples of the Philippines were compared with the North American Indian tribes in terms of their heterogeneity, lack of political unity, and general low level of civilization. However, this analogy was problematic as a guide for policy, as we shall see in chapter 5.

69. The Bureau of Non-Christian Tribes was in charge of the ethnographic research. David Barrows, director of the bureau, rejected the theory that all peoples in the Philippines were basically of Malay stock. Barrows stated his working hypothesis in a most schematic manner. The Negritos, considered to be racially distinct from all other groups, were viewed as both the original inhabitants and the most backward. Next were the Malay, "of low culture broken up in many tribes," principally inhabiting Luzon. The southern islands (Mindanao and the Sulu Archipelago) were inhabited by tribes classified as Malay or Indonesian. Finally, the civilized Malay had been "formerly affected by Hindu culture, Christianized by Spain and now [were] approaching the plane of western civilization." David Barrows, "Circular of Information: Instructions for Volunteer Field Workers" (Manila: Bureau of Non-Christian Tribes, 1901), 7–8. National Archives, Record Group 350, 3833. See also Philippine Commission (Schurman), *Report*, vol. 1.

70. Olivares listed these sources in Bryan, *Our Islands*, 609. In addition, he had access to the opinions of official observers—namely, Leonard Sargent and W. B. Wilcox, Joseph Wheeler, George Becker, and Professor O. C. Marsh of Yale (ibid., 641, 658–659).

71. Paul Kramer argues that the Filipino elite, in its bid for political recognition, had to continuously struggle against the tendency to identify the "primitive tribes" with "Filipinos" in general. This was especially important during the St. Louis Exposition in 1904, in which the fascination with "savages" dominated the organizers and the general public despite protests of the Filipino elite. By the time of the 1915 San Francisco Exposition, however, the elite had achieved recognition as the "representative men" of the Philippines. See Kramer, *The Blood of Government*, chs. 4, 6.

72. Dean Worcester, "Notes on Some Primitive Philippine Tribes," *National Geographic Magazine* 9, no. 6 (1898): 284–301. Worcester was later a member of the Philippine Commission and served as secretary of the interior.

73. Dean Worcester: "Field Sports among the Wild Men of Northern Luzon," *National Geographic Magazine* 22, no. 3 (1911): 215–267; "Head-Hunters of Northern Luzon," *National Geographic Magazine* 23, no. 9 (1912): 833–930; and "The Non-Christian Peoples of the Philippine Islands: With an Account of What Has Been Done for Them under American Rule," *National Geographic Magazine* 24, no. 11 (1913): 1157–1256. These articles contained high-quality black-and-white and colored photographs.

74. In Bryan, *Our Islands*, 660.

75. Worcester, "The Non-Christian Peoples of the Philippine Islands," 1228. Emphasis in original.

76. Kramer, *The Blood of Government*, chs. 3–4.

77. See "Two Bagobo Musicians and Their Instruments, Davao, Mindanao, P.I.," n.d. (National Archives, Record Group 350-P Box 9 Bab-1-5), and "Young Bagobo in Regalia Costume, Davao, Mindanao," n.d. (ibid., Bab-1-3).

78. Bryan, *Our Islands*, 744. On the same page, there was a photograph of "A Dato, or Moro Chief, on Board an American Warship."

79. Ugarte, "'Qualifications Most Necessary to Rule.'"

80. Wheeler in Browne, *The New America*, vol. 2, 217.

81. Vergara has argued that inferior racial traits were marked by squatting, full or partial nudity, small stature, etc. See Vergara, *Displaying Filipinos*. It should be noted that these were most likely Tagalog peasants, and it would seem that the men were dressed in their working clothes.

82. Letter from Elihu Root to Senator Morgan, 8 July 1902. National Archives, Record Group 350, 5749.

83. In Bryan, *Our Islands*, 560.

84. Halstead, *Pictorial History*, 330–331.

85. Wheeler in Browne, *The New America*, vol. 2, 297–298. Aguinaldo demanded independence for his country with protection by the United States from foreign intervention. Wheeler called this proposal "unfair" to the United States (299).

86. The Filipinos' response to colonial rule was complex and varied; see Michael Cullinane, *Ilustrado Politics: Filipino Elite Response to American Rule, 1898–1908* (Quezon City: Ateneo de Manila University Press, 2005). For a comparative view of Filipino resistance and accommodation, see Vince Boudreau, "Methods of Domination and Modes of Resistance: The U.S. Colonial State and Philippine Mobilization in Comparative Perspective," in Go and Foster, *The American Colonial State in the Philippines.*

87. Sixto Lopez, *The "Tribes" in the Philippines* (Boston: New England Anti-Imperialist League, 1900), http://www.boondocksnet.com/ai/vof/sl_tribe.html. In Jim Zwick, ed., *Anti-Imperialism in the United States, 1898–1935,* http://www.boondocksnet.com/ai/. Retrieved 26 February 2002.

88. The "single tribe fiction" was refuted by Edward Pierce in his anti-imperialist tract, *The "Single Tribe" Fiction,* Liberty Tracts, No. 14 (Chicago: Anti-Imperialist League, 1900).

89. Lopez, *The "Tribes" in the Philippines,* 7. Emphasis in original.

90. Ibid., 4. See also the message of Felipe Buencamino to the Congress and the interview with Sixto Lopez reproduced in "Civil Government for the Philippine Islands," 57th Cong., 1st sess., Senate, 2 June 1902; *Congressional Record* 35, nos. 6–8, 6168–6187. Kramer has demonstrated the complexity and amplitude of this struggle for the Filipino elite to be recognized as "representative men" in *The Blood of Government.*

Chapter 4
Strategies for Americanization

The Family of Man and the Infant Metaphor
One of the most prevalent tropes of the nineteenth century was that of the "family of man." It provided an image of legitimate and intimate social hierarchy based upon unequal relationships among races, genders, and classes. The normative middle-class nuclear family of the nineteenth century—understood as the subordination of women and children under the authority of the husband and father—provided a model for the male authority over social inferiors, including peoples of other cultures or races. The science of zoology provided the theoretical basis for this metaphor by means of the principle that "ontogeny recapitulates phylogeny"—that is, the lineage of human evolution corresponded to the stages of a child's growth. All races had to pass through the stages of growth from the most infantile state of savagery to the highest adult stage of civilization. The white race had, for the most part, attained highly advanced civilization. Moreover, every child recapitulated the process of human evolution, although only the white male child could progress through the complete process.[1] At the same time, the metaphor of family designated the responsibilities of white men to promote the common interest of humanity: to educate and guide the maturation of their own children and the civilization of those lowly races that were like children.

The metaphor of the family of man offered a very powerful analogy for evaluating and ranking other peoples because it provided both a justification for hierarchy and the hope for improvement for the reputedly inferior groups. If the adults of inferior groups were like children, then white male "fathers" must exercise their authority and guidance over them. The infant metaphor was used widely throughout the nineteenth century to describe both peoples within the territorial jurisdiction of the United States—especially American Indians and Afro-Americans—and those of other regions, including Latin America. In June 1898, immediately prior to the signing of the Treaty of Paris, the U.S. commissioner of education published a detailed analysis of the backward condition of public education in Cuba, Puerto Rico, and the Philippines and recommended that the U.S. government promote the improvement and expansion of public schools. The commissioner prefaced his discussion by stating a familiar principle—ontogeny recapitulates phylogeny—although he did not explicitly use this phrase: "The child of an American citizen, in a favorable locality, between the years of 1 and 20 passes through all the stages of culture between the savage and the highest civilization." This process of acculturation could only occur in a "favorable locality," where the child had access to "eight years of elementary studies" along with "four years of secondary or higher study." Education prepared youth for "understanding and using the instruments of civilization."[2] Without the proper education, children would never progress beyond savagery or barbarism. In Kipling's infamous phrase, it was the "white man's burden" to educate the uncivilized.

The elaboration of the idea of civilization was central to colonial discourse since it permitted both a description of the current state of affairs and a projection of future strategies concerning the new possessions. What, then, were the specific criteria of civilization? What were its signs? What must be done in order to civilize? The commissioner of education offered a succinct and pointed analysis with clear policy recommendations:

> We must emancipate them [the uncivilized] from tribal forms and usages and train them into productive industry and individual ownership of land. We must take them out of the form of civilization that rests on tradition and mere external authority and substitute for it a civilization of the printed page, which governs by public opinion and by insight rather than by mere authority. Such a civilization we have a right to enforce on this earth. We have a right to work for the enlightenment of all peoples and to give our aid to lift them into local self-government. But self-government can not exist where there is no basis of productive industry and book-learning.[3]

This passage suggested that civilization was measured by the degree of individual ownership of land, the extent of advanced technology, and the level of literacy. Furthermore, the commissioner continued, civilization, understood as technological knowledge, allowed "man to conquer nature and make it his servant." The indicators of advanced civilization were commerce; railroads; steam engines; and the "knowledge of the uses of minerals, chemical substances, and the natural forces, such as heat, light, electricity, gravitation." The commissioner went on to explain that all cultures could be ranked along a continuum from the lowest tribal forms to the glorious exemplars of advanced civilization, specifically the modern nations of Great Britain, France, Germany, and the United States. Advanced technological knowledge was, of course, completely beyond the capacity of the tribes, due to their small size, their lack of cooperation with other peoples, and the absence of communication with the outside world. In between the tribe and the modern nation were those "other forms of civilization above the tribe [that] take rank as higher or lower according to the degree in which they realize this ideal of conquest over nature and complete intercommunication with the rest of the world."[4] Although this text did not in fact rank the new possessions, its implications were clear. The Philippines, with its host of widely dispersed tribes, fell among the least civilized. In contrast, Hawaiʻi, with its expansive commerce and extensive public school system, was among the more advanced. Cuba and Puerto Rico fell in between these two extremes: private property was well established, although agricultural production languished due either to war, in the case of Cuba, or limited markets and investment in Puerto Rico. In both of these islands, revitalization and modernization of the economy awaited capital investment and the expansion of commerce with the United States. Literacy was quite inadequate, but the deprived children were anxious to learn.

Embedded in this discussion of the criteria for civilization was a political principle of utmost importance to the conceptualization and justification of imperial rule: "self-government can not exist where there is no basis of productive industry and book-learning." In other words, self-government could not exist, by this reckoning, where there was no advanced civilization. More concretely, this meant that the peoples of Cuba, Puerto Rico, and the Philippines could not adequately exercise self-government until they had visibly progressed in industry (and, by implication, commerce) and education. This document, then, suggested an integral connection between civilization and self-government, with special emphasis on the role of education and technology. First, civilization was understood in a technological and commercial sense. Second, education plus material advancement provided the basis for self-government. Finally, the uncivilized were like children, so they were capable of education and material progress through tutelage.

What were the best ways to civilize? A practical guide was provided in a mundane congressional document with a clumsy title: "Monthly Summary of Commerce and Finance of the United States, Colonial Administration, 1800–1900." It was accompanied by an annotated bibliography prepared in 1901 by A. P. C. Griffin, who sought to present "the world's best judgment of to-day's requirements in the government of a people differing in race characteristics and

climatic environment from that of the governing people, and occupying noncontiguous territory."[5] The "Monthly Summary" raised the question of the most
effective means of introducing and extending "civilization and enlightenment"
to the colonies. It described how the great European countries of the nineteenth
century had done it:

> [They civilized their colonies through the] introduction of roads, railways, irri-
> gation works, river and harbor improvements, and through them the devel-
> opment of production and thus of material prosperity; the encouragement of
> commerce and the adoption of improved conditions of life; the establishment
> of reliable and permanent forms of currency, with proper banking facilities for
> the encouragement of thrift among the natives; the establishment of postal
> and telegraph service for the encouragement of intercommunication among
> the people of the colony and between them and the outside world; the estab-
> lishment of steamship lines to connect the colony with the home country and
> the civilized world, the encouragement of education through schools, colleges,
> newspapers, libraries, and churches; the establishment and proper administra-
> tion of laws and regulations by which public safety and order are assured.[6]

William Taft summed up this idea as follows: "Civilization follows material development."[7] This description of the means of civilization emphasized
primarily the criteria of technology (production, transportation, and communication); economy (savings, commerce, and material prosperity); education
(schools and literacy); and administration (law and order). The lack of these elements signaled backward civilization. The technological and economic criteria
established the relative backwardness of the people, while the educational and
administrative criteria established their incapacity for self-government. In this
way, official reports, censuses, and popular books could demonstrate, through
textual description and photographic illustration, the absence of "civilization
and enlightenment" and thus justify and even prescribe one form or another
of colonial government. Furthermore, the justification of empire was premised
upon the ability of the United States to improve the infrastructure, to foster economic expansion, to educate the common people, and to guide the local leaders
on the path to self-government.[8]

What, then, was self-government, and how might it be achieved? In 1901,
Woodrow Wilson delivered a speech, "The Ideals of America," that one year later
appeared in the *Atlantic Monthly*. In it, Wilson argued against the immediate
independence of the Philippines and repeated the familiar motif that the Philippines did not have the characteristics of a nation: "You cannot call a miscellaneous

people, unknit, scattered, diverse of race and speech and habit, a nation, a community." More original, however, was Wilson's general definition of self-government,
his outline of the history of its origins in England, its full realization in the United
States, and its further dispersal by means of colonization. Citing the English political philosopher Edmund Burke, Wilson argued that liberty must be balanced with
obedience to the state. In the Philippines, only a colonial power could establish a
stable, ordered government and achieve this balance: "This is what Burke meant
by combining government with liberty,—the spirit of obedience with the spirit
of free election. Liberty is not itself government. In the wrong hands,—in hands
unpracticed, undisciplined,—it is incompatible with government. Discipline must
precede it,—if necessary, the discipline of being under masters."[9]

Liberty should not be granted hastily, Wilson argued, because there were
neither adequate leaders nor democratic traditions in the Philippines. Obedience and discipline must be first established by "masters"—that is, the U.S.
colonial administrators. In order to bolster this argument, Wilson used a trope
of immaturity; he infantilized the Filipino leaders and their country just as he
masculinized the colonial administrators. Aguinaldo was but a "winning, subtle
youth now a prisoner in our hands at Manila"; he was not "a second Washington."
Furthermore, the peoples of the Philippines had limited experience in responsible government: "They are children and we are men in these deep matters of
government and justice." Regarding self-government, Wilson wrote, "Liberty is
the privilege of maturity, of self-control, of self-mastery and a thoughtful care for
righteous dealings,—that some peoples may have it, therefore, and others may
not." Wilson believed that the Philippines, unlike Cuba, was not yet ready for
independence because, first, it did not constitute a nation, and its leaders and
peoples were too immature for responsible self-government. Most striking was
his argument that the building of the nation and the maturation of its people
were premised upon prior colonization by a people with traditions of liberty
and responsible government. This was so of the United States, colonized by the
English, and it was so of the Philippines, to be colonized by the United States.
In contrast, "We fought but the other day to give Cuba self-government." Cuba
was ready for self-government, but the Philippines was not.[10]

Wilson rounded off his article with a discussion of public education and
political tutelage, which he considered to be the twin responsibilities of the colonial power and the only means of achieving self-government. Public education
must make informed citizens out of literal children. At the same time, colonial administrators must tutor the figurative children, the local political leaders,
in the practical ways of responsible government. ("We are old in this learning
and must be their tutors.")[11] Wilson directed this discussion of education and

tutelage to the situation in the Philippines and Puerto Rico. Even though he suggested that the United States was committed to the eventual independence of the Philippines, no such promise was suggested or implied for Puerto Rico.

In this symbolic world, then, to suggest that Puerto Ricans, Filipinos, or anyone else were like children was to argue that they were not fully civilized and therefore not prepared for full political rights or responsibilities. They would require not only formal education and economic development, but also tutelage by the United States in all matters of government. The infant analogy was especially important because it both established the incapacity of peoples to govern and provided the paradigm for the tutelage of these peoples; limited, but progressively more autonomous, self-government would accompany the expansion of public education and technological development. Thus, the infant metaphor articulated a political principle and a rough outline for imperial rule.

Likewise, to suggest that people were technologically backward was to argue that they were fundamentally incapable of self-government. Charles Magoon asserted the plenary power of the Congress over the new possessions and disavowed their capacity for self-government precisely in these terms. The peoples of Puerto Rico, Guam, and the Philippines were "unable to distinguish the difference between the Constitution of the United States and a map of the country, and [were] as incapable, at present, of properly applying its complex provisions and diverse agencies as they would be those of the switchboard of a union railway station."[12] Using a technological analogy, he reasoned that a people incapable of controlling a railway switchboard could not manage the mechanics of a constitution.

These combined criteria of civilization deprecated the complex social structures and symbolic systems of the diverse cultures throughout the imperial archipelago. As noted, many authors have argued that the imperial project was inherently "racist," suggesting that this dimension was even more fundamental than the issue of technological backwardness.[13] However, this argument underestimates the strategic importance of the projected improvements in technology, infrastructure, and education. The imperial governments had to justify their actions both in the United States and throughout the imperial archipelago. Racial superiority alone was not sufficient justification for domination, nor did the notion of racial inferiority alone provide an adequate strategy for the civilization project.[14] Without the stated goal of improvement and without evidence of the progress of civilization under U.S. dominion, the imperial project could find little justification. Furthermore, the connection between racism and imperialism was both complex and ambiguous. On the one hand, the most blatantly racist thinkers were most often against imperial expansion because of their fear of degeneration through contact with tropical climates and their inferior peoples.

On the other hand, imperial expansion was premised upon a Darwinian notion of competition and survival of the fittest.[15] This notion applied both to the rivalries among imperial powers and the peoples they subordinated. A notion of superiority was inherent in any imperialist project; the explicit goal of uplifting or civilizing inferior peoples was common among the European powers. As a result, imperialists of the late nineteenth century claimed legitimacy based upon a civilizing mission.[16]

The civilization project was understood in specifically "American" terms: U.S. markets, commodities, and ways of doing business; U.S. capital investment and technology; and widespread public schools in the English language. Only political tutelage could provide these requisites. How were these general ideas regarding civilization to be applied in the different sites? What were the particular tactics of Americanization?

The Problem of Americanization without Settlement

As we have seen, by the late nineteenth century Hawai'i had been thoroughly Americanized through the immigration of European Americans, who quickly established economic, political, and cultural hegemony. Upon the U.S. acquisition of the former Spanish territories of Puerto Rico and the Philippines, many began to speculate upon the possibilities for their Americanization. The Hawaiian Commission, which had submitted its report pursuant to the establishment of civil government in Hawai'i, expressed its concern about the possible precedents that the annexation of Hawai'i and its future territorial government might establish for rule over the new possessions. The commission explicitly rejected the idea that the peoples of Puerto Rico and the Philippines were prepared for self-government to the same degree as in Hawai'i:

> Much has been said to the effect that the policy or scheme of government for the Hawaiian Islands will be taken and accepted as an index or precedent to be followed in the plan of government for Porto Rico and the Philippines. In view of this apparent expectation or belief on the part of many good people in the United States, the commission deem it proper to say that the people of Hawaii are capable of self-government, and have proven this by the establishment of the Republic of Hawaii and the adoption of a constitution and code of laws which will compare favorably with those of any other government, and under such constitution and laws have maintained a stable government for several years worthy of a free people. The people of those islands are more or less familiar with the institutions and laws of the United States, while the laws of the little Republic are largely taken from the laws of this country.

It can not be said that either the Porto Ricans or the Philippinos are at all
familiar with our system of government, or with any other based on the principles of liberty.

The underlying theory of our Government is the right of self-government, and
a people must be fitted for self-government before they can be trusted with the
responsibility and duties attaching to free government. These remarks are made
to negative [i.e., reject] the idea that because the people of the Hawaiian Islands
can, in the judgment of the commission, be consistently given self-government to
an extent almost equal to that given to the people in the States, it can not be safely
inferred that other insular possessions which the United States have, or may
acquire by treaty with Spain, can be granted equal freedom in government.[17]

Both the renowned expansionist author Murat Halstead and the high-
ranking official George Davis quoted this influential recommendation, and they
concurred.[18] Only slightly beneath the surface of this recommendation was the
distinction between the American settlers of Hawai'i and the former Spanish
colonial subjects. The "free people" of Hawai'i had established a constitutional
republic, and they had effectively governed for several years. The "little Republic" was modeled upon the institutions and laws of the great republic. Its people
were familiar with the "principles of liberty," as well as the "responsibilities and
duties" of a free government; in short, they were "fitted for self-government."
Who specifically were these "free people" who were worthy of a system of self-
government "almost equal" to that enjoyed by the citizens of the United States?
They were not the native Hawaiians, although they were also citizens of the
republic. They were neither the Japanese nor the Chinese; most were not even
citizens. Instead, these were the European American settlers who had over-
thrown the constitutional monarchy and established the republic.

As we have seen above, the principal narrative of Hawai'i was of Americanization and political evolution under the guidance of U.S. settlers. If the
former Spanish colonies were ever to attain self-government, they too would
have to be Americanized. But exactly how were they to learn the American way
of self-government? Given the absence of American settler populations in the
new possessions, authors, colonial administrators, and prospective colonists
tentatively considered the possibility of migration to Cuba, the Philippines, and
Puerto Rico. However, they soon concluded that there were few opportunities
for colonization. Americanization by means of settlement, a deeply ingrained
idea derived from historical experience, would have very little practical application in the former Spanish colonies. Referring specifically to Cuba and Puerto
Rico, Olivares observed that there were no opportunities for the "small capitalist

or enterprising citizen whose only capital consists of the usual American pluck and good health."[19] For large-scale capital investment, however, the opportunities were considerable:

> During the progress of this marvelous development, which has already commenced, there will be opportunities for American enterprise and the profitable investment of capital greater than were ever known in the whole previous history of our century. At the same time it must be admitted that these advantages cannot be enjoyed by the masses of the people to the same degree that characterized the settlement of territories that were contiguous to the older States, because the islands are not so accessible. The citizen seeking a home or investment in these new possessions [Cuba and Puerto Rico] cannot take his rifle, or his ox-wagon and his "yellow dog," and depending upon wild game for sustenance, journey into the wilderness to clear a field and build a cabin for his wife and children. He must have the means to pay the cost of an ocean voyage, more or less expensive according to the location of his objective point, and still have some left on his arrival to purchase a title from some previous owner. For it must not be forgotten that the islands are already owned and occupied by a population in many instances more dense than our own, and neither humanity nor good policy will permit the dispossession of these people. Still, in every one of the principal islands there are vast tracts of unoccupied lands as fertile as the sun ever shown upon, and these may be purchased, now before the era of general improvement sets in, for a mere song in comparison to their real value.[20]

Olivares established a clear distinction between settlers, on the one hand, and large capitalists, on the other. The new possessions presented opportunities unlike those afforded by the previous continental expansion. First, the new islands were relatively inaccessible and required an expensive journey. Second, most productive land was either occupied or owned and "neither humanity nor good policy" permitted the outright dispossession of the local population. Therefore, settlement "by the masses" would not be possible. However, land was both relatively cheap and marvelously fertile, so large-scale investments could be both extensive and profitable. Unlike the continental experience, in which Americanization was driven by settlement, in the new possessions capital investment would initiate the process of Americanization, especially through the use of American technology. This idea was implicit in the following comment: "Numerous enterprises in the way of railroads and street car lines are under way or contemplated, and in this respect Porto Rico will soon be thoroughly Americanized."[21]

The idea of Americanization by means of capital investment was quite popular and was repeated in both popular books and official publications. The principle that American capital would bring American civilization constituted the first pillar in the strategy of Americanization.[22] In 1902, a group of distinguished colonial administrators published a book detailing the economic opportunities in Puerto Rico and the Philippines—the "colonies"—and Cuba. These authors emphasized, above all, the considerable possibilities for large-scale investment of capital in agriculture. According to them, technological improvements, in combination with the extensive employment of cheap local labor, provided excellent investment opportunities. However, only limited numbers of U.S. professionals—lawyers and doctors, engineers and mechanics, civil servants and teachers—would be able to find gainful employment. Unskilled laborers or small-scale farmers would not find any opportunities at all.[23]

The second pillar of Americanization was public education, which would have a civilizing effect. In the words of Olivares,

> One of the most remarkable features that has developed in connection with the islands that have come under American influence, is the earnest desire of the people, and particularly of the children, to acquire knowledge. It was so in Cuba and Porto Rico, and we see the same manifestation in the Philippine Islands. Little naked or halfclad savages crowd into the sweltering schoolrooms and pursue their studies with an eager persistence that is truly wonderful. In Hawaii we found a population already educated even above our own high standard, for there are scarcely any of the natives of those islands who cannot read and write; and yet even there we perceive the same earnestness of desire to advance to the higher planes of knowledge.[24]

This passage expressed a dichotomy that ran throughout the sources of the period: the former Spanish colonies were fundamentally different from Hawai'i. Olivares found the "little naked and halfclad savages" of the former Spanish possessions to be both woefully ignorant and genuinely motivated to learn. These children were admirably persistent in their efforts to attend the new schools. In contrast, he did not describe the Hawaiian population as children; rather they were "already educated even above our own high standard" in American-style public schools with instruction in English. Protestant missionaries had successfully established these schools decades earlier. Despite a decided interest in the more exotic aspects of Hawai'i, the illustrated books agreed that it was an example of successful Americanization by means of settlement and the establishment of U.S.-style public institutions—namely, public education and constitutional government.

However, the general populations of Puerto Rico and the Philippines were unfamiliar with the American theory and practice of these institutions. Therefore, a period of tutelage was required. Public schools would provide the basic education necessary for efficient workers and literate citizens. In addition, local leaders would take part in the new governmental institutions. In this sphere, colonial administrators would be tutors in the art of self-government. This was the third pillar in the strategy of Americanization.[25] William Willoughby explained that the general policy regarding the insular territories was to entrust the dependent peoples with the management of public affairs to the extent possible given the particular local conditions. This policy, from a practical standpoint, encompassed "a dual problem: that of colonial government proper, and that of the education of the colonists in the art of self-government." The colonial government was the school of self-government: "There is no other known way that this instruction in the principles and methods of government can be imparted than in the practical school of experience." The local peoples were given a voice in the determination of policy and participated in the administration process but always under the supervision and guidance of imperial officials who were responsible for "pointing out errors," correcting "misconduct," and "encouraging higher ideals." According to Willoughby, the school of self-government was implemented at all levels: national, provincial (in the case of the Philippines), and municipal.[26]

These three basic principles—capital investment, public education, and political tutelage—would find their particular expression in each site. Let us now to turn to the analysis of the strategies for the Americanization of the sites that lay beyond the pale of settlement: Cuba, Puerto Rico, and the Philippines.[27]

Revitalization of Cuba

Perfecto LaCoste, former mayor of Havana and then secretary of agriculture in Cuba, was quite optimistic regarding the economic situation given the past and future investment of U.S. capital:

The amount of American capital already invested in Cuba is very large. Previous to the late war this capital was absorbed almost entirely by the vast sugar plantations, but the trend of investment to-day is toward more diversified interests, such as copper mines, tobacco, fruit and vegetables and the cattle industry. Cuba's geographical position, practically at the door of the United States, and her undoubted agricultural and mineral wealth offer a field for American enterprise, which is bound to attract not only an enormous amount of capital, but that which is equally essential, Yankee energy and brains.[28]

The fundamental contribution of the United States was to be capital investment, directed by "Yankee energy and brains." The fundamental contributions of Cuba were to be ample natural resources and the abundance of cheap labor. Yet LaCoste still held out the hope of settlement of smallholders from the United States. Even so, the smallholder would need inducements to migrate, although the author never outlined what these might be.[29]

White also believed that an influx of "American colonists" would "correct that which has been its [Cuba's] greatest disadvantage from our own point of view, the absence of a congenial American society." Notwithstanding his expressed hope for American immigration as the basis of the transformation of Cuban society and its integration into the United States, White had little to say about this possibility.[30] Instead, he continuously emphasized the economic changes brought about by the influx of capital: "It remains for industry and wisdom applied through the channels of labor and capital to make Cuba one of the garden spots of earth." White invoked the well-known notion of Manifest Destiny to refer not to the territorial expansion of a people, but rather to the expansion of U.S. commerce and capital: "It is manifest destiny that the commerce and the progress of the island shall follow American channels and adopt American forms."[31] In his discussion of economic expansion, White stressed three principal factors of production: the abundant natural resources of the island, cheap Cuban labor, and American capital: "The reorganization of peace and prosperity in the island of Cuba is a problem which should not be difficult of solution in an island where nature has such marvelous recuperative power. . . . The climate and nature's bounty will be the greatest contributor to this condition. Next will come the prompt and generous introduction of American capital and American enterprise, which are already beginning to make themselves felt. Finally will come the labor of the Cubans, applied to the latent resources of the island."[32]

Such was the division of labor as envisioned by White and his contemporaries. The United States would provide the capital for technological improvement, while Cuba would supply the land and labor. There was nothing in this scheme that required the establishment of an American community in Cuba. Instead, soldiers, tourists, and investors would introduce piecemeal U.S. "customs": beefsteak and buttered bread, baseball, and the English language.[33]

White published a photograph of a well-kept sugar mill, noting in the caption that this "factory was typical of the sugar mills in Cuba, though by no means the largest" (figure 4.1). He devoted an entire chapter to the production of sugar and tobacco. His description was both detailed and very favorable regarding the quality of the product, the fertility of the soil, and the technology. Unfortunately, the war had devastated much of the sugar industry, and many of the mills were "but wrecks of their former greatness."[34] Olivares also lamented the destruction of agricultural properties during the war but chose to publish several photographs of large sugar mills in full production. He also included detailed photographs of plowing, harrowing, harvesting, and replanting. The tone of his descriptions was optimistic, emphasizing the productivity of the soil and quality of the agricultural produce. Aside from the problems caused by the war, his only negative comment regarded agricultural implements, which were frequently made locally since the implements imported from Spain required an "excessive embargo." As a result, the implements used throughout Cuba were "of the most primitive character," as illustrated in figure 4.2. The plow in the photograph was

Figure 4.1. Sugar Mill near Culea, Island of Cuba. White, *Our New Possessions.*

Figure 4.2. Manufacturing a New Plow. Bryan, *Our Islands.*

hand- and homemade entirely of wood and had a single handle. Olivares looked forward to the near future, when the people would have the opportunity to purchase iron implements from the United States.[35]

Olivares foresaw that Cubans would buy not only U.S. manufactured goods, but also foodstuffs, in exchange for the tropical products of Cuba, especially sugar and tobacco. Figure 4.3 was one of a series of photographs from the Vuelta Abajo tobacco district in the province of Pinar del Río. It showed the strings of tobacco leaves that had been cut and were ready for curing. Olivares also included photographs of extensive tobacco fields, drying houses, and cigar workshops. Finally, he presented a photograph of workers fencing tobacco plots with barbed wire taken from the Spanish fortified defenses. The message was clear: Cubans would turn the land devastated by war into an agricultural paradise.

Olivares wrote glowingly of the Cubans, their country, and their promising future. They were dedicated to their country and their homes, and they expected and deserved good government. The productivity of the land and the energy of the people would soon be recuperated:

Figure 4.3. Cutting and Stringing Vuelta Abajo Tobacco. Bryan, *Our Islands*.

To-day Cuba is quiet, expectant, preparing for the great destiny which her people rightfully believe to be in store for her. Their heroism in war, and their patient endurance of the ills of bad government, that would have driven a more turbulent people into voluntary exile, prove them to be a race entitled, to a larger meed of praise than has sometimes been accorded them. They love their island homes with an intensity of devotion that is truly commendable, and under the blessings of a stable government, and its encouragement of honest industry, their prolific fields will soon blossom with nature's richest bounties. The more closely one studies Cuba and its possibilities, and the recuperative energy of its people, the more favorable will be the verdict as to the future greatness of this incomparably rich and beautiful island.[36]

However, this "future greatness" could be accomplished only with the help of the United States. Cuba would remain dependent upon its political guidance, capital investment, and commercial exchange. In figure 4.4, a black child, called a "mascot," appeared with the photographer Walter Townsend. According to the

Figure 4.4. The Artist and His Mascot. Bryan, *Our Islands.*

text, the child accompanied Townsend during his travels in western Cuba. By the photographer's own admission, the child was a hero of the Cuban revolution. Thanks to his young age and considerable ingenuity, the child, who remained nameless, managed to smuggle badly needed medicines, sewn into his clothes, to sickly *reconcentrados* in the town of Batabanó, at the request of a local doctor.[37] He managed to slip through Spanish lines, traveling roughly thirty miles north to Havana and back in less than a week. The caption of this photograph stated that his brave exploits deserved to be immortalized. Instead, the child—and by extension all Cubans—suffered an indignity unwarranted by his status as a patriotic hero. In the photograph, the child posed like a beggar, while Townsend, towering over the youngster, struck a haughty pose with a cavalier smile. Townsend appeared as a potential benefactor, paternal and proud, but none too sympathetic, although somewhat amused. He had entered into an unequal relation with the child, who was patriotic and resourceful, yet in need. He then arranged this deprecating and self-serving photographic caricature in which the hero was pictured as dependent and the interloper as benefactor.[38]

Was the relationship depicted in figure 4.4 much different from the relationship that the United States was establishing with the Cuban nation? The United States offered assistance in the economic reconstruction of the country but assured that large investors would benefit. It offered to better the basic infrastructure but thought principally in terms of the hygiene of its own troops and the safety of export agriculture. It promised political stability but insisted upon the right to intervene in Cuban affairs. Although the U.S. flag was not destined to fly over the presidential palace for long, the predominant narrative established Cuba's need of the United States as a paternal protector and guide. Faced with the economic ruin of the countryside and the exhaustion of the revolutionary army, the Cuban elite accepted civilian positions in the provisional military government and helped to reorganize the armed forces as a rural guard. By collaborating with the military government, the Cuban elite assured their political power, economic gain, and social position. In exchange, they pledged loyalty to the United States. In order to negotiate a speedy transition to civilian rule, they accepted the provisions of the Platt Amendment, which compromised the sovereignty of the country.[39]

Assimilation of Puerto Rico

In his discussion on the various problems in the transition from Spanish to American rule, George Davis, then military governor of Puerto Rico, concluded, "The Puerto Ricans can not be absorbed through the immigration of Americans, for the country is already more densely populated than India or any

State of the Union, and there is no room for any large influx of outsiders from anywhere."[40] Davis expressed the position held generally by colonial administrators: there were very few opportunities in Puerto Rico for immigrants from the United States. The island would never be a settler colony. This presented a difficulty: how could the island become Americanized without American settlers? For Commissioner Henry Carroll, the answer was clear: Americanization could be accomplished by the influx of capital from the United States: "The difference between Oklahoma and Porto Rico is chiefly geographical. The former provided for an overflow of population from surrounding States, the latter will furnish a field for American capital and American enterprises, if not for overflow of population. It is American and must and will be Americanized."[41]

This passage expressed a common theme with clear simplicity. The difference between the Oklahoma territory and Puerto Rico was merely "geographical"— that is, the island was not contiguous to the other states. Therefore, immigrants from those states would not establish settlement communities there. Instead, American capital, highly mobile and expansive, would Americanize the island by means of the establishment of productive and commercial enterprises. The island was "American"—that is, it belonged to the United States—and economic integration would promote "Americanization"—th at is, American investment and consequent American ways of doing business. Implicitly, rule by the United States would provide the platform for the establishment of the companies that, in turn, would provide the foundation for "Americanization."[42]

Charles Allen, the first civil governor of Puerto Rico, succinctly stated the argument regarding the former Spanish colonies in general and Puerto Rico in particular: "With American capital and American methods, the labor of the natives can be utilized to the lasting benefit of all parties and the general good of the commonwealth."[43] Allen asserted that the island needed "men with capital, energy, and enterprise to develop its latent industries and to reclaim its sugar estates; to build factories and railroads, and make the country hum with the busy sound of commerce." Such development would promote the common good of both Puerto Rico and the United States. Allen was not entirely clear whether he anticipated absentee owners or whether small numbers of investors would actually take up residence in Puerto Rico. At any rate, he did not envision widespread settlement by Americans. Opportunities even for professionals were quite limited since knowledge of the Spanish language was essential in the practice of law, medicine, and local commerce. The island already had "plenty of laborers and poor people generally" to work on the plantations and in the factories.[44] Therefore, Americanization would take place not by the hegemonic presence of "colonists," but rather by means of the widespread investment of American capital: "The peculiarities of the people and the distinct individuality of the island will for some time be a decided disadvantage, but with the introduction of American machinery and improvements, great changes will be effected, and with the thrift and industry that follows the Anglo-Saxon, in time this very individuality will disappear, and American capital, energy, and intelligence, will find a wide and favorable field for their successful exercise."[45]

According to this vision of the future, Puerto Rico would become more like the United States due to the improvements brought about by modern technology and the Anglo-Saxon way of "thrift and industry." The people of Puerto Rico would lose their "peculiarities" and the island its "individuality." In sharp contrast to both the recognition of Cuban independence and the promotion of future Filipino nationhood, the Americanization of Puerto Rico was understood as assimilation to the United States. This assimilation was to be based solidly upon capital investment in production and commerce. In addition, Americanization would be advanced by means of public education, including instruction in English, and through political tutelage, which would eventually lead the people to some unspecified form of local self-government closely tied to the United States.

In this respect, the child, often black and naked, was one of the most important representations of the peoples in Puerto Rico. In this context, "child" referred to someone who was immature, dependent, unfledged, and untutored. However, it also connoted innocence, loyalty, and potential and suggested eventual adulthood. Accordingly, this "child" must go to public school, receive instruction in English, be employed in factories and plantations, consume U.S. goods, and so gradually become Americanized. Nakedness expressed the poverty and backwardness of the population, the remedy for which only the new regime could provide by means of schools and economic development. Bryan published a photograph of a teacher and her students in Cataño (figure 4.5). However, the photograph did not follow the style of a school photograph; children were not grouped together in any orderly fashion, and there were several adult women with babies. There were not more than a dozen school-age children in the group, but they were all fully dressed, except that many lacked shoes. It was not clear which of the buildings (which appear to be suburban houses) was the school. Indeed, this appears as an informal picture of the residents in one of the many suburban neighborhoods throughout the island. Obviously, the local schools needed to be larger, better organized, and more prevalent, but it would take U.S. guidance to accomplish that. In contrast, Bryan also published a picture of the "first American school in Porto Rico"

Figure 4.5. Group of Schoolchildren and Their Teacher at Catano. Bryan, *Our Islands.*

in "Cangrejos" (that is, Santurce, a suburb of San Juan). Because of its rather poor quality, I have not reproduced it in this book. However, the contrasts were notable. According to the caption, an American teacher organized the school in Cangrejos. It was on the second floor of a substantial commercial establishment in the center of town. Dozens of children of roughly the same age (judging by their height) were lined up along the second floor balcony. The caption stressed that the children, "who manifest an eagerness to acquire knowledge, are rapidly advancing."[46]

The conclusion that Puerto Rican children were eager to learn was repeated by many authors. For example, Frederick Ober, who was one of the few authors to journey to Puerto Rico before the war, returned afterwards to report on the conditions there. He quoted the observations of a missionary who had ventured through the mountainous countryside on horseback: "The Rev. Father Sherman, who traveled over the island shortly after we took possession, reported the children as quick to learn, precocious even, and very susceptible of becoming Americanized."[47]

The image of the child was put to many uses. In figure 4.6, the photographer (Townsend) represented the presence and hegemony of the United States. He grabs the children, not with affection as toward his own, but rather as if they were possessions. Their nakedness, listlessness, and distended bellies evoked abject necessity and profound dependency. This photograph imitated the caricatures of the pickaninnies recently acquired by Uncle Sam (see the cartoon in

Figure 4.6. Our Artist in Puerto Rico.
Bryan, *Our Islands*

figure 1.1). In contrast to the photograph of the Cuban boy in figure 4.4, these children were not young heroes, but rather they appeared as wards.

According to these books, not only the school, but also the factory and the plantation would modernize the country and provide the basis for limited self-government. A photograph of the U.S. customs house at the bustling port of Ponce and its agricultural exports—coffee, rum, sugar, and tropical fruits—was a clear sign of progress and an indicator of the future thriving economy that would develop with the addition of U.S. capital, organization, production, and commerce (figure 4.7). "From this time forward is anticipated that Porto Rico's trade will be mainly with the United States."[48]

In contrast, White was rather ambiguous regarding opportunities for Americans in Puerto Rico. On the one hand, investment opportunities in wholesale commerce, retail stores, agriculture, banking, and manufacturing would be available to those willing to buy out existing businesses or properties, especially from Spanish owners who would soon be leaving the island. On the other hand,

Figure 4.7. U.S. Customs House at Ponce. Bryan, *Our Islands.*

Puerto Ricans were not accustomed to doing business with Americans. Still, White concluded, there was "nothing about the people of this island which makes the prospect of adapting them to American methods and manners a dubious one." Regarding retail trade, White warned that only a few stores would be able to sustain American consumption patterns. However, he believed that Puerto Rican consumption patterns would rapidly change under the influence of an "American population," which "by contact will teach the people of Puerto Rico to want things of the same sort."[49]

Halstead, the arch-imperialist, was both hopeful and condescending regarding the assimilation of the Puerto Ricans. He suggested that it would take some time for them to "assimilate Americanism," but the combined effects of the military government and capital investment would lead to the general well-being of the inhabitants. Any notion of Puerto Rican political participation, however, was entirely mistaken. Halstead wrote the following:

> The people of Porto Rico are of mixed races, and it is probable it will take them some time to assimilate Americanism even under the weighty expression of military authority. The dealings of the people of Porto Rico have been rather with Europeans than with ourselves. They will, we hope, and we base expectation founded upon ordinary human experience, trust, they will grow fonder of us as they find us out. It is an important point in our duty to make them feel at home under our flag and to soothe them if we observe restlessness in their manner when the novelty of being free Americans ceases to have an impressive fascination. Some of them may think reading certain interpretations by eloquent men of our Constitution, that it is a part of the contract implied when we took them in charge that they are to soon have a call to be heard in our general government. We have firmly but kindly to make known to them that they are mistaken.
>
> However, we have confidence they will be reasonable and "consent" to be governed without seeking trouble along lines of theory, promulgated in a spirit of benevolence by some of our eminent men in behalf of the Filipinos when they assaulted the American lines at Manila. We would advise friends in the colonies not to place a great deal of reliance upon the emotional element of patriotic gentlemen whose information is deficient, being radically erroneous. The people of Porto Rico, we are sure, will contentedly remain with us, partake of the bounty of our good will, consent to the investment of our capital in the improvement of the island, and be taught by us that they have not alienated but gained by our expansion including them in a liberal sense in the rights of man and an excellent opportunity of generous guidance in the better ways and

means, in the language of the Declaration of Independence, for the pursuit of happiness.[50]

This passage expressed a thoroughly imperial mentality. Puerto Ricans would enjoy some limited civil rights, especially the "pursuit of happiness," presumably in the economic sense. Real political rights, however, should not be forthcoming. While Halstead was more imperialist than most, his basic principle was shared by all. Puerto Rico would become Americanized primarily by means of material, economic improvement, specifically through the investment of capital, the expansion of commerce, and the American way of doing business. The Puerto Ricans, except perhaps for certain "patriotic gentlemen," would be quite content with this arrangement and would quickly "feel at home under our flag." Halstead's view was extreme only in that he did not anticipate the participation of Puerto Ricans in civil government. Most observers, including colonial administrators like Charles Allen, recommended limited participation in the government of the island: "At least as far as the exercise of the privilege of suffrage is concerned, citizenship should and, in this island at least to some extent, does depend on education."[51]

In sum, the Americanization of Puerto Rico was to be the result of capital investment, commerce, and public education, but without extensive settlement. Only Dinwiddie held out the possibility of extensive immigration. His formula for Americanization was as follows: ten years of capital investment plus ten years of public education (to increase literacy) plus the immigration of one hundred thousand Americans would make Puerto Rico—possibly—ready for statehood. Unlike other authors, he believed that American settlers would eventually control the government. The basic elements of his argument were the same, but instead of excluding settlers from the formula, he included a considerable contingent of them. This calculus led him to hold out the possibility of eventual statehood.[52] Other authors were less certain about the degree of assimilation that could be achieved in Puerto Rico without settlement. Notwithstanding, all were optimistic about the positive effects of economic integration and public education upon the gradual establishment of local self-government. Only the persistent view that Puerto Ricans continued to be a foreign, backward people prevented the island's full political incorporation as a territory of the federal union.

The Puerto Rican elites embraced at least two of the three projects of Americanization: capital investment and public education. However, political tutelage was a source of conflict. Both the colonial administrators and the Puerto Rican elites were in favor of an autonomous, but not an independent, government. Still, the meaning and practice of autonomy led to political conflicts. The Puerto

Rican elites complained that they were treated as children, yet they sought to be treated as brothers. They sought privilege, respect, and economic advantage and received, in many cases, reprimands for corruption, favoritism, and party politics. Nevertheless, the conflicts did not lead to direct challenges to the legitimacy of the colonial state or its policies of Americanization.[53]

Civilization of the Philippines

President McKinley's first proclamation to the Philippine people, in December 1898, assured them that the "mission of the United States is one of benevolent assimilation, substituting the mild sway of justice and right for arbitrary rule." He also promised the "bestowal of the blessings of good and stable government upon the people of the Philippine Islands under the flag of the United States."[54] Although the president's proclamation was ambiguous with regard to the meaning of assimilation or the form of government, it was clear in its claim to sovereignty over the Philippines. Indeed, the military governor, General Elwell Otis, recognized that the U.S. claim to sovereignty would be inflammatory to the Filipinos, and he refused to diffuse it until it had been edited.[55] In April 1899, after fighting had already commenced, the proclamation of the First (Schurman) Philippine Commission outlined a program of civilization, not assimilation. The commission stated that its mission was "the well being, the prosperity, and the happiness of the Philippine people and their elevation and advancement to a position among the most civilized people of the world." It mentioned specifically the guarantee of civil and religious freedom; the establishment of a just legal system; the promotion of "letters, science and the liberal and practical arts"; and the expansion of industry, trade, commerce, transportation, and communication. Instead of "assimilation," the commission proposed to ascertain the forms of government "best adapted to the Philippine peoples, most apt to conduce their highest welfare, and most conformable to their customs, traditions, sentiments, and cherished ideals."[56]

The Schurman Commission rejected the option of immediate independence because it predicted internal anarchy and inevitable foreign intervention by rival states. It also rejected the proposal of a protectorate. However, the ultimate goal was a "free, self-governing, and united Philippine commonwealth." The commission asserted that this ideal was attainable only through American occupation and temporary, albeit indefinite, colonial government.[57] This assertion was entirely consistent with Woodrow Wilson's argument, discussed above, that historically self-government was the direct result of colonization by those with profound traditions of liberty and obedience to the state. The Filipino nation, such that it was, could never develop these traditions on its own without tutelage. One year later, McKinley's instructions to the Second (Taft) Philippine Commission concerned the establishment of order, civil government, and a corps of Filipino civil servants. He repeated the idea that government must conform to local customs and added that the first civil governments should be established at the municipal level as soon as the area was pacified. He wrote that the Taft Commission "should bear in mind that the government which they are establishing is designed not for our satisfaction, or for the expression of our theoretical views, but for the happiness, peace and prosperity of the people of the Philippine Islands, and the measures adopted should be made to conform to their customs, their habits, and even their prejudices, to the fullest extent consistent with the accomplishment of the indispensable requisites of just and effective government."[58]

Nevertheless, certain principles were "inviolable," and McKinley instructed the Taft Commission to maintain them "however much they may conflict with the custom of laws of procedure with which they are familiar." In general, McKinley stated that "no person shall be deprived of life, liberty, or property without due process of law" and went on to specify the particulars.[59] The task, then, in the Philippines was the civilization of the people while taking into consideration their particularities.

As in all of the former Spanish colonies, the civilization of the Philippines would have to take place in the absence of U.S. settlement. In his contribution to the volume on opportunities in the colonies, M. E. Beall, of the Division of Insular Affairs in Washington, saw the Philippines as entirely inhospitable for American immigrants due to "differences in climate, the unusual crops, the foreign languages, [and] the strange people." He wrote that settlement would be impossible "unless a colony were formed which could take in a great measure its own customs and institutions along, and then the venture would be a hazardous one." A few professionals, especially in law and medicine, might find success in cosmopolitan Manila, but the man "without a useful trade cannot hope to compete in that climate with the native or Chinese laborers." Beall cautioned that "anyone who goes to the Philippines without a definite purpose, hoping that something will turn up, will make a serious mistake." He concluded that the opportunities in the Philippines, principally in agriculture, commerce, banking, and transportation, would require considerable "capital and skilled direction."[60]

Likewise, White deemed the tropical climate to be an impediment to the migration of Americans, especially for manual workers and their families. Such a climate would be "a very trying one for white women and children." Furthermore, the white man might "enjoy good health" only if he refrained from "all the excesses," including hard liquor, and if he "avoids violent physical exertion, does not expose himself to the hot sun in the middle of the day, and exercises proper care as to his diet." White advised that it would be "folly for the white mechanic or laborer or farmer to emigrate to these islands with the expectation of laboring at this occupation." American men simply could not work in that climate nor compete with cheap native labor. Commerce would be the most lucrative investment for U.S. capital. White noted that even though European companies controlled the large-scale commerce, there would soon be "opportunity for ample commercial enterprise for the American investor" once trade restrictions were reduced.[61] However, European American settlement would not be an important factor in the equation for controlling the Philippines.

Furthermore, the civilization project in the Philippines confronted an obstacle unique in the imperial archipelago: sustained armed resistance to the U.S. colonial regime. The illustrated books included many photographs of the Filipino "insurgents" and their commanders. On the one hand, this suggested that they were capable of organizing and fighting for their political rights and were determined to defend them. On the other hand, the authors found ways of deprecating their abilities and motivations.[62] Figure 4.8 shows General Gregorio Pio del Pilar in full uniform. The caption described him as both "aristocratic" and a "mere boy in age," even though it recognized his "vast influence among his people." At the time of the photograph, the general was twenty-three or twenty-four years of age and had considerable military experience; he had proven his bravery and leadership in the revolution of 1896 and later joined Aguinaldo in exile in Hong Kong. He returned in 1898, leading his troops in battle in several military engagements. He died in 1899 while defending the rearguard of General Aguinaldo, who was retreating through a mountain pass. On the page facing this large photograph, Olivares, quoting the report of W. B. Wilcox and Leonard Sargent, described the insurgent officers they met in Luzon in the following manner: "All of these officers are very young, a large proportion being minors."[63] Likewise, White described Aguinaldo, in a photographic caption, as a "man of slight physique," even though he recognized his "great ability as a leader and commander of men."[64] In addition, almost none of the Filipino officials had facial hair, while virtually all U.S. officials, following their military and social norms, had striking beards, both abundant and carefully groomed. In the minds of the elder, corpulent, bearded U.S. officers, the younger, slight, beardless Filipino commanders seemed but mere boys. The armed conflict in the Philippines resulted in the widespread characterization of Filipinos as uncivilized and unruly "children" who had dishonored the United States and now required disciplining and order.[65] Images such as these, when anchored by commentary, reinforced these stereotypical characterizations.

Figure 4.8. General Pio del Pilar. Bryan, *Our Islands.*

In the Philippines, then, the beginning of the civilization process was to subdue militarily the revolutionaries and then proceed immediately with the organization of municipal governments and public schools. Toward the end of the armed
conflict, Beall wrote that the "school book is taking the place of the cartridge as a
civilizer."[66] William Taft explained the process to the National Geographic Society:
"As the army pacified the islands we followed closely with civil government and
with schools."[67] First, military control was established simultaneously with educational and governmental efforts. The army was responsible for organizing both
the first English language schools and the new municipal governments. Municipal governments were organized as soon as imperial control was established,
beginning in the mountainous areas of Luzón, where the hill tribes had offered no
armed resistance. In the Christian municipalities, colonial administrators organized municipal governments as soon as the areas were subdued militarily. In
the southern Muslim areas, political reorganization did not begin until after the
Christian areas had been pacified. The military was deployed in the south only
after 1902 to put down armed rebellion, which was considerable in the Muslim
areas. Again, the strategy was to subdue the population by means of military force
and then organize municipal governments with both elected and appointed local
officials, all of whom were responsible to provincial imperial authorities.

Second, Taft understood the civil municipal and provincial governments as
the training grounds for self-government. According to him, it would have been
easier to simply appoint colonial administrators at the upper levels to govern,
but the Filipinos would not have learned anything about self-government: "They
would not be subject to scolding at every mouth by the officers above them, they
would not find out what it is to be responsible for the government of others, and
they would not be enjoying the education or partial education—or, rather an
education in partial self-government—which our system gives them."[68] Indeed,
Taft was simply following the recommendation of the Schurman Commission
to fill civil service positions as soon as possible with Filipinos. Soon, Filipinos
were active in all levels of government: municipal, provincial, and central. To be
sure, these positions were under the supervision of U.S. administrators; nevertheless, this Filipinization was a means of ensuring support for the elite and
quieting dissent.

Third, public schools were established, not only to teach Filipino children,
but also to "teach the Filipino teachers how to teach their Filipino children." Taft
included a photograph in his article adapted from a stereograph by the Underwood and Underwood Company (figure 4.9). The students in the photograph
were identified as boys in the normal high school in Manila—that is, they were
to be the teachers of Filipino children, although they appeared but children

themselves. This normal school, orderly and well appointed, was the "right road to Filipino freedom." It is true, Taft admitted, that the people of the Philippines were "less educated" and "more like children" than in the English colonies, but he strongly disagreed that they were incapable of learning self-government. They need only to be taught administrative responsibility, to be supervised closely, and to be scolded when necessary—in short, to receive an "education in partial self-government." The caption to the photograph suggested that the "right road" was public education and political tutelage, not rebellion.[69]

In addition to public education and political tutelage, technological development was understood as a key factor to civilization. Olivares contrasted the great "natural wealth" of the Philippines with the almost complete lack of

Figure 4.9. Right Road to Filipino Freedom. Taft, *National Geographic.*

technological development: "In a commercial sense, they are probably worth more than any other region of the same size in the world; and their riches are practically undeveloped."[70] However, backward technology resulted in the lack of economic development and was a sign of the low level of civilization. Most of the illustrations and descriptions in the official reports and popular books were devoted to this theme. White displayed two photographs on the same page (figure 4.10). Both were composed in the ethnographic style: posed profiles close to a plain background, either a wall or high bamboo fence. The first was of a Filipino "freight train"—that is, a *carabao* pulling a sled loaded with a very large basket. White commented that there existed ample opportunity for investment in transportation, with the implication that railroad development would be a priority. The second photograph was of an adult driving a *carabao* with a type of harrow used in wet-rice cultivation. In the caption, White stated that the development of agriculture would progress greatly by the introduction of "improved methods." Although he admitted that the people were "quite successful" in wet-rice production, he described their methods as "crude": they planted rice shoots by hand and cut the ripe heads of grain one at a time with a short knife; threshing was done either by treading or with wood flails; husking was done with big mortars; winnowing was done with flat baskets. In general, no machinery was used, except for the infrequent homemade husker or winnower. White suggested that manufactured farm implements and machinery from the United States would produce striking results: "The Filipinos have a surprise awaiting them in the introduction of American agricultural implements."[71]

The three pillars of the civilization project also applied to the most backward tribes, which were the object of much interest and scrutiny. In 1901, the Philippine Commission established the Bureau of Non-Christian Tribes in order to undertake ethnographic research, including the description of the current conditions and the classification of various tribes. It was to provide the knowledge base for the establishment of municipal and provincial governments in areas inhabited by animist and Muslim peoples.[72] In Washington, D.C., the Bureau of Insular Affairs collected photographs that showed the process of civilization of the wild tribes in the Philippines, principally through all kinds of before-and-after photographs, including people, roads, bridges, and houses. Dean Worcester also used this method of illustrating progress in his appropriately titled book, *The Philippines Past and Present*, in which he attempted to contrast the backward past with the improvements of the colonial regime.

Although imperial officials held out little hope for the nomadic Negritos, most of the hill tribes practiced sophisticated agricultural techniques, includ-

A FREIGHT TRAIN IN THE PHILIPPINES
Primitive methods of transportation still prevail in the islands, and there is ample opportunity for American development of this industry.

A HARROW IN THE PHILIPPINES
An observation of the rude agricultural methods employed in these islands is convincing of the fact that even greater riches await the development of the industry by modern improved methods.

Figure 4.10. Freight Train and Harrow. White, *Our New Possessions.*

ing the extensive use of terraces, especially among the Bontoc and the Ifugao. Albert Jenks, a leading ethnographer in the Philippines, stated, "On agriculture hangs his claim to the rank of barbarian—without it he would be savage."[73] Officials quickly established schools and local governments under imperial control. They also sought to end internecine feuds among and within tribes through the establishment of the Philippine Constabulary and the recruitment of young men as constables. A series of photographs showed the "evolution" of a Bontoc who in 1901 was a "head-hunting savage" (figures 4.11–4.13).[74] This series used one of the ethnographic styles of photography, a close-up profile against a neutral background, although usually a frontal view was also provided. This technique permitted close, comparative examination of physical characteristics—in this case, the difference between before and after the Bontoc's joining the constabulary.[75] In the first photograph (figure 4.11), the man was shown in profile, naked to the waist, with a traditional cap worn on the back of his head. He was unshaven, his hair was long, and he sat with a slouch. After one year in the constabulary he had lost his slouch and brought his hair up under his cap. He now dressed in dark pants and a white long-sleeved, but-

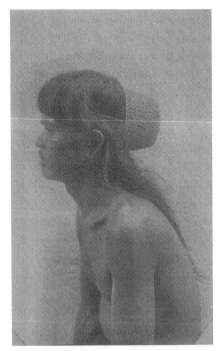

Figure 4.11. Evolution of a Bontoc Igorot Man. In 1901 a Head-Hunting Savage. National Archives, Record Group 350-P.

Figure 4.12. Evolution of a Bontoc Igorot Man. After One Year in the Constabulary. 1902. National Archives, Record Group 350-P.

toned jacket (figure 4.12). The final photograph (figure 4.13), taken in 1903, after the man had been in the constabulary for two years, showed his complete transformation. He was now in full uniform, with his rank of lieutenant on his long-sleeved jacket, and he was sporting a military cap. He was clean-shaven, with his hair closely cropped. His posture was now very straight. Superficially, the transformation was evident by changes in clothing, but the posture and the grooming of the constable implied a more profound change in the discipline of the body and mind. Perhaps more than any other images discussed in this book, one can see in this series the creation of a colonial subject: the physical and mental transformation of a person by means of an institution of the colonial state. As Paul Kramer observed, this series expressed "a narrative of imperial masculinization, of a child-race developing into erect, martial manhood."[76]

Moreover, this photographic series suggested that only the colonial state, in this particular case through the constabulary, could produce a civilizing effect in

Figure 4.13. Evolution of a Bontoc Igorot Man. After Two Years in the Constabulary. 1903. National Archives, Record Group 350-P.

individuals and in the collectivity. Colonial discourse in the Philippines established the following proposition: the Filipino leaders were but boys; the rest were mere savages. Further, it posed a rhetorical question: how could boys govern savages? The warrant for this rhetoric was established descriptively. First, the Filipinos were only an aggregate of tribes. Second, only the most civilized were capable of limited self-government, and they were too immature and inexperienced to govern the whole country on their own. Third, the lack of compact nationhood presented problems of sovereignty locally and in the international context. Finally, special problems were attendant upon the uncivilized hill tribes and the savage Muslims. According to this colonial discourse, only a paternalistic colonial state could discipline, contain, and transform this complexity into a civilized nation. The presence of both military and civilian government officials provided the political leadership and tutelage to put the peoples of the Philippines on the road to self-government.

Capital investment, public education, and political tutelage became fundamental strategies of civilization in the Philippines. The mission of the schools was to both educate and civilize the new generation. Political tutelage began at the level of the municipality, followed by the province, and finally the central government. European Americans would, of course, establish and oversee these institutions, although native peoples were to gradually take them over and make them their own. The municipal, provincial, and central governments were understood as "schools" for self-government on a national scale. The vastness of the Philippine archipelago meant that the local elites would play an important role; essentially they became clients to the colonial patrons, although there were some conflicts over this issue. Early on, the appointment of Filipinos to positions in civil government was a fundamental tactic for establishing the legitimacy of the colonial state and its strategy of tutelage. U.S. administrators depended upon the local elites for all kinds of practical matters and to legitimate imperial rule. The elites, in return, depended upon the U.S. authorities for resources.[77]

* * *

The general notion of "civilization" defined the fundamental strategy for the transformation of the economy, government, and culture of the imperial archipelago. More specifically, however, "civilization" was understood as "Americanization." The master narrative of successful Americanization distinguished Hawai'i from the former Spanish colonies. This narrative emphasized the civilization of the Hawaiian Islands by means of European American settlement and consequent hegemony. This had resulted in the political evolution from a feudal monarchy to a small insular republic modeled on the great continental republic.

Protestantism and the English language prevailed, thanks to missionary zeal and public schools. Agricultural exports assured economic integration with the United States. According to this narrative, Hawai'i was already Americanized in 1898 and would continue to enjoy the advancement that would result from even greater integration with the United States. This was a discursive narrative that corresponded with annexation and territorial government. It reflected the interests of the annexationists in Congress and the hegemonic elites in Hawai'i, just as it elided the protests of the monarchy and its supporters.

In contrast, the former Spanish colonies would have to be Americanized in the absence of European American settlement. The Americanization of Cuba, Puerto Rico, and the Philippines was conceived in metaphors: to cultivate the paradise, educate the child, and tutor in the ways of self-government. Aside from Hawai'i, which was already substantially Americanized through settlement, these former Spanish colonies would require three general strategies: (1) capital investment and expanded commerce (including development of infrastructure, especially roads and communication); (2) public education; and (3) political tutelage. The displacement of the Spanish and the arrival of the European American administrators, both military and civilian, led to the creation of a new political and economic order. Since both rational economic activity and representative government were founded upon literacy, public education was a central concern. While Americanization meant economic control by American capital, the introduction of American technology and goods, and American ways of doing business, it also meant the education of children, both literal and metaphorical. The literal children were the new generations that would be brought up in public schools. The metaphorical children were the adults who would benefit from new technologies, consume new products, and be apprentices in the arts of self-government. In general, this was the narrative that justified imperial dominion.

These goals required strong and stable governments with varying degrees of imperial control. The representations of the needs of the children (again both literal and metaphorical) in the imperial archipelago were not uniform, however. Less direct control was required in Cuba, and the United States guaranteed to maintain its independence as a protectorate. Cuba suffered from the devastation of war but not from an abject lack of civilization or from absolute agricultural backwardness. The expansion of capital investment and commerce, as well as public education, would soon remedy what seemed to be only temporary setbacks caused by the war. Cuba was a nation that needed to be revitalized. The Cuban elite negotiated control of the state apparatus in exchange for more limited national sovereignty than they had hoped.

In Puerto Rico, children were naked, poor, and dusky but deprived rather than savage. These were a special class of children—they were quick studies entirely disposed to education. Puerto Rico was not living up to its economic potential, but it was not entirely devoid of civilization: private property was firmly established, and export crops abounded, both actually and potentially. Puerto Rico showed the greatest potential for profound assimilation both culturally and economically to the United States, but its progressive integration into the United States was not certain. Here political tutelage, along with capital investment and public education, were understood as the means of assimilation. The local elites fully embraced these strategies and strove to accommodate themselves in the new regime, although not without political conflicts over the issue of autonomy.

The problems of rebuilding Cuba or uplifting Puerto Rico were not of the same order as the great obstacles faced in the Philippines, where the signs of savagery were ubiquitous: primitive, uneducated peoples and the lowest levels of technology. It was a foregone conclusion: the Philippines needed a more profound process of civilization. This too would be accomplished with the influx of capital and manufactured goods. The development of infrastructure would promote the expansion of markets. However, these unruly children, who had risen up in revolt, needed to be subdued before proceeding to public education and political tutelage in order to build a "civilized" nation out of an aggregate of tribes. Still, the Philippines was destined, after a long and indeterminate period of tutelage, for independence. Again, imperial authorities adopted a strategy of political tutelage as the means of effective control over the whole country and of cementing loyalty to the regime. Filipino elites managed to accommodate themselves within the regime and, much to the consternation of imperial authorities, expand their patronage system. The elites were both resourceful and necessary to the functioning of the colonial regime.

In general, then, the strategies were understood as revitalization, assimilation, and civilization. In all sites, this meant increased capital investment and the expansion of markets. With regard to political control, in Cuba a protectorate would suffice; in Puerto Rico and the Philippines, more direct political control, by means of political tutelage, was established. However, Puerto Rico and the Philippines were to follow distinct political trajectories, the former toward greater assimilation and the latter toward independence. It was incumbent upon Congress to establish the precise legal structures that would support these strategies and their trajectories. Let us now turn precisely to the legal debates and the establishment of civil governments throughout the imperial archipelago.

Notes

1. Anne McClintock, *Imperial Leather: Race, Gender, and Sexuality in the Colonial Contest* (New York: Routledge, 1995), 42–51. McClintock elaborates on the analysis of Stephen Jay Gould, *The Mismeasure of Man* (New York: Norton, 1981).

2. U.S. Department of the Interior, "Report of the Commissioner of Education," in *Annual Reports of the Department of the Interior for the Fiscal Year Ended 30 June 1900;* 56th Cong., 2nd sess., House of Representatives, 1901, House Document 5, vols. 1–2, chapter 29; U.S. Serials 4114–4115: xl.

3. Ibid., xlii.

4. Ibid., xli.

5. A. P. C. Griffin, *A List of Books, with References to Periodicals, Relating to the Theory of Colonization, Government of Dependencies, Protectorates, and Related Topics.*

6. "Monthly Summary of Commerce and Finance of the United States," 1199, 1278.

7. "Address by Taft in Manila before the Union Reading College, Manila, 17 December 1903," 58th Cong., 2nd sess., 1904, Senate Document 191, 7.

8. Michael Adas has emphasized the importance of technology in the "civilizing mission" of the United States; see *Dominance by Design: Technological Imperatives and America's Civilizing Mission* (Cambridge, Mass.: Belknap Press, 2006).

9. Woodrow Wilson, "The Ideals of America," *Atlantic Monthly* 90, no. 6 (December 1902): 721–734. Retrieved 9 January 2009 from http://www.theatlantic.com/issues/02dec/wilson.htm.

10. Ibid. Wilson only briefly mentioned Cuba and did not seem to be entirely convinced it was ready for complete self-government. By avoiding an explicit discussion of Cuba, he steered clear of the contradictions in his argument. On the one hand, if Cuba was ready for self-government, it was so without the colonization by England or the United States; this would contradict his argument regarding the Philippines. On the other hand, if Cuba was not ready, then it would have to be colonized; this would contradict the policy of independence for Cuba.

11. Ibid.

12. Magoon, *Legal Status*, 45–46. I will discuss this document at length in chapter 5.

13. For example, Vergara has argued that for the Americans technological inferiority was less important than the imputed racial inferiority of the "Filipinos." See Vergara, *Displaying Filipinos.*

14. According to Vergara, the imperialists argued that racial inferiority, combined with the negative effects of the tropical climate, were the root cause of the inferiority of the local civilization in the Philippines. Physical characteristics, habits, and customs (height, beauty, scowling, squatting, smoking, clothing, and so forth) were but outward

signs of racial character. Even though any race was susceptible to the improvement of character, and that was the goal of imperial rule, racial inferiority could never be overcome. In contrast, I agree with Go's argument that a Lamarckian scheme of racial improvement predominated in the Philippines. See Go, "Racism and Colonialism."

15. George Frederickson, *Racism: A Short History* (Princeton, N.J.: Princeton University Press, 2002), 107–109.

16. At least one author, Eric Love, has argued that racism had very little to do with the justification of the imperial project and most advocates of expansion avoided the "race question" so as not to further antagonize the anti-imperialist opposition, which was concerned about contact and complications with inferior races. Love argues that the civilization project was not an integral part of the justification of expansionism. Instead, expansionists appealed to less controversial economic and strategic interests and avoided, whenever possible, the race question. However, Love fails to distinguish, on the one hand, the expressed reasons for expansion in general, and on the other hand, the underlying rationale for imperial control in the various sites. Love's argument cannot explain the variegated systems of political control or the rationale for ruling the new possessions. The "race question," I would argue, was unavoidable. See Love, *Race over Empire*.

17. Hawaiian Commission, *Report*, 17–18.

18. Halstead, *Pictorial History*, 235; Davis, *Civil Affairs* (1899), 17–18.

19. In Bryan, *Our Islands*, 287.

20. Ibid., 285.

21. Ibid., 379.

22. The Hawaiian Commission questioned this principle and urged the establishment of conditions for the migration of smallholders.

23. Wood et al., *Opportunities*. I will discuss the recommendations for each country in the sections that follow.

24. In Bryan, *Our Islands*, 690.

25. Julian Go has analyzed the strategies of political tutelage in Puerto Rico and the Philippines. See his article "Chains of Empire" and his book *American Empire*.

26. Willoughby, *Territories and Dependencies of the United States*, 13–16.

27. For the most part, Guam lay outside the domain of Americanization. Of these three pillars, the navy would be interested only in public education, as we shall see in chapter 6.

28. In Wood et al., *Opportunities*, 268.

29. Ibid., 271.

30. Although the popular books did not mention them, other schemes for the colonization of Cuba existed. In an attempt to flee the resurgence of racial discrimination in the United States, some Afro-Americans organized migration ventures to Cuba.

Supposedly there was more opportunity for middle-class Afro-Americans because there was no color line, one of the most pernicious elements of U.S. racial stratification. However, all of these schemes failed. It seems that local populations did not accept these "foreigners" with open arms, and even though the constitution did not follow the flag to the new possessions, U.S. officials did bring their prejudices along. See Willard Gatewood, *Black Americans and the White Man's Burden, 1898–1903* (Urbana: University of Illinois Press, 1975), 323–324.

31. White, *Our New Possessions*, 623, 461.

32. Ibid., 582.

33. Bryan, *Our Islands*, 30–31.

34. White, *Our New Possessions*, 599. White's photograph did not detail the harvest activities; see p. 594.

35. Olivares's comments regarding implements accompany a photograph of workers harrowing a cane field; in Bryan, *Our Islands*, 100.

36. Ibid., 127.

37. *Reconcentrados* were rural Cubans who had been interned in garrisoned towns or detention camps by the Spanish military authorities during the war of independence (1895–1898).

38. Ibid. The story appeared on page 89, the photograph on page 80. A photograph of another child beggar appeared on page 78. I presume that Olivares took the picture of Townsend and the Cuban youngster.

39. Pérez, *Cuba between Empires*.

40. Davis, *Civil Affairs* (1900), 36.

41. Carroll, *Report*, 61.

42. Pedro Cabán compares and contrasts the "Americanization" of Puerto Ricans and that of European immigrants to the United States in "Subjects and Immigrants during the Progressive Era," *Discourse* 23, no. 3 (2001): 24–51.

43. In Wood et al., *Opportunities*, 298.

44. Ibid., 327, 366.

45. Ibid., 369.

46. See Bryan, *Our Islands*, 304. The census of 1899 also published three exterior photographs of large urban schools with carefully grouped children and teachers lined up in front; see U.S. War Department, *Report on the Census of Porto Rico, 1899*.

47. Frederick Ober, *Puerto Rico and Its Resources* (New York: Appleton, 1899), 238.

48. In Bryan, *Our Islands*, 274.

49. White, *Our New Possessions*, 371, 439.

50. Halstead, *Pictorial History*, 36–37.

51. In Wood et al., *Opportunities*, 323–324.

52. Dinwiddie, *Puerto Rico*, 249.

53. Carmen Rafucci de García, *El gobierno civil y la ley Foraker* (Rio Piedras: Editorial Universitaria, 1981); Go, *American Empire*.

54. William McKinley, "Benevolent Assimilation Proclamation," 21 December 1898. Retrieved 27 October 2009 from http://www.humanitiesweb.org/human.php?s=h&p=c&a=p&ID=23008.

55. Frank Hindman Golay, *Face of Empire: United States-Philippine Relations, 1898–1946* (Quezon City: Ateneo de Manila University Press, 1997), 47.

56. Cited in Dean Worcester, *The Philippines Past and Present* (New York: Macmillan, 1914), vol. 2, 977–979.

57. Philippine Commission (Schurman), vol. 1, 183. For an excellent comparative analysis of the British protectorate and the U.S. colonial model, see Donna Amoroso, "Inheriting the 'Moro Problem': Muslim Authority and Colonial Rule in British Malaysia and the Philippines," in Go and Foster, *The American Colonial State in the Philippines*.

58. Cited in Worcester, *The Philippines Past and Present*, vol. 2, 985. See also Philippine Commission (Taft), *Reports of the Taft Philippine Commission*, 56th Cong., 2nd sess., Senate, 1901, Senate Document 112; U.S. Serials 4040: 1–333.

59. Ibid., 985–986.

60. In Wood et al., *Opportunities*, 113, 120–121. At least one scheme for the colonization of the Philippines by Afro-Americans was envisioned but was short-lived. Senator John Morgan of Alabama proposed to recruit both Afro-American soldiers and homesteaders from the South. The secretary of war, Elihu Root, requested from his officers an evaluation of the feasibility of the senator's proposal. George Davis, in a report to his commanding officer, Adna Chaffee, concluded that this scheme would not be successful for many reasons, too numerous to mention here. See "Letter of Gen. George Davis to Gen. Adna Chaffee, 17 April 1902," National Archives, Record Group 350, 5749-1.

61. White, *Our New Possessions*, 163, 268.

62. After more that fifteen years of research and administrative experience in the Philippines, Dean Worcester maintained in 1914 that Filipinos were still not capable of independence and opposed the proposal of a protectorate. Calling upon a well-known rhetorical tradition, he made his argument by means of an infant metaphor:

It has been urged by one class of our citizens that we abandon the islands because they are a source of military weakness, and that we guarantee their independence, which in plain English means that we hold ourselves ready to fight for them! They insist that with our Caucasian origin and our years of hard-earned experience, we are not fit to govern them, but that their Filipino inhabitants, who are the Malayan savages of the sixteenth century, plus what

Spain has taught them, plus what they so recently have learned from us, are fit to govern themselves and must be allowed to do so under our protection. In other words, having brought up a child who is at present rather badly spoiled, we are to say to the family of nations: "Here is a boy who must be allowed to join you. We have found that we are unfit to control him, but we hope that he will be good. You must not spank him unless you want to fight us."

Worcester stressed the importance of political strength and unification in an international context. The United States had raised an unruly child that was still "spoiled"; only recently had these "savages of the sixteenth century" learned a bit about government. In the "family of nations," Filipinos were but children: difficult to control even by means of the current imperial government and decidedly unfit for self-government. For Worcester, Filipino independence would result in an unacceptable contradiction: the United States would be forced to defend a child (i.e., an aspiring yet immature nation) that it could not control and discipline (i.e., rule directly). According to Worcester, the United States, still responsible for its "ward," should not relinquish authority over the Philippines until its people had proven to be faithful, well behaved, and capable of defending themselves. Worcester, *The Philippines Past and Present*, vol. 2, 961. Worcester criticized the proposal for Philippine independence introduced in the Congress. Kramer analyzed the continued resistance to Filipino independence in *The Blood of Government*.

    63. In Bryan, *Our Islands*, 656. For the original report, see Wilcox and Sargent, *Affairs in the Philippine Islands*, 24–44.

    64. White, *Our New Possessions*, 19.

    65. This lack of sympathy for the Filipino people also led to descriptions of unattractive and sullen women, as we have seen in chapter 2. Charles Hawley shows how the representations of Filipinos in Hollywood movies changed in response to the political transition from colonial commonwealth to neocolonial independence. Furthermore, certain images of Filipinos were favored in Hollywood's propaganda efforts during World War II. Charles Hawley, "You're a Better Filipino Than I Am, John Wayne: World War II, Hollywood, and U.S.-Philippines Relations," *Pacific Historical Review* 71, no. 3 (2002): 389–414.

    66. In Wood et al., *Opportunities*, 6.

    67. William Taft, "The Philippines," *National Geographic Magazine* 16, no. 8 (1905): 365.

    68. Ibid.

    69. Ibid., 365–366. The photograph appears on page 369. Also included were photographs entitled "Primary Pupils in a Municipal School, Manila" and "Young Filipinos." Taft responded to English critics of U.S. policy, John Foreman, A. R. Colquhoun,

and Alleyne Ireland. Later works included considerably more about the development of transportation (especially roads) and the civilizing aspects of education. In particular, Worcester used the technique of before-and-after photographs of water wells, streets, roads, prisons, hospitals, homes, schools (including teachers, pupils, nurses, and athletic teams), and constabulary officers. The second volume of Worcester's *The Philippines Past and Present* included the frontispiece of Pit-a-pit, a young, smiling, half-naked, long-haired Bontoc boy who was completely transformed in nine years into a medical student in a white suit and shoes. Vergara argued that this before-and-after picture was emblematic of the fundamental narrative of the book: the primitive Filipino past followed by the civilized future under imperial supervision. Vergara, *Displaying Filipinos*.

70. In Bryan, *Our Islands*, 691.

71. White, *Our New Possessions*. The two photographs appeared on page 98. The description of rice production was on pages 260–261. A photograph in the same style (farmer with *carabao* and plow in front of bamboo fence), along with the caption quoted here, appeared on page 115. These same photographs are also found in Neely, *Panoramic Views*. Neither White nor any of his contemporaries mentioned or pictured the magnificent rice terraces found in the mountainous areas of Luzon.

72. Worcester, *The Philippines Past and Present*. Paul Kramer provided a history of the bureau in *The Blood of Government*, ch. 3.

73. Albert Jenks, *Philippines: The Bontoc Igorot* (Manila: Department of the Interior, Ethnological Survey, 1904), 88. This book is a very extensive ethnography with many high-quality pictures taken by Dean Worcester; Charles Martin, the government photographer; and Albert Jenks. Martin took most of the ethnographic photographs now stored in the Still Picture Collection, Bureau of Insular Affairs, in the National Archives, College Park, Maryland. This book formed a part of the library of the bureau: Record Group 350, 142.1, Library Materials vol. 1562, entry 95.

74. This series was probably produced as a part of the Ethnological Survey. Captions were attached to the photographs. National Archives, Record Group 350-P Box 8 Bb-2-12; Bb-2-23; Bb-2-24.

75. Vergara also analyzed this series, which was published in Frederick Chamberlain, *The Philippine Problem, 1898–1913* (Boston: Little, Brown, 1913).

76. Kramer, *The Blood of Government*, 320.

77. Ibid.; Go, *American Empire*.

Chapter 5
Legal Foundations of Colonial Rule

Alterity and Government

This chapter will explore the connections between representations of alterity as a means to conceive, mobilize, and justify imperial rule and the concrete forms of government established throughout the imperial archipelago. I will argue that the elaboration of cultural difference was fundamental in the conceptualization and establishment of different governments, in particular the civil governments for the Philippines and Puerto Rico. Throughout the legal debates, official reports, court decisions, and congressional debates, participants used the metaphors of femininity, childishness, and race to evaluate the capacity of the various subject peoples for self-government. These representations expressed the cultural contrasts of the various peoples and served to devise and justify particular strategies of government. First, the contrast between the regions (states and territories) settled by European Americans and the new possessions inhabited by "alien" peoples effectively set the limits of the republic's body politic and led to imperial rule beyond. Second, the evaluation of cultural differences among the subject peoples of the imperial archipelago resulted in variations in the structure of government for each site. This chapter will examine how legal scholars, Congress, colonial administrators, and the Supreme Court devised the means of governing overseas possessions based upon notions of difference not only *between* the United States and the subject peoples but also *among* the subject peoples themselves. It will concentrate on the second part of the imperial problem: how to rule.

Hawai'i: A Distant Frontier

Hawai'i had been a frontier of European American settlement since missionaries, sailors, and merchants had arrived in the 1820s. As early as the 1850s

these immigrants and their descendants, known as haoles, controlled the leading economic interests and exercised considerable power behind the throne
of the Hawaiian monarchy. In 1893 they seized political power, overthrew the
monarchy, and created a provisional government with annexationist aspirations.
The Hawaiian monarchy protested the usurpation of power. President Grover
Cleveland also questioned the legitimacy of the "revolution" and opposed annexation. Although Congress demonstrated some interest in Hawai'i for strategic
reasons, there was not enough support for annexation at this time. In 1894,
haoles created the Republic of Hawai'i but did not abandon their movement
for annexation. In June 1898, during the military operations against Spain, the
annexation of Hawai'i once again became an issue. William McKinley, elected in
1896, was now president, and Republican expansionists dominated Congress.
The debate regarding the Newlands Resolution (Joint Resolution 259), which
proposed the annexation of the Republic of Hawai'i, anticipated many of the
objections that subsequent opponents would raise against the acquisition and
possible annexation of the islands ceded to the United States by the Treaty of
Paris. Hawaiian annexation seemed to pose many of the same problems later
raised by the acquisition of the former Spanish islands.[1]

The annexation of Hawai'i raised considerable controversy in Congress. In
his polemic pamphlet directed at Congress, Lorrin Thurston, an ardent annexationist and instigator of the "republican revolution," listed twenty commonly
expressed objections to Hawaiian annexation.[2] The principal objections were,
first, that it was a distant, noncontiguous island territory, and second, that it was
densely populated by peoples of different languages, customs, and races. The
lack of continental contiguity supposedly diminished the geopolitical merits of
annexation since it made Hawai'i difficult to defend from foreign powers and
would require excessive naval expenditures. More important, Hawai'i was populated largely by *kanaka* (native Hawaiians), Chinese, and Japanese who were,
according to opponents, unfit for citizenship and self-government. Other issues
included the competition that Hawaiian sugar posed for domestic producers,
the questionable future of statehood for the territory, and the precedent statehood might establish for future overseas acquisitions—namely, the Spanish
colonies.

How did the proponents of Hawaiian annexation refute the objections
raised by their opponents? Thurston claimed that Hawai'i was already a well-
established and successful American colony. In his spirited pamphlet, he advo-
cated Hawaiian annexation on the grounds that it had been successfully Americanized according to the following criteria: (1) its American-style legal system
and constitutional government; (2) its extensive public school system and high

literacy rates; (3) the use of English in the courts, schools, and commerce; (4) the use of American technology and standards in production and commerce; and (5) the use of the dollar as the official currency.[3] Americanization had been achieved through the continuous presence on Hawaiian soil of European Americans. They controlled the economy and had integrated it with U.S. shipping and trade. They held political power and maintained cultural dominance, especially through the use of the English language. This hegemonic presence of European American settlers established the crucial difference between Hawai'i and the former Spanish colonies acquired by the Treaty of Paris.

The congressional debates similarly emphasized the Americanization of Hawai'i by means of colonization. Representative Robert Hitt of Illinois, speaking in favor of annexation, referred to Hawai'i as "the only true American colony."[4] A Republican from Iowa, S. M. Clark, also spoke in favor of annexation. In his refutation of one of the most serious objections to annexation—the incorporation of *kanaka*, Chinese, and Japanese into the United States without their consent—he reminded his colleagues that earlier continental expansion had also involved the domination of subject peoples. He presented the following interpretation of U.S. history:

> It is said we should not annex Hawaii because its native people are not homogenous with us and have not voted in favor of joining this Republic. This statement involves a strange forgetfulness of the facts of American history. Every American State was made by dispossessing the native Indians. When and where did the two peoples become homogenous? When and where was the formation and conduct of this Government or the admission of a State into the Union made dependent upon a vote of the native American Indians? There are millions of colored people in this country. The majority opinion of the Supreme Court, after the Republic had existed seventy-five years, said the negroes were not citizens. And for twenty years past our Democratic friends in the Southern States have been making constitutions and laws eliminating the negroes out of the citizenship by depriving them of the suffrage.[5]

For Clark, the annexation of Hawai'i was but a continuation of the time-honored traditions of continental expansion, settlement, and racial exclusion. The majority of Congress agreed, and the resolution passed easily in the House and the Senate. On 7 July 1898, President McKinley signed the resolution that annexed the Hawaiian Islands "as part of the territory of the United States" and made them "subject to the sovereign dominion thereof."[6] The resolution left intact the current government but made provision for a commission to make recommendations regarding future congressional legislation to establish a local government. The resolution also prohibited Chinese immigration to Hawai'i and from there to the United States in accordance with the Chinese Exclusion Act.

The Hawaiian Commission, presided by Shelby Cullom, presented its report to President McKinley in December 1898 after a visit to Hawai'i that included public hearings. One of the most important tasks of the commission was to make recommendations regarding the future government of the "territory of Hawaii," and for this reason it had to determine the capacity of the population to assume "the responsibilities and duties of free government." The commission was confident that the "entire population . . . is dominated, politically, financially, and commercially, by the American element," although it comprised a minority of about 4,000 persons of a total population of 110,000. On the one hand, Hawaiians (39,000, including mixed blood) were described as "a kindly, affectionate people, confiding, friendly, and liberal, many of them childlike and easy in habits and manners, willing to associate and intermarry with the Europeans or other races, obedient to law and governmental authority." One the other hand, "the Chinese and Japanese do not now possess political power, nor have they any important relation to the body politic, except as laborers." The commission was particularly impressed with the constitution and the laws of the former Republic of Hawai'i and its system of public education and the high levels of literacy. It suggested Hawai'i was ready and prepared for a territorial government.[7]

Despite the controversy over annexation, Congress resolved the issues of Hawaiian government in a manner entirely consistent with the previous model of continental territorial expansion. The United States had expanded during the nineteenth century by means of migration, settlement, and a territorial scheme of making new states. Congress organized districts, then territories, and later admitted these as states with some regularity, following the model outlined in the Northwest Ordinance of 1787. First, Congress would create a temporary district government for a designated region. This district government was composed of an appointed governor, secretary, and several judges. The governor had extensive autocratic powers. Second, upon reaching a specified "white" population, Congress would organize a territorial government, consisting of an appointed governor, an appointed legislative council, and an elected legislative assembly. Third, the process culminated with the territory's incorporation as a state of the federal union with full representation in Congress.[8]

By the end of the nineteenth century, most of the continental acquisitions had been converted to states of the union. The remaining organized territories on the continent were New Mexico, Arizona, and Oklahoma, where governments had been organized in 1850, 1863, and 1890 respectively.[9] In addition, Congress had established a district government for Alaska in 1884.[10] In 1830 all of the Louisiana Purchase, except for the states of Louisiana and Missouri and the Territory of Arkansas, was considered "free Indian territory" or "Indian country." The gradual organization of these lands into territories and states reduced the area of "Indian country," and by the 1850s, "Indian Territory," now an official designation, occupied only the area roughly corresponding to present-day Oklahoma. Due to pressures from European American settlers, the western half of Indian Territory was opened to settlement in 1889, and one year later Congress organized the Territory of Oklahoma, conserving the eastern half as Indian Territory.[11] Thus, in 1898, in addition to the states, the United States comprised three organized territories, two districts (Alaska and the District of Columbia), and Indian Territory. These regions, with the exception of the District of Columbia, constituted the final frontiers of European American settlement on the continent. Of these regions, only Alaska was not contiguous with the other states and territories. Hawai'i was an overseas extension of this frontier of white settlement, unique in many ways but sharing this important attribute.

Two years after the annexation of Hawai'i, Congress organized a territorial government following the well-established legal precedents of continental expansion established during the late nineteenth century.[12] Although there had been considerable debate regarding the desirability of Hawaiian annexation, its new territorial government presented no constitutional problem whatsoever. The territorial government of Hawai'i consisted of a presidentially appointed governor, who in turn appointed his cabinet; a bicameral legislature of elected representatives; and a local supreme court appointed by the president. Hawai'i sent a nonvoting delegate to the House of Representatives in Washington. Furthermore, Hawai'i was fully incorporated into the United States with respect to the federal judiciary, customs, and currency. All legal statutes applied, including the collection of internal revenue. U.S. citizenship was granted to all former citizens of the Hawaiian republic—that is, to all male European American and native Hawaiian residents. Chinese and Japanese residents were excluded from citizenship, and future immigration from China and Japan was either prohibited (in the first case) or restricted (in the second). As noted above, the law also prohibited the emigration of Chinese from Hawai'i to any other state or territory (see table 1, p. 204).[13]

Cuban (In)dependence

Like Hawai'i, Cuba did not present major constitutional problems but for an entirely different reason. Shortly before the declaration of war on Spain, the Teller Resolution formalized the ideal of Cuban nationhood and guaranteed formal independence upon the conclusion of hostilities with Spain and the political stabilization of Cuba. The resolution, adopted by Congress in April 1898, stated that "the people and the Island of Cuba are, and of right ought to be, free and independent." It further outlined the duty of the United States to both demand and, if necessary, force Spain to "relinquish its authority and government" over Cuba and to "withdraw its land and naval forces." Finally, it disclaimed any disposition or intent of the United States to "exercise sovereignty, jurisdiction or control" over Cuba, "except for the pacification thereof," and swore to "leave the government and control of the Island to its people." The resolution justified the intervention of the United States according to the principles of the Monroe Doctrine.[14] The idea that Spain had unjustly denied Cuba its rightful independence legitimized the military intervention of the United States and its declaration of war against Spain in 1898. After all, the island was home to a very strong and militant nationalist culture. It had fought two wars of independence. The first, beginning in 1868, lasted for ten years without success. The second armed struggle began in 1895, ending in 1898 with the withdrawal of Spain and the military occupation of the United States. The Treaty of Paris, between Spain and the United States, reiterated the guarantee of the expeditious independence of Cuba.

Although Cuba successfully achieved its long-sought independence from Spain, Congress did not respect the letter of the Teller Resolution that disclaimed any intention to exercise any control over the island. Instead, Congress attached the Platt Amendment to the military appropriation bill of 2 March 1901. The Cuban constitutional convention, unsuccessfully resisting political pressure, ratified the provisions of the Platt Amendment and signed a permanent treaty with the United States on 22 May 1902. The amendment compromised the sovereignty of the new nation by providing legal justification for military intervention by the United States into the internal affairs of Cuba. It granted to the United States the right to intervene "for the preservation of Cuban independence" and for the "maintenance of a government adequate for the protection of life, property, and individual liberty." It also obligated the Cuban government to sell or lease coaling stations and naval bases within Cuban territory. Finally, the amendment prohibited Cuba from making any treaty or compact with any other country that would impair its own independence or authorize the establishment of military or naval bases on the island. In effect, the Platt Amendment and the subsequent treaty between the two countries made Cuba a protectorate of the United States.[15] Congress treated Cuba as a formally independent country under the protection of the United States.

The Imperial Problem: Legal Opinion

Although there was considerable discussion regarding the peoples and governments in both Hawai'i and Cuba, neither constituted an imperial problem as such. As we have seen, the imperial problem comprised two related dimensions. First, since the "dependencies" were inhabited by peoples of different cultures, they required political systems different from those of the territories. Second, significant cultural differences within the "dependencies" made any uniform political system unworkable. The temporary military occupation and subsequent independence of Cuba did not present any substantial constitutional problems. Nor did the annexation of Hawai'i and the subsequent organization of a territorial government raise any legal problems. However, beginning in 1898, legal scholars debated two issues regarding the outright acquisition of overseas territories from Spain from a strictly legal point of view. First, by what constitutional principle could the United States govern the new possessions of Puerto Rico and the Philippines?[16] Second, exactly what sort of government should Congress establish therein? The leading law reviews devoted considerable attention to the issues of constitutional authority and the kinds of government and citizenship most appropriate for the dependencies and their inhabitants. These debates concentrated on the issue of how to rule without ever losing sight of the issue of the character of the peoples in question.[17]

A minority of legal scholars adopted the doctrine of *ex proprio vigore*. This doctrine held that the Constitution applied in the territories "by its own force"— in other words, the "Constitution followed the flag." The doctrine asserted that Congress had the power to acquire territories, establish temporary military rule, organize civil territorial governments, and admit territories eventually as states. However, the Constitution permitted neither permanent colonies nor subjects. Scholars who adhered to this doctrine assumed that eventually all territorial possessions would become states of the federal union. Consequently, all personal and civil rights guaranteed by the Constitution must also apply to the European American inhabitants of the territories, although full political participation at the federal level was to be extended to these inhabitants only after statehood. The paradox of the doctrine of *ex proprio vigore* was that the Constitution would extend to the new dependencies, but the present inhabitants of the islands were supposedly not fit for self-government under the Constitution. By implication, direct rule over the islands would have to be relinquished shortly, following the precedent of Cuba. This was a conclusion entirely unacceptable for the expansionists of the day.[18]

In contrast, the majority of scholars in the legal debate adopted a doctrine of plenary powers, which stated that Congress could legislate for U.S.

possessions or territories as it saw fit, with little or no constitutional restrictions. These scholars asserted the legitimacy of the cessions of the Treaty of Paris and sought the utmost political expediency in ruling them. They were concerned that the inhabitants of the former Spanish colonies were not prepared for self-government, that they were not culturally assimilable to the United States, and that the lands would never be sites for migration and settlement by European Americans. These scholars ruled out the possibility of repeating the historical sequence of cultural inclusion envisioned by the Northwest Ordinance.[19] The paradox of the doctrine of plenary powers was that by granting virtually unrestricted sovereignty to Congress to deal with the insular territories abroad, it implied that Congress had these same unlimited powers at home, even in the existing continental territories and districts.

In an effort to resolve this paradox, the legal debates produced a third view, the doctrine of incorporation, which proposed a simple and effective distinction between the new possessions and the territories as such. Abbott Lowell was the first to present this third view. After reviewing legal precedents, he asserted that "possessions acquired by conquest or cession do not become a part of the United States." Rather, "the incorporation of territory in the Union" is a question to be considered by the "legislative or the treaty-making authorities," which have two options. First, a "territory may be so annexed as to make it a part of the United States, and that if so all the general restrictions in the Constitution apply to it, save those on the organization of the judiciary." Second, "possessions may also be so acquired as not to form part of the United States, and in that case constitutional limitations, such as those requiring uniformity of the taxation and trial by jury, do not apply." Therefore, the new territories ceded by the Treaty of Paris were "possessions," according to this third view, but they did not "form a part of the United States"—that is, they were not fully incorporated to the United States. Although the language was subdued, the meaning was clear: Not all constitutional principles necessarily applied to possessions. Indeed, many constitutional principles were "inapplicable except among a people whose social and political evolution has been consonant with our own."[20] The third view granted plenary powers to Congress over the new possessions and their inhabitants, while it left intact the constitutional guarantees and congressional limits in the incorporated territories and districts that were part of the body politic.

Some of the same language of the "third view" was also found in Charles Magoon's official report to Elihu Root, the secretary of war. On 12 February 1900, Magoon delivered his extensive study concerning the legal status of the territory and inhabitants of the islands of Puerto Rico, the Philippines, and Guam, recently acquired from the United States from Spain. The report responded to four specific questions of law raised by Root.[21] The first question was the following:

> 1. Have the territorial boundaries of the United States been extended to embrace the islands of the Philippine Archipelago, the island of Guam, and the island of Puerto Rico?

Magoon responded to this question by denying that the territorial boundaries of the United States had been extended upon the acquisition of the islands. When the United States acquired a territory, whether by conquest, treaty, or discovery, it became initially a "possession appertaining or property belonging to the United States."[22] Magoon argued that congressional assent was necessary to extend the geographical boundaries of the United States through the incorporation of new territory. The Treaty of Paris did not extend the boundaries of the United States; rather it ceded Puerto Rico, the Philippines, and Guam to it. This territory was not a part of the union, but rather property of the United States to be disposed of by the Congress as it wished. This language followed Lowell's argument concerning the "third view" and anticipated the doctrine of incorporation expressed by the Supreme Court the following year. Magoon concluded that the islands of Puerto Rico, the Philippines, and Guam were both "outside the boundaries of the United Sates" and were territories "appertaining to the United States, to which the sovereign people of the United States had acquired sovereign title."[23]

The second question addressed by Magoon was the following:

> 2. Are said islands and their inhabitants bound and benefited, privileged and conditioned by the provisions of the Constitution of the United States?

Regarding the extension of the Constitution, Magoon argued that any territory beyond the boundaries of the United States was neither bound nor privileged by the Constitution because it was not a part of the body politic. *Sovereignty* followed the flag, but not all the provisions of the Constitution. Subsequently, the Congress could establish any political entity or local government, whether state or territory, and might bestow citizenship upon its inhabitants as "acts of grace on the part of the new owner or sovereign." Magoon developed an extensive critique of the doctrine of *ex proprio vigore,* to which he referred as the "transmigration of the Constitution" and the "doctrine of squatter sovereignty."[24]

The third question was the following:

3. Has the Congress of the United States jurisdiction to legislate for said islands and their inhabitants?

Magoon stated that previous decisions of the Supreme Court regarding acquisition and government of new territory had established two propositions. First, the United States, as a sovereign nation, could acquire and govern new territory. Second, the government of this territory belonged primarily to the Congress and secondarily to any institutions it might establish.[25] Magoon argued that the Congress had the power to legislate for territories appertaining to but outside the boundaries of the United States, such as the uninhabited "guano islands," which were a source of fertilizer. Furthermore, citing a number of precedents, Magoon emphatically argued that the power of Congress over the territories is general and plenary.[26] In this regard, Magoon moved away from the measured position of the "third view," which sought to protect the already established continental territories from the arbitrary powers of Congress, and toward the doctrine of plenary powers.

The fourth question was the following:

4. Must such legislation conform to the constitutional requirements regarding territory within the boundaries of the United States and citizens domiciled therein?

Just as Congress had plenary powers over the territories, it also had the powers to determine the personal and political rights of the inhabitants of the territories, whether organized or unorganized. Magoon wrote the following justification in the form of a long rhetorical question:

If this is the rule as to organized Territories, peopled as they are by immigration from the older communities of the nation, by our own citizens who at home possessed the rights of citizenship and participated in the sovereignty, many of whom entered the Territory to avail themselves of special privileges bestowed upon them by the nation in recognition of their valor in defense of the nation, is a more advantageous rule to be applied to unorganized territory, largely peopled by an alien race, ignorant of our laws, customs, and institutions, unable to distinguish the difference between the Constitution of the United States and a map of the country, and as incapable, at present, of properly applying its complex provisions and diverse agencies as they would be those of the switchboard of a union railway station?[27]

This argument was based upon the legal distinction of an organized territory, with a local government organized by Congress, and an unorganized territory appertaining to and governed directly by the United States. Most important,
a racial and cultural distinction ran parallel to this legal distinction. On the one
hand, there were the Euro-American settlers, who were honorable and valiant
citizens migrating from the previously colonized areas of the United States. This
implied continuity, contiguity, and homogeneity between the "older communities of the nation" and those new settlements founded by "our own citizens who
at home possessed the rights of citizenship and participated in the sovereignty."
On the other hand, there were alien races ignorant of the Constitution, geography, and even modern industrial technology. If the former citizens did not
enjoy full political rights in the territories, much less so the native inhabitants
of the insular possessions.[28] Magoon employed a powerful rhetorical device to
discredit the political rights in the possessions: if their peoples knew nothing of
modern technology, if they could not even operate a railway switchboard, how
could they possibly manage the machinery of a constitutional government? This
rhetoric was effective precisely because of the predominant technological notion
of civilization. The many reports and photographs of the technological backwardness in the islands lent quiet support to this argument (see chapter 4).

The inhabitants of the territories owed allegiance to the United States, and
they would receive protection from the imperial power. However, they would
not enjoy citizenship rights. According to Magoon, this was not a novel concept
since many persons who were not full citizens of the United States still owed
complete allegiance to the country: "Many soldiers in our Army, sailors in our
Navy, seamen in our merchant marine, travelers, temporary sojourners, Indians,
Chinese, convicted criminals, and, in another and limited sense, minors and
women belong to this class."[29] Furthermore, the inhabitants of the territories did
not have the right to free entry into United States since they were not citizens.
Finally, the products of the territories did not enjoy the right of commerce free
of trade restrictions or duties since they were considered foreign commerce.
Although Magoon argued strongly in favor of the doctrine of plenary powers,
he used some of the language of the "third view" in his distinction between a
territory that was merely a possession and one that was a part of the body politic.
However, he did not make any specific recommendations for government in the
new possessions. Instead, his report justified the actions of Congress to legislate
governments and citizenship as it saw fit with few constitutional limitations.[30]

In addition to the strictly constitutional question, the legal debate produced a range of opinions regarding civil government even before Congress
commenced its deliberations. Proponents of the doctrine of *ex proprio vigore*

argued that the only tradition compatible with the Constitution was the organization of a territorial government in the near future, which implied eventual statehood. However, this argument led to the conclusion that the new possessions should not be annexed because the inhabitants were not suited at present for territorial government and would never be suited for statehood. Carman Randolph, for example, concluded that the United States should not annex any country "unfit for statehood because of the character of its people," especially if there was little hope that "Americans will migrate to it in sufficient numbers to elevate its social conditions and ultimately justify its admission as a state."[31] Randolph also ruled out the possibility that the inhabitants be governed either as "dependent nations" or as "wards," using the congressional precedents in dealing with American Indians. Only a minority of the inhabitants of the Philippines could be considered to be "tribal Indians," but the majority could not be denied the privileges of citizenship on the mistaken premise of their tribal organization. Simeon Baldwin reached similar conclusions for Puerto Rico and Hawai'i: eventually the inhabitants must be conceded the same right to suffrage as was afforded to "white men of civilized races." Since neither permanent colonies nor dependencies were permissible under the Constitution and since the inhabitants of the new possessions were not suited for statehood, Congress would have to relinquish the territories.[32] This anti-imperialist conclusion was not acceptable to the expansionists of the period.

Proponents of the doctrine of plenary powers produced two basic alternatives for civil government. The first, pursued by Lebbeus Wilfley, among others, was to treat Puerto Rico and the Philippines as the British treated their crown colonies. He distinguished "temperate colonies," inhabited by English or European immigrants who enjoyed "responsible governments" with elected legislatures, from "tropical colonies," inhabited by native, colored populations incapable of self-government. He argued that climate determined the racial attributes of the population, in turn dictating the appropriate form of government.[33] The second strategy, which stayed explicitly within the confines of U.S. constitutional tradition, was to treat the new possessions as unorganized territories to be ruled directly by Congress. John Beach argued that legal precedents provided for three kinds of territories—organized, unorganized, and Indian—and for five "degrees of relationship" between the individual and the federal government—full citizenship in the states, limited citizenship in the organized territories, minimal citizenship in the unorganized territories, subjects, and wards.[34] He concluded that Congress should treat the new possessions as unorganized territories and treat its peoples as either subjects or wards of the United States with no political rights and only a minimum of personal rights. To Beach, the most appropriate models were the district of Alaska and the ward status of American Indians in general.

Critics identified considerable problems with each of these imperial alternatives. Most members of Congress were loath to accept outright that the United States possessed colonies like the British, especially in light of the persistent anti-imperialist stance many congressmen had taken. In addition, the United States did not possess a well-developed legal, political, or institutional tradition of administering imperial possessions in the manner of European empires. At the same time, Congress did not want to treat the possessions as either organized territories—which implied eventual statehood—or as Indian territory—which implied some kind of tribal organization and loyalty that did not exist, except perhaps in some isolated areas of the Philippines. Instead, congressional leaders wanted to organize civil governments with some representative institutions in order to promote limited self-rule within the confines of imperial sovereignty. Although the legal debate had produced a workable distinction between the territories that were a part of the United States and those that were possessions, it would be colonial administrators, rather than legal scholars, who produced the institutional models for civil government in Puerto Rico and the Philippines.

Rule in Puerto Rico and the Philippines

While the lawyers discussed the doctrine of plenary powers and its subtle variant, the "third view," Congress proceeded pragmatically to establish authority over Puerto Rico, the Philippines, and Guam. It would effectively treat these islands as if they were possessions belonging to but not a part of the United States. As a whole, then, Congress treated the new possessions—later known formally as "unincorporated territories"—differently from the "incorporated" territories, including Hawai'i. Despite this common legal foundation, however, Congress would not deal with the unincorporated territories in uniform fashion when it came time to organize local governments. Effective control over the new possessions required not only a fundamental exclusion based upon a radical difference *between* possessions and the states and territories, but also an elaboration of the differences *among* the possessions. The legal debates over the constitutional issues over the status of the territories and their inhabitants did not resolve the administrative problem of how they should be governed.

After the ratification of the Treaty of Paris, Congress began to consider legislation for civil government for the newly acquired possessions of Puerto Rico and the Philippines. Under instructions from the Treasury Department, Henry Carroll visited Puerto Rico two times as special commissioner. He arrived on the island on 15 October 1898 and stayed one month, undertaking a study of customs, currency, and civil government. He returned on 31 December 1898 and toured the island during January 1899, conducting interviews and inquiries regarding the political aspirations and capabilities of the Puerto Ricans. On the basis of these interviews, Carroll concluded that the Puerto Ricans desired the following:

> They expect under American sovereignty that the wrongs of centuries will be righted; that they will have an honest and efficient government; the largest measure of liberty as citizens of the great Republic under the Constitution; home rule as provided by the Territorial system; free access to the markets of the United States and no customs duties on goods coming from our ports; a school system modeled after that of the United States; the adoption of the English language in due time and the general adaptation to the island of all those institutions which have contributed to the prosperity, progress, and happiness of the American people.[35]

According to Carroll, the elites in Puerto Rico were generally in agreement and were clear in their expectations: U.S. citizenship, territorial government, free trade with the United States, public schools, and the gradual adoption of the English language. However, were the elites, as well as the general population, ready, able, and willing to put into practice a territorial government like that of the other organized U.S. territories? "The question of capacity for self-government"—wrote Carroll—"lies at the threshold of the whole subject." He argued that the Puerto Ricans freely admitted that they had had little opportunity to show their capacity for self-government. They were, however, very familiar with U.S. institutions and principles of government and possessed a strong desire to assume the responsibilities of local self-government. Carroll also pointed out the obvious deficiencies in education, evident in the low rates of literacy among the people. The commissioner had no hesitation in affirming, however, that the people had good claims to self-government—namely, their moral conduct, their loyalty and obedience to the United States, their respect for the law and peaceable conduct, the relative absence of criminal behavior, and their industriousness. Carroll found that they did not have any "customs or prejudices" that would "prevent them from becoming good American citizens," and he found them to be more politically capable than the republics of Central and South America. He did not ascribe to the people any onerous or defective racial characteristics. The "existing institutions and laws, usages, and customs" required only moderate reforms. The people, he anticipated, would soon learn English and improve their Spanish.[36]

Carroll concluded his report on Puerto Rico with recommendations for U.S. citizenship and territorial government "similar to that of Oklahoma." However, these recommendations were problematic in their avoidance of several key issues. First, Carroll did not directly address the promise of future statehood that the nature of territorial government implied. Instead, he simply asserted that a territorial government in itself did not guarantee future statehood. Second, he argued that the Americanization of Puerto Rico could occur by means of overseas investments and enterprises just as it had occurred in Oklahoma by means of immigration and settlement (see chapter 4). He apparently believed that the Americanization of Puerto Rico could take place by means of economic development and the voluntary adoption of "American culture," which would serve, somehow, as a substitution for immigration and settlement. Finally, he opposed a colonial state or any form of political "tutelage which proclaimed their inferiority."[37] In a deft play on words, he stated that Puerto Rico was "American" (it was a possession) and would be soon "Americanized" (would adopt U.S. institutions, language, and culture). It was not clear to most observers, however, that this might occur without either settlement or political tutelage.

Carroll's recommendations, submitted to President McKinley in October 1899, were among the first but were not the most influential. Indeed, his vision of an organized American territory in the Caribbean would not prevail. Among the most influential recommendations were those of George Davis, then military governor of Puerto Rico, who drew upon both U.S. territorial experience and British colonial models. He began with an overview of governance in the independent nations and British colonies in the Caribbean. He quickly rejected the model of the independent nation, giving a decidedly unfavorable review of the Dominican Republic. Then he turned to the colonial arrangements in the British Empire, which he classified as of three types: (1) those with a responsible parliament and appointed governor (like Canada); (2) those with an appointed governor and executive council but with an elected legislature (like Barbados); and (3) those with an appointed governor and executive council, without an elected assembly (like Jamaica). He suggested that the colonial model most appropriate for Puerto Rico was the crown colony of Trinidad, which was a variant of the Barbados model. The government in Trinidad had a partially elected legislature: a fully elected house and an appointed executive council, which had both executive and legislative functions. His specific recommendations for Puerto Rico provided for an appointed governor and executive council, but with a legislative assembly eventually to be fully elected.[38] Davis summed up as follows:

> The degree of autonomy that this project [for a civil government] contemplates is very much broader than that accorded now to the English Crown colonies and approaches to that accorded to Canada, Australia, New Zealand, and the

Cape Settlements. It provides for as large a measure of self-government as the Puerto Ricans are capable of using wisely. . . . While this proposed scheme bears some resemblance to that under which some English colonies are now administered, there are many points in which it differs. The bill "To provide a territorial government for Hawaii" . . . supplied some features which have been incorporated, but as a whole it does not bear close resemblance to any existing system of government.[39]

Thus, Davis recommended that the civil government in Puerto Rico should at first resemble a British crown colony (Trinidad) but should assume, as soon as possible, the form of a colonial government with responsible representative institutions (Canada), combined with elements of U.S. territorial government (Hawai'i). According to his scheme, Puerto Rico would be a "dependency" and decidedly not a territory destined for "final incorporation within the American Union"—that is, statehood. Davis stated emphatically that neither the annexation of Hawai'i nor the Senate proposal for a Hawaiian territorial government established precedents for either Puerto Rico or the Philippines regarding incorporation or eventual statehood. "We have no American precedent," he commented, "to which we can refer as an aid to decide the form of civil government that should be set up."[40]

In its discussion of a suitable government for the Philippines, the Schurman Commission also considered the varied colonial governments established throughout the British Empire: the crown colony, the colony with representative institutions, and the self-governing colony with an autonomous local government. The commission rejected the crown colony because it did not promote the development of "home rule"—that is, local self-government. The commission also rejected the self-governing colony because there was no "community of blood, race, and language," and the island populations in general were considered entirely unfit for self-government at the moment. The model of a colony with representative institutions, furthermore, did not provide for a clear division of governmental functions between the sovereign power and the colony that might enable the further development of representative institutions. Thus, the commission argued that the most applicable model for governing the Philippines was the U.S. model of territorial government, which itself was a modified version of the British colony with representative institutions:

> The [colonial] governor might, indeed, be given a qualified veto power on local legislation; and in such a case the whole subject should be referred for final disposition to the legislature of the sovereign power, in which, however, the

colony should have a representative to present its side of the case. In this way, without doing any violence to representative institutions, the rights of the local legislature and the supremacy of the sovereign power could be easily adjusted and reconciled. But in these suggested modifications of the British colony having representative institutions but not responsible government has developed substantially into the American scheme of Territorial governments.[41]

Furthermore, according to the commission, this model of territorial government had two variants: a "first-class" territorial government with an elected legislature and a "second-class" territorial government with a presidentially appointed legislature.[42] Citing Thomas Jefferson on self-government among people who were "as yet as incapable of self-government as children," the commission recommended a lower house of elected representatives and an upper house of appointed officials:[43] "The changes suggested in the Jeffersonian scheme of government for Louisiana, in the light of the ideals formulated by prominent and progressive Filipinos—that is, an elected lower house with an upper house half elected and half nominated—would practically convert the scheme into a Territorial government of the first class. And this, after due consideration of circumstances and conditions in the Philippines, is what the commission earnestly recommends."[44]

Despite the different reasoning of General Davis and the Schurman Commission, the recommended forms of government were remarkably similar: an appointed imperial governor, an executive council with legislative functions (fully appointed in Davis's scheme and half elected in the commission's proposal), and an elected legislative assembly. In other words, both provided a representative institution—the legislative assembly—under the watchful eye and firm control of the appointed imperial officials in both the executive and the legislative branches. These recommendations incorporated some elements of U.S. territorial traditions within an overall imperial framework borrowed chiefly from the British. As we shall see below, these recommendations would have considerable influence in Congress.

* * *

Several bills regarding trade with Puerto Rico and its civil government were presented, and amended, in the House and the Senate. The principal points of contention were free trade with the United States and the question of citizenship. Early versions of the bills, submitted by Sereno Payne in the House and Joseph Foraker in the Senate, treated Puerto Rico as a part of the United States with regard to economic matters and extended citizenship to the population. However, the debates expressed concern over the possible precedents that Puerto

Rico might establish for future legislation for the Philippines.[45] The more fundamental issue was whether the legislative power of Congress was limited by the Constitution in the new possessions or whether it was plenary. In his report from the Committee on Pacific Islands and Puerto Rico, Foraker made several key points. First, he supported the doctrine of plenary powers, arguing that Congress could legislate as it wished in both Puerto Rico and the Philippines. In addition, he argued that Puerto Ricans should be classed as "citizens"—that is, persons "owing allegiance to a government and entitled to protection from it." Citizenship in Puerto Rico did not limit the plenary powers of the Congress and did not "extend" the Constitution to the territory. In this way, Foraker argued that citizenship did not imply political equality or Constitutional rights, only loyalty to the United States. Finally, he also supported free trade since Puerto Rico was a possession of the United States, not a foreign country.[46]

Because of concerns regarding the Puerto Rican precedent, congressmen regularly deployed a discourse of difference in order to distinguish it from the Philippines. Representative Thomas Spight argued that Puerto Rico was a "contiguous territory" that was "part of the American continent." In addition, "its people are, in the main, Caucasian blood, knowing and appreciating the benefits of civilization, and are desirous of casting their lot with us." In contrast, the Philippines was far away, and its "inhabitants are of different races of people from ours." Further, "they have nothing in common with us and centuries can not assimilate them."[47] Spight highlighted differences in proximity, racial character, civilization, and disposition to argue for a close, integrated political and economic relationship between Puerto Rico and the United States. On the floor of the Senate, Albert Beveridge deployed feminine metaphors in arguing for the bill to establish Puerto Rico's civil government:

> This island of beauty and natural wealth came to us like a bride to the arms of her beloved. . . . Porto Rico came to us like Ruth, saying, "Entreat me not to leave thee, or to return from following after thee; for whither thou goest I will go, and where thou lodgest I will lodge; thy people shall be my people, and thy God my God." Thus comes this little land, pleading, like Ruth, only that she may glean in the harvest after the reapers. And she is hungry; we will feed her. She asks for the liberty to live; we will free the hands of her industry. She is bruised and wounded and weak; we will soothe her bruises, heal her wounds, strengthen her weakness.[48]

According to Beveridge, this Puerto Rican Ruth sought the freedom to work and to make a living, not to acquire political liberty and self-determination. The pressing issue, then, was agriculture, industry, and commerce under U.S. political tutelage. But the imagery was not unsympathetic: the Puerto Rican Ruth was like a bride who might become a part of "thy people."

In the House of Representatives, Sereno Payne similarly deployed the metaphor of childhood throughout his speech: "Keep them all in leading strings until you have educated them up to the full stature of American manhood, and then crown them with the glory of American citizenship."[49] In the nineteenth century, children would hold on to leading strings in order to learn how to walk unassisted. In this regard, the Puerto Rican child had not achieved manhood, although with education and political tutelage, he might one day deserve U.S. citizenship. Likewise, Congressman Joseph Graff, in his support of legislation for civil government in Puerto Rico, recognized the abject poverty and lack of education among the majority of Puerto Ricans. Notwithstanding, he described them as "kindly" and "not inclined to be belligerent or hostile to the United States." Indeed, they seemed willing to conform to any conditions determined by Congress. "They are willing pupils in the school of self-government, but the transformation from their present condition into the high stature of our ideal of American citizenship can not be accomplished in a day or in several years."[50] These Puerto Rican children, when provided with adequate schools and leadership, were very promising wards and might even be candidates for American citizenship in a far distant future.

In these debates, we see the metaphorical importance of a child's education in relation to imperial strategy. Together, the sympathetic images of femininity and childhood served to promote the integration of the island into the U.S. economic and judicial systems, but their decidedly negative connotations simultaneously excluded Puerto Rico from complete political integration into the United States.[51] Sympathy did not translate into political equality. Congress regularly expressed concerns over the high levels of illiteracy and the Spanish heritage, especially in the realm of the political. After considerable debate and several amendments, the Foraker bill was approved. It established a temporary tariff on trade with the United States. Finally, as we shall see below, Congress avoided the possible legal entanglements of granting U.S. citizenship.

The congressional debates over legislation for the Philippines were long, high spirited, and complex. The principal measures dealt with tariffs and civil government but were complicated by the issue of the ongoing war. The main legislative disagreement was whether Congress was to grant independence or whether it would organize a colonial government for the Philippines. Several measures and amendments conceding independence were rejected by the majority. There were also alternate House and Senate bills regarding the details of civil government, including the elective assembly, the banking system, the currency, and the use of public lands for investment. There was no question that there would be no free trade between the Philippines and the United States; the discussion centered around the preference rates and the use of tariffs to fund the colonial government.[52] Throughout the debates, members of Congress regularly used singularly negative terms to describe the Philippines as a vast, culturally diverse archipelago that could never be assimilated or settled by European Americans. The debates stressed that the problem was a lack of "civilization." The principal narrative was of the evolution of an aggregate of diverse tribes, ranging from the most primitive to the more civilized. The participants in the debates were highly aware of the power of language and frequently questioned the particular words and phrases used by others. An advocate of speedy independence for the Philippines, Senator Edward Carmack, who favored independence, complained that his opponents who favored a colonial government unfairly characterized the Filipino people in degrading terms: "Now, sir, the first and worst offender in this respect is the President of the United States. 'Savages,' 'barbarians,' 'a savage people,' 'a wild and ignorant people,' 'Apaches,' 'Sioux,' 'Chinese Boxers,' these are the words habitually employed by him to describe a people nine-tenths of whom are sufficiently educated to read his bitter and scornful and contemptuous words!"[53] Carmack contrasted the images of savages with another: Filipinos as literate and capable of self-government. Filipino leaders similarly asserted their status as a "civilized nation" against the prevalent image of a "collection of tribes," as did Sixto Lopez in 1900 in his anti-imperialist tract for Filipino nationhood:

> As a matter of fact, with the exception of the few uncivilized tribes in Central Mindanao and the Sulus, and the semi-civilized Igorrotes and Negritos of Luzon . . . the Filipinos are a homogenous people belonging to the Malayan race. They speak several dialects, but they are one people. They constitute an overwhelming majority of the inhabitants of the Philippines. They are opposed not solely to American but to any foreign rule; and they are united in the desire for independence and for the purpose of maintaining a stable, independent government. In conclusion, I again assert without fear of contradiction, that the alleged antagonisms between the inhabitants of the provincial districts, or between the so-called "tribes," have arisen not in the minds of the Filipinos themselves, but in the minds of those who do not understand our peoples and who have reached conclusions in no way warranted by the facts.[54]

Virtually the whole Congress agreed that assimilation of the Philippines to the United States was impossible; the basic disagreement was whether Congress would commit itself to an independent government in the near future. Democrats portrayed the Filipinos' capacity for self-government as similar to that of the Cubans, while Republicans, who favored a long, indefinite period of tutelage, stressed that the Philippines was inhabited by a heterogeneous aggregate of tribes that did not constitute a civilized nation. Senator John Spooner, in his defense of the organic bill, argued that "It takes more than land and inhabitants to constitute 'a people.'" Since there was no unified "people," there was no justification for an independent government.[55] Buttressed by diverse photographic images and deprecating descriptions, Republicans denied that the peoples of the Philippines constituted a nation, and national sovereignty therefore had no cultural basis. Indeed, Republicans conceived the colonial project in the Philippines as the creation of a nation through political tutelage over the long term. The analogy of tribes, articulated within the narrative of evolution, was a powerful argument for the establishment of colonial rule.

* * *

On the basis of the official reports, Congress passed organic acts to establish civil governments in Puerto Rico and the Philippines.[56] The acts created in each locale an executive branch composed of a presidentially appointed governor and an executive commission, plus a legislative branch composed of the same executive commission and a lower house of elected representatives.[57] Contrary to the constitutional principle of the separation of powers, the executive commission served both as the governor's cabinet and as the upper legislative body, limiting the autonomy of the elected assembly. Thus, both executive and legislative branches were firmly under the control of appointed colonial administrators who were supposedly tutors in the art of self-government. In addition, the president appointed justices to the local supreme court, while the governor appointed judges to the district courts. In short, the president of the United States exercised control over the local governments by means of appointments to the executive, legislative, and judicial branches (see table 1).

According to the organic acts, the inhabitants of neither Puerto Rico nor the Philippines became U.S. citizens. Instead, they became "citizens of Porto Rico" and "citizens of the Philippine Islands." As such, they were entitled to the protection of, and owed allegiance to, the United States. The law did not grant the "citizens of Porto Rico" a bill of rights, but the "citizens of the Philippine Islands" were explicitly granted rights of life, liberty, property, due process of law, religious freedom, and freedom of speech and of the press.[58] Puerto Ricans elected, by popular vote, a "resident commissioner" to serve in Washington, D.C. In the Philippines, the legislature selected and sent two resident commissioners to Washington. In both cases, these commissioners had no clearly defined rights

Table 1 Governments of Hawai'i (1900), Puerto Rico (1900), and the Philippines (1902) Established by Congress

	HAWAI'I	PUERTO RICO	THE PHILIPPINES
Executive	Governor and territorial secretary appointed by president. Other executive officials appointed by governor.	Governor and executive council, both appointed by president.	Governor-general and Philippine Commission, both appointed by president.
Legislature	Two houses, a senate and a house of representatives, both comprised of elected delegates.	A legislative assembly comprised of the executive council and a house of elected delegates.	A legislative assembly comprised of the Philippine Commission and the Philippine Assembly of elected delegates.
Local judiciary	Local supreme court appointed by president. U.S. Supreme Court had arbitrament.	Local supreme court appointed by president. U.S. Supreme Court had arbitrament.	Local supreme court appointed by president. U.S. Supreme Court had arbitrament.
Federal judiciary	Judge, district attorney, and marshal appointed to federal district court by president.	Judge, district attorney, and marshal appointed to federal "district court of the United States for Porto Rico."	Not a part of the federal judiciary.
U.S. statutes	All applied, except those not locally applicable; collection of internal revenue applied.	All applied, except those not locally applicable and excluding internal revenue.	Did not apply.
Congressional representation	One elected delegate to the House with voice but no vote.	None (one resident commissioner was entitled to official recognition in Washington).	None (two resident commissioners were entitled to official recognition in Washington).
Citizenship	Citizens of former Hawaiian republic became U.S. citizens (including native Hawaiians).	Citizens of Puerto Rico not U.S. citizens.	Citizens of the Philippines not U.S. citizens.
Customs	U.S. customs district.	Temporary duties on trade between United States and Puerto Rico (until 1902), followed by free trade.	Foreign port.
Currency	U.S. dollar.	U.S. dollar.	Philippine peso.
Language stipulations	Proceedings of legislature in English. Voters required to speak, read, and write English or Hawaiian.	Proceedings of district court in English. Delegates to legislature required to read and write English or Spanish. Resident commissioner required to read and write English.	None.

Table 1   *(continued)*

	HAWAI'I	PUERTO RICO	THE PHILIPPINES
Racial exclusion	Chinese immigration to Hawai'i or from Hawai'i to the states or territories prohibited. Chinese and Japanese residents denied citizenship.	None.	Special provinces for Muslims and animist tribes ruled by appointed officials without representation in the Philippine Assembly.

Sources: U.S. *Statutes at Large:* vol. 31 (12 April 1900), 71–86; vol. 31 (30 April 1900), 141–162; vol. 32 (1 July 1902) 691–697.
Note: All presidential appointments required the approval of the Senate.

or duties; both organic acts simply provided for their "official recognition" in the federal departments in Washington. In 1902, however, the House of Representatives amended its internal rules of procedure and granted the Puerto Rican commissioner access to the floor of the House and, two years later, the right to participate in debates and in committees but *not* the right to vote. Shortly thereafter, the House began to pay the salary and transportation costs of the Puerto Rican commissioner. This made the status of the Puerto Rican commissioner practically the same as that of a territorial delegate: a nonvoting, second-class member of the House of Representatives.[59] In 1907, the commissioners from the Philippines also gained the right to speak in the House of Representatives but could not vote. The House soon became a forum for the presentation of Filipino nationalist views regarding independence.[60]

Despite the important similarities in the executive and legislative structures of local government, the laws pertaining to Puerto Rico and the Philippines were quite different in their judicial and economic provisions. Puerto Rico's organic act provided a much greater incorporation of the island to the United States. First, the act extended U.S. statutes (except those regarding internal revenue) and the federal judiciary to Puerto Rico, which became a new district in the federal court system. In contrast, U.S. statutes did not automatically apply in the Philippines, which was not a part of the federal court system, even though the U.S. Supreme Court had final jurisdiction over decisions of the local courts. Second, Puerto Rico became a domestic port with regard to tariff duties and customs, while the Philippines continued to be designated a foreign port.[61] Finally, in Puerto Rico, U.S. currency replaced Spanish money, while in the Philippines the law created a new legal tender, the Philippine peso.

The Supreme Court and the Insular Cases

No sooner had Congress approved the Foraker Act (1900), which created the civil government of Puerto Rico, than a series of nine "Insular Cases" was brought before the Supreme Court. Decided in 1901, these cases dealt with various constitutional issues in Puerto Rico, Hawai'i, and the Philippines.[62] The most important case was undoubtedly *Downes v. Bidwell*, which concerned the uniform tariff clause of the Constitution.[63] In 1900, Samuel Downes, the plaintiff, sued George Bidwell, the customs collector at the port of New York, for having levied an import tax on a cargo of oranges from Puerto Rico. The customs collector had followed the provisions of section 3 of the Foraker Act, which established tariffs on trade between Puerto Rico and the United States with the purpose of providing revenues for the new civil government until the establishment of a Puerto Rican treasury along with the means of appropriating revenues. The plaintiff appealed to the uniform tariff clause of the Constitution, which stated that "all duties, imposts, and excises shall be uniform throughout the United States." In order to decide this case, the Supreme Court had to determine whether Puerto Rico was indeed part of the United States and thus subject to the uniform tariff clause. In the process, the court was also compelled to clarify the constitutional powers of Congress with respect to the territories. Thus, a seemingly mundane tariff dispute over charges to a shipment of oranges—which totaled $659.35—became a fundamental precedent in territorial law, in effect establishing for the first time the legal distinction between incorporated and unincorporated territories.

Downes v. Bidwell took up many of the same issues discussed earlier in the *Harvard Law Review*, the *Yale Law Journal*, and several official documents, especially the recommendations of Davis and Magoon. In the exceptionally long decision, one finds the justices juggling the same issues and producing similar alternatives. Five separate opinions were delivered in the case, but they may be grouped into three major legal positions coinciding with those that emerged from the legal debate: the doctrines of extension (coinciding with the doctrine of plenary powers), *ex proprio vigore*, and incorporation (coinciding with the "third view"). The crucial difference was that *Downes v. Bidwell*, decided by the Supreme Court, became the law of the land. It remains the most important legal precedent in territorial law up to this very day.[64]

Legally speaking, two issues were involved: first, the extension of constitutional provisions, including the uniform tariff clause, to the territories, and second, constitutional limitations to the power of Congress in the territories, including the determination of personal, civil, and political rights. Politically speaking, there were also two issues. The first was that the insular possessions had not been, and most likely would not become, areas of Euro-American settlement, but rather were inhabited by "alien races." The second, which followed from the first, was how to justify congressional power over these new territories in a manner that distinguished them from the existing territories and districts.

Justice Henry Brown (with Justice Edward White and three other justices concurring) delivered the decision of the majority. According to Brown, the Constitution applied primarily to the states, their citizens, and their representatives. In contrast, plenary power to acquire and govern territories was vested in Congress and was derived from the power to make treaties, declare war, and conquer territories, which were all aspects of national sovereignty. Brown was quite emphatic in his defense of the right of conquest of territory and the subjugation of native populations: "We are also of opinion that the power to acquire territory by treaty implies not only the power to govern such territory, but to prescribe upon what terms the United States will receive its inhabitants, and what their status shall be in . . . the 'American Empire.'"[65]

Indeed, Brown argued, all previous treaties had made special provisions for the citizenship of the inhabitants upon the annexation of territories. Furthermore, it would have been "extremely dangerous" to automatically admit these new subjects as citizens, with all rights and privileges.[66] Congress should have the power to decide whether the inhabitants of the annexed territories would be accepted as U.S. citizens. Indeed, Brown argued, it was doubtful if Congress would ever assent to the annexation of territory upon the condition that its inhabitants, quite possibly unaccustomed to the "habits, traditions, and modes of life" of the United States, should become at once citizens.[67] Citizenship had always been a consideration upon the annexation of territory, and this was especially the case for the new insular possessions. Justice Brown contrasted the previous continental expansion with the new insular possessions in this way: "It is obvious that in the annexation of outlying and distant possessions grave questions will arise from differences of race, habits, laws and customs of the people, and from differences of soil, climate and production, which may require action on the part of Congress that would be quitted unnecessary in the annexation of contiguous territory inhabited only by people of the same race, or by scattered bodies of native Indians."[68]

The previous continental expansion, Brown recounted, involved the incorporation of contiguous territory, settled by "people of the same race"—that is, Anglo-Saxons. At most, the previously annexed continental territory might have included sparse indigenous populations, to whom were excluded the rights of citizenship. Thus, his ruling was based upon and perpetuated the frontier myth of Euro-Americans settling unpopulated, or at least unused, lands. For Brown, however, the new possessions reflected a fundamentally different situation. First of all, these possessions were "outlying and distant" and were noncontiguous. Second and more important, there were differences of race, culture, law, soil, climate, and economic production. These new possessions, as implied, were already inhabited by peoples that were quite different from Euro-Americans and would not be assimilated or displaced easily by settlers. The new possessions were not, in other words, an extension of the frontier.

In the decision of the Supreme Court, Brown affirmed the judgment of the circuit court and ruled that the Foraker Act was constitutional insofar as it imposed duties upon imports: the uniform tariff clause did not apply. This ruling was based upon the notion that Puerto Rico was an appurtenant territory of the United States but not part of the body politic of the republic and thus not subject to all the provisions of the constitution.[69] This ruling established a precedent for the differential treatment of the territories on the basis that they were possessions, but not a part, of the United States. The inhabitants of these areas were subjects but not citizens. The reasoning was clearly based upon the principle that the annexation of "alien races" was something to be strictly avoided, even in the process of overseas expansion:

> Patriotic and intelligent men may differ widely as to the desirableness of this or that acquisition, but this is solely a political question. We can only consider this aspect of the case so far as to say that no construction of the Constitution should be adopted which would prevent Congress from considering each case upon its merits, unless the language of the instrument imperatively demand it. A false step at this time might be fatal to the development of what Chief Justice Marshall called the American Empire. Choice in some cases, the natural gravitation of small bodies towards large ones in others, the result of a successful war in still others, may bring about conditions which would render the annexation of distant possessions desirable. If those possessions are inhabited by alien races, differing from us in religion, customs, laws, methods of taxation and modes of thought, the administration of government and justice, according to Anglo-Saxon principles, may for a time be impossible; and the question at once arises whether large concessions ought not to be made for a time, that, ultimately, our own theories may be carried out, and the blessings of a free government under the Constitution extended to them. We decline to hold that there is anything in the Constitution to forbid such action.[70]

This passage was exceptionally clear in stating that the "administration of government and justice according to Anglo-Saxon principles" could be denied to any peoples differing in terms of "religion, customs, laws, methods of taxation and modes of thought." Free government and constitutional rule were consistent with "our own" principles and should not be automatically extended to the "alien races" of the new possessions. Thus, Brown ruled that the right to govern the territories was a power granted to Congress by the territorial clause of the Constitution. In addition, he suggested that only the states constituted by European American settlers were guaranteed a free government under the Constitution. In principle, then, he argued that "we" (read Congress) had the right to govern "them" (read the subjects of the new possessions).

Nevertheless, Justice Brown did grant that some constitutional rights did indeed apply in the new possessions: "We suggest, without intending to decide, that there may be a distinction between certain natural rights enforced in the Constitution by prohibitions against interference with them, and what may be termed artificial or remedial rights which are peculiar to our own system of jurisprudence."[71] In this way, he argued that some constitutional rights coincided with natural or universal rights, but others were particular and exclusive to "our own system of jurisprudence." Although he was unwilling to determine exactly which rights were "natural" and which were "remedial," he suggested the following. Natural rights included religious freedom; personal liberty; individual property; freedom of speech; freedom of the press; due process and equal protection under the law; and immunities from unreasonable searches and seizures, as well as from cruel and unusual punishments. Remedial or "artificial" rights included citizenship; suffrage; and the methods "peculiar to Anglo-Saxon jurisprudence," such as trial by jury.[72] Brown was not clear as to exactly which rights should be granted to the inhabitants of the new territories, but he suggested that even if they were regarded as "aliens," they would be entitled to protection of "life, liberty, and property."[73] Nevertheless, it was at the discretion of Congress which rights would be extended to the territories; hence his was a "doctrine of extension." Indeed, the Treaty of Paris assured the inhabitants of Puerto Rico and the Philippines the freedom of religion and the rights of life, liberty, and property, but any remedial rights were at the discretion of Congress. In addition, there was no basis whatsoever for the application of the uniformity clause of the Constitution. Thus, the Foraker Act was constitutional. Mr. Downes failed to recoup the tariff paid at the port of New York.

The ruling of Justice Brown was very much in line with the arguments made by the proponents of plenary powers in the legal debate, especially those of Langdell and Thayer; the latter in fact expressed his agreement with the decision.[74] The decision expressed very clearly the expansionist motives and the logic of racial exclusion; however, the doctrine of extension was not the best legal solution. Strangely enough, the decision of the Supreme Court was the expressed point of view of one lone justice, Brown. Justice White had concurred, but he offered a different legal basis for the decision. White, the author of the second opinion, introduced the "doctrine of incorporation." He began by forcefully arguing that even though the Constitution granted to Congress the power to dispose of and govern the territories, Congress did not stand above or outside the Constitution. The Constitution granted powers, with certain restrictions, to Congress, just as it prohibited absolutely other powers.[75] Thus, the United States had the constitutional powers to impose local taxes or to organize a government in Puerto Rico, but it was absolutely prohibited from denying "liberty and justice."[76] In order to determine whether the Foraker Act violated the uniformity clause the sole question was whether Puerto Rico had been incorporated to the United States.

Thus, in one way or another, the Constitution applied to all territories, but not in exactly the same fashion since the territories were not equal. In a long review of the territorial precedents, Justice White argued strongly against the notion that all territories were automatically incorporated to the United States. The terms of annexation had been determined always by treaty, and Article 9 of the Treaty of Paris had explicitly stated that: "The civil rights and political status of the native inhabitants of the territories hereby ceded to the United States shall be determined by the Congress." To deny Congress this power of treaty would have had undesirable consequences. If incorporation were automatic, any war and conquest could result in the admission to territorial status and eventual statehood of "an alien and hostile people," precisely the case of the Philippines at that time.

Indeed, the constitutional rights of self-government and citizenship were historically granted only to "Whites," but not to African Americans or American Indians in either the states or the territories. The issue was not the annexation of territories inhabited by alien peoples, for this had been done before. The problem was the means of control over these peoples without European American settlement and hegemony. White argued that an alien people should not be incorporated to the United States by mere cession of a territory without the express approval of Congress. Thus, he based his distinction of incorporated and unincorporated territories upon the principle of avoiding the admission of alien peoples as citizens of the United States.[77] His much-cited conclusion regarding Puerto Rico was as follows: "The result of what has been said is that while in an international sense Porto Rico was not a foreign country, since it was subject to the sovereignty of and was owned by the United States, it was foreign to the United States in a domestic sense, because the island had not been incorporated into the United States, but was merely appurtenant thereto as a possession."[78]

According to White, Puerto Rico (and by extension the Philippines and Guam) were not incorporated to the United States by the Treaty of Paris; rather they were unincorporated territories belonging to, but not a part of, the United

States. The doctrine of incorporation conformed to the intents and purposes of the imperial project but managed to create a more elegant legal solution based upon the same racial exclusions expressed by Brown. According to the doctrine, the plenary powers of Congress extended only to the unincorporated territories.

Chief Justice Melville Fuller delivered the dissenting position, with three justices concurring. Fuller criticized White's doctrine of incorporation, arguing that Puerto Rico had become an organized territory pursuant to the Foraker Act, which "has created a civil government for Porto Rico, has constituted its inhabitants a body politic, has given it a governor and other officers, a legislative assembly, and courts, with right of appeal to this [Supreme] court."[79] According to Fuller, this did not mean necessarily that the people of Puerto Rico were citizens of the United States; it did definitely mean that the uniformity clause of the Constitution applied. The chief justice also argued that the Constitution did not permit Congress to establish governments throughout the world at will since this was contrary to the republican system. Nevertheless, the doctrine of incorporation "assumed that the Constitution created a government empowered to acquire countries throughout the world, to be governed by different rules than those obtaining in the original states and territories, and substitutes for the present system of republican government a system of domination over distant provinces in the exercise of unrestricted power."[80] Of course, Congress and the executive branch had embarked precisely on this kind of imperial project, to acquire colonies and establish governments therein that were distinct from those of the states and the republic. This anti-imperialist dissent would not prevail.

However, neither the doctrine of extension, which was the decision of the court, nor the doctrine of incorporation, which was the concurring variation, answered the question of precisely how the possessions were to be governed. Instead, the Supreme Court decisions of 1901 legitimated what was a *fait accompli;* already Congress had created a civil government in Puerto Rico in 1900. Still, by legitimizing the organic act for Puerto Rico, the court prepared the way for the organic act for the Philippines. Thus, the decision provided Congress with a general justification for excluding Puerto Rico, the Philippines, and Guam from the body politic and authorized its plenary powers over these new possessions. It left the decisions regarding the specific structures of government to Congress.

Special Provinces in the Philippines

Even though the imperialists used the narrative of tribes in a most general fashion, it was also apparent that not all tribes were the same. Cultural difference led to divergent provincial governments *within* the Philippines, according to a cultural—specifically religious—criterion.[81] The organic act denied representation in the Filipino legislature to provinces "inhabited by tribal Indians" or where the local government was conducted by "sultans, datos [sic], or chiefs." Colonial administrators categorized the diverse ethnic groups according to three basic categories: Christian, animist, and Muslim, with the latter two often referred to as "non-Christian" or "uncivilized tribes." President McKinley instructed the Second Philippine Commission to apply to the latter the same general policy that Congress had adopted for the American Indians:

> In dealing with the uncivilized tribes of the islands the commission should adopt the same course followed by Congress in permitting the tribes of our North American Indians to maintain their tribal organization and government, and under which many of those tribes are now living in peace and contentment, surrounded by a civilization to which they are unable or unwilling to conform. Such tribal governments should, however, be subjected to wise and firm regulation; and, without undue or petty interference, constant and active effort should be exercised to prevent barbarous practices and to introduce civilized customs.[82]

McKinley's directive suggested that the "uncivilized tribes" were comparable with the American Indians and therefore subject to similar policies, especially with regard to the maintenance of their tribal organization and government.[83] Along these lines, the organic act provided for the gradual establishment of civil government in pacified provinces with Christian majorities while excluding areas "inhabited by Moros or other non-Christian tribes."[84] For "Christian" provinces, the act granted limited municipal self-government, organized partially elected provincial governments, and provided for elected representatives to the national legislature, known as the Philippine Assembly. In contrast, the governor-general and the Philippine Commission governed the "non-Christian tribes" directly by means of appointed officials. In 1900, the Philippine Commission established the Bureau of Non-Christian Tribes, which was assigned to conduct ethnographic research, including the description of the current conditions and the classification of various tribes. The bureau was to provide the knowledge base for the establishment of municipal and provincial governments in areas inhabited by animist and Muslim peoples. In 1901, it was renamed the Ethnological Survey.[85]

To comply with McKinley's directive, David Barrows, first chief of the bureau, spent several months visiting American Indian reservations and schools in the United States. The "Indian policy" to which McKinley referred was not entirely clear since during the previous decades Congress had worked to abandon the reservation policy, allot land to individuals, and dismantle tribal organizations.[86] Barrows understood "Indian policy" to mean the system of reservations, the maintenance of tribal governments, and the establishment of boarding schools to promote acculturation. However, he was not impressed with the policy of reservations since it recognized tribal organization and provided for the allocation of communal lands to the "tribes," also known as "domestic dependent nations." He also felt that boarding schools were inadequate since they provided the students with an education that they could seldom use when they returned home. His general conclusion, contrary to McKinley's directive, was that "the policy of the United States in dealing with the American Indian contains little that can be followed in governing the backward races here [in the Philippines]."[87] In this statement, Barrows thus rejected the comparison of American Indian tribes with the tribes of the Philippines. To the contrary, he suggested that the United States should take into consideration the particular culture, religion, and political organization of the local tribes. It is important that instead of recognizing local tribal authorities, Barrows sought to undermine their power.[88] The Philippine Commission, following the advice of Barrows, organized two "special provinces" under the control of appointed officials: Moro Province, created in 1903, and Mountain Province, created in 1908.

The Bates Agreement, signed in 1899 by the United States and the Sultan of Sulu, Jamalul Kiram II, granted considerable political autonomy to the various sultans and *datus* in the southernmost areas of the Philippines.[89] The agreement, which resembled the previous Spanish treaties with the sultans, achieved a momentary peace in the region while the war raged in the northern regions. Upon the defeat of the Philippine Army and the virtual elimination of guerrilla resistance in the northern provinces, the Philippine Commission turned its attention to the rule of the island of Mindanao, the second largest of the Philippines group; the Sulu Archipelago; and the island of Palawan (then known as Paragua), which were officially under U.S. military rule but for all practical purposes controlled by the sultans. Prominent army officers, such as General Davis (the former military governor of Puerto Rico) and General Leonard Wood (the former military governor of Cuba and the first governor of Moro Province), opposed the Bates Agreement because of the autonomy it granted to the sultanates. In this way, the Bates Agreement was a treaty similar to those made—and broken—by Congress with the various American Indian tribes throughout the nineteenth century. Moro Province was created in 1903 precisely to destroy the traditional political authority of the Muslim sultans and *datus*. The province was simultaneously a civil government and a military district. In practice, military officers held the highest positions of civil government. It was divided into municipalities and "tribal wards" delimited by ethnicity. The provincial governor appointed local officials to the municipal governments and loyal "headmen" to supervise the tribal wards. This structure of loyal governor-appointed local officials undercut the centralized political authority of the sultans and *datus*. One year after the creation of Moro Province, President Theodore Roosevelt abrogated the Bates Agreement and thus officially revoked the political authority of the sultans and *datus*.[90]

The creation of Moro Province led to widespread revolts that, over roughly ten years, were systematically suppressed by the U.S. Army. In 1913 Moro Province, then fundamentally under military rule, became the Department of Mindanao and Sulu, with a civil government made up of seven provinces. All tribal wards were replaced with municipal districts with appointed officials. This new civil government still fell under the direct supervision of the governor-general and the Philippine Commission. The Jones Law of 1916, which eliminated the Philippine Commission, created a new Bureau of Non-Christian Tribes to oversee the government of these provinces.[91] If "Indian policy" provided any guidance for governing the Muslim peoples, it was only during the first few years of transition. Instead of maintaining "tribal organization," the policy over the long term was directed at the complete elimination of traditional centralized authority.

Likewise, tribal organization was not the operative principle for the governing of the hill tribes of northern Luzon. In 1908 the Philippine Commission, after much experimentation with civil municipal governments and a good deal of gerrymandering in order to group together the northern hill tribes, created Mountain Province in the mountainous north-central areas of the island of Luzon. The new Mountain Province was divided into subprovinces, roughly corresponding to "culture areas." Barrows noted that the term "tribe" was not entirely adequate because he felt that it implied a more centralized tribal political organization than what he had found in the province. According to him, political capacity did not extend beyond the community or village. For this reason, he preferred the term "culture area," although the term "tribe" was still widely used. At no point did the Philippine Commission recognize any kind of unified tribal government apart from particular village "headmen" and "councils." Instead, the commission organized municipal or township governments under the guidance of provincial or subprovincial imperial authorities. The Township Government Act (1905) allowed the appointment of local officials by the provincial governor in the "least civilized areas" or the election of such officials (except secretary-treasurers) by "manhood suffrage" in areas that had shown progress in governmental capacities. Neither provincial nor subprovincial positions were elected. The Philippine Commission, furthermore, promulgated laws that supplanted customary laws.[92] Thus, while imperial authorities initially recognized traditional village authority, they did so only as a means of transition to the organization of township governments. Unlike Moro Province, Mountain Province did not have a military government.

It is doubtful, therefore, that U.S. policy toward American Indians provided much guidance for policy in the Philippines, even with respect to the animist and Muslim peoples in the two special provinces. Colonial administrators explicitly departed from President McKinley's directive to maintain tribal organization and government, although at first traditional authorities were recognized. The Philippine Commission did not organize reservations; rather it established municipal and provincial governments that supplanted traditional authority. While the Bates Agreement was analogous to congressional treaties with American Indian tribes, the imperial government abrogated this agreement and created Moro Province as soon as U.S. authority was clearly established in the rest of the Philippines. Despite the presidential directive, colonial administrators concluded that the animist tribes of the Philippines were different from American Indians and that the recognition of Muslim political systems threatened the sovereignty of the imperial government. Thus, while not entirely abandoning the analogy of tribes, colonial administrators began to distinguish different kinds of tribes on the basis of religion. Christian Filipinos were favored as the participants and representatives of colonial democracy.[93]

* * *

Congress *adopted* for Hawai'i the standard territorial government, according to the model it had already used in the various continental territories, including New Mexico, Arizona, and Oklahoma (the district of Alaska, however, had to wait until 1912 for a territorial government). The organic act provided for an appointed governor and a fully elected bicameral legislature. European American and Hawaiian residents became citizens of the United States. Of the insular territories, only Hawai'i approximated the continental experience of European American settlement and local hegemony. For this reason, Hawai'i was the only new territory to be incorporated into the United States and eventually (1959) admitted as a state. Hawai'i, then, was a distant frontier of European American settlement, and this distinguished it from the former Spanish colonies acquired in 1898. In contrast, Congress *adapted* the territorial model for Puerto Rico and the Philippines in quite flexible ways. Their governments were adaptations of the territorial model used in the continental territories and Hawai'i, but their organic laws marked a shift in U.S. expansionism: from colonialism via settlement to imperialism via political dominion. The basic structure of these imperial governments resembled that of a territorial government, but one firmly under the control of appointed European American administrators. The executive branch comprised a presidentially appointed governor and an appointed executive commission. The legislative branch was composed of the same executive commission, which functioned as the upper house, and a lower house of elected representatives. The organic act for Puerto Rico provided significant integration to the United States, principally through the extension of U.S. statutes and the federal judiciary, the use of a common currency, and the treatment of the island as a domestic rather than foreign port. While Congress integrated Puerto Rico into the commercial and judicial systems of the United States, it excluded the Philippines as a foreign port, with its own currency, and did not make it subject to U.S. statutes or courts. Such decisions followed from the conclusion that Puerto Rico might eventually become "Americanized" but that the Philippines could never be assimilated. Furthermore, special provinces were created in the Philippines for tribes considered to be both "uncivilized" and "non-Christian."

The discussions in the law reviews and the decisions of the Supreme Court produced the legal language to justify and normalize the division between territories that were explicitly incorporated by Congress and those that were not incorporated—namely, Guam, the Philippines, and Puerto Rico. The latter belonged to, but were not a part of, the body politic of the republic. This distinction followed from the conclusion that these islands were inhabited by peoples of fundamentally different races and civilizations who were not fully capable of constitutional self-government. It was premised upon the notion of the cultural difference, or "otherness," of the inhabitants of the islands. Specifically legal discussions were permeated by, and contributed to, an elaboration of presumably relevant differences that also appeared in descriptions and photographs in illustrated books, law journals, reports and recommendations by government officials, debates on the floor of Congress, and the decisions of the Supreme Court. Repeatedly, we find the observation that the new possessions were tropical islands, thickly populated by "alien races." These were places with few, if any, possibilities for immigration and settlement by "Americans." The absence of opportunities for European American settlers is a recurring theme in the congressional debates. While the list of adjectives—distant, noncontiguous, tropical, densely populated, inhabited by alien races—was equally applicable to Hawai'i, the decisive divergence stemmed from the conclusion that the new insular territories were inhospitable to European American immigrants while Hawaii was an "Americanized" settlement.

The principal narrative for Hawai'i described this "Americanization" by means of widespread public education, the use of English in government and business, the close economic relationship with the United States, the establishment of U.S.-style political institutions, and the presence of a strong annexationist movement. A central theme was the transition from a monarchical government, led by Hawaiian royalty, to a democratic republic, led by hegemonic settlers resolutely loyal to the United States. In contrast, the narratives for Puerto Rico, the Philippines, and Guam presented the inhabitants as quite incapable of the kind of self-government the United States supported in Cuba (a dependent republic) or established in Hawai'i (an incorporated territory). First, their local elites were viewed as either weak and lacking political will (Puerto Rico and Guam) or incapable of ruling a vast and culturally heterogeneous archipelago (the Philippines). Second, there was no history of "Americanization" through European American settlement, nor was there any possibility for future assimilation by the same means. According to these political and cultural evaluations, Congress created a third kind of political status for Puerto Rico, the Philippines, and Guam that was distinct from that of either Cuba or Hawai'i. So these islands became unincorporated territories—possessions—of the United States, distinct from either an independent country or an incorporated settler territory.

Notes

1. Political processes are treated in Roger Bell, *Last Among Equals: Hawaiian Statehood and American Politics* (Honolulu: University of Hawai'i Press, 1984), and in two volumes by William Adam Russ: *The Hawaiian Revolution (1893–94)* (Selinsgrove, Pa.: Susquehanna University Press, 1959), and *The Hawaiian Republic (1894–98) and Its Struggle to Win Annexation* (Selinsgrove, Pa.: Susquehanna University Press, 1961). Cultural aspects are treated in Buck, *Paradise Remade*, and Haunani-Kay Trask, *From a Native Daughter: Colonialism and Sovereignty in Hawai'i* (Monroe, Maine: Common Courage Press, 1993). Trask is explicit in her characterization of Hawai'i as a "settler society." An excellent account of the resistance of the Hawaiian monarchy and its loyal citizens is provided by Silva, *Aloha Betrayed*.

2. Lorrin Andrews Thurston, *A Handbook on the Annexation of Hawaii* (St. Joseph, Mo.: A. B. Morse, 1897), 27–44.

3. Ibid., 31. Compare Alfred Hartwell, "The Organization of a Territorial Government for Hawaii," *Yale Law Review* 9, no. 3 (1899): 107–113.

4. In *Congressional Record,* 55th Cong., 2nd sess., 11 June 1898, 5773.

5. S. M. Clark, "Proposed Annexation of Hawaii," *Congressional Record,* 55th Cong., 2nd sess., 14 June 1898, appendix, 510. Compare Mr. Bromwell in ibid., 5919

6. "Joint Resolution to Provide for Annexing the Hawaiian Islands to the United States," *U.S. Statutes at Large*, vol. 30, 750, res. 55 (7 July 1898). For a detailed account of the congressional debates, see Russ, *The Hawaiian Republic*.

7. Hawaiian Commission, *Report*. For an excellent discussion of the importance of law in the transformation of traditional Hawaiian culture, see Sally Engle Merry, *Colonizing Hawai'i: The Cultural Power of Law* (Princeton, N.J.: Princeton University Press, 2000).

8. For a comprehensive treatment of the importance of the Northwest Ordinance in the process of state making, see Onuf, *Statehood and Nation*. Jack Eblen has argued that this model went through some changes during the nineteenth century. During the period of the "first empire" (1787–1848), the autocratic district government was the normal predecessor to the territorial government. During the "second empire" (1848–1898), the district government was skipped in favor of an immediate establishment of territorial governments, in which Congress expanded the powers of the elected legislature—frequently bicameral—and reduced those of the appointed governor. Eblen characterized the third phase as an "oceanic empire" and grouped Hawai'i along with Puerto Rico, the Philippines, and Alaska for reasons of geography, population, and historical period. Contrary to Eblen's classification, the evidence presented in this chapter suggests that the territorial government and the eventual trajectory of Hawai'i clearly follow the model established in the "second empire." See Eblen, *The First and Second United States Empires: Governors and Territorial Government, 1787–1912* (Pittsburgh: University of Pittsburgh Press, 1968), 7–9. Rafucci contrasts the Puerto Rican organic and the continental territorial governments in *El gobierno civil*.

9. Luis Dávila Colón, *Breakthrough from Colonialism: An Interdisciplinary Study of Statehood*, 2 vols. (Río Piedras, Puerto Rico: Editorial de la Universidad de Puerto Rico, 1984).

10. "An Act Providing a Civil Government for Alaska," *U.S. Statutes at Large*, vol. 23 (17 May 1884), 24–28. Congress did not organize a territorial government until 1912. See "An Act to Create a Legislative Assembly in the Territory of Alaska, to Confer Legislative Power Thereon, and for Other Purposes," *U.S. Statutes at Large*, vol. 37 (24 August 1912), 512–518.

11. Roy Gittinger, *The Formation of the State of Oklahoma (1803–1906)* (Berkeley: University of California Press, 1917). The state of Oklahoma, admitted in 1906, comprised the former Territory of Oklahoma and the former Indian Territory.

12. William Willoughby argued that the only important difference between the government of the Territory of Hawai'i and that of the continental territories was the absence of municipal governments in Hawai'i. As a result, the government of the islands was highly centralized. I should add that this situation facilitated control by a

haole minority over the whole of Hawai'i. See Willoughby, *Territories and Dependencies of the United States*, 60–70.

13. The territorial government of Hawai'i was created by "An Act to Provide a Government for the Territory of Hawaii," *U.S. Statutes at Large*, vol. 31 (30 April 1900), 141.

14. H.R. Joint Resolution 24, 55th Cong., 2nd sess.; 30 Stat 738, 1898.

15. Philip Foner, *The Spanish-Cuban-American War and the Birth of American Imperialism*, 2 vols. (New York: Monthly Review Press, 1972), vol. 2, 559–632; Eric Williams, *From Columbus to Castro: The History of the Caribbean* (New York: Vintage Books, 1970), 419–421.

16. The debaters consistently ignored Guam in their discussions, perhaps because they never considered the possibility of a civil government there.

17. See José Trías Monge, *Historia constitucional de Puerto Rico*, 4 vols. (Río Piedras: Editorial Universitaria,1980), vol. 1, 236–241. I follow Trías's division of the debaters into three fundamental groups.

18. The main proponents of the doctrine of *ex proprio vigore* were Elmer Adams, "The Causes and Results of Our War with Spain from a Legal Standpoint," *Yale Law Journal* 8, no. 3 (1899): 119–133; Carman Randolph, "Constitutional Aspects of Annexation," *Harvard Law Review* 12, no. 5 (1898): 291–315; and Simeon Baldwin, who published several articles, including "The Constitutional Questions Incident to the Acquisition and Government by the United States of Island Territory," *Harvard Law Review* 12, no. 6 (1899): 393–416, and "The People of the United States," *Yale Law Journal* 13, no. 4 (1899): 159–167. The Teller Amendment to the Joint Resolution of Congress (1898) disclaimed any "intention to exercise sovereignty, jurisdiction, or control" over Cuba and proclaimed its right to a free and independent government. However, the United States recognized the new government of Cuba in 1903 only after imposing the provisions of the Platt Amendment, which in fact limited Cuban sovereignty. Cuba could not sign treaties with other countries, it ceded territory for a U.S. naval station, and it conceded to the United States the right to intervene militarily in Cuban affairs. See L. Pérez, *The War of 1898*, 28–36.

19. Among the proponents of the doctrine of plenary powers were C. C. Langdell, "The Status of Our New Territories," *Harvard Law Review* 12, no. 6 (1899): 365–392. The territorial clause of the Constitution stated simply that Congress had the "power to dispose of and make all needful rules and regulations respecting the territory or other property belonging to the United States." U.S. Constitution, article IV, section 3, clause 2. Others, like Horace Fisher, proposed that the new possessions be designated "colonial dependencies" to distinguish them from the "territories." However, Fisher's terminology was not easily accommodated within either the political climate or the legal doctrine of the day. Fisher, *Principles of Colonial Government*.

20. Abbott Lowell, "The Status of Our New Possessions: A Third View," *Harvard Law Review* 13, no. 3 (1899): 176.

21. Magoon, *Legal Status*. The questions were posed on page 3.

22. Ibid., 3.

23. Ibid., 13.

24. Ibid., 3, 17, 33–41, 46–67.

25. These two propositions were derived principally from *Mormon Church v. United States*, 136 U.S. 1.

26. Magoon, *Legal Status*, 45.

27. Ibid., 45–46.

28. In addition, Magoon states that the right of trial by jury enjoyed by the citizens of the District of Columbia was not a constitutional right, but rather one deriving from "our civilization and racial [Anglo-Saxon] inheritance." He used a contrast of temperate and tropical regions to stress his point: "The rights of the citizens of the District of Columbia are as far removed from those of the varied races in the Philippines as are the degrees of longitude marking their geographical locations." See ibid., 67.

29. Ibid., 71.

30. Cabranes suggests that the doctrine of plenary powers was the guiding principal of congressional legislation for Puerto Rico and the Philippines. See José Cabranes, *Citizenship and the American Empire: Notes on the Legislative History of the United States Citizenship of Puerto Ricans* (New Haven, Conn.: Yale University Press, 1979), 24.

31. Randolph, "Constitutional Aspects of Annexation," 304.

32. S. Baldwin, "The Constitutional Questions," 393–416.

33. Lebbeus R. Wilfley, "How Great Britain Governs Her Colonies," *Yale Law Journal* 9, no. 5 (1900): 207–214. Compare James Thayer, "Our New Possessions," *Harvard Law Review* 12, no. 7 (1899): 464–485.

34. John Beach, "Constitutional Expansion," *Yale Law Journal* 8, no. 8 (1899): 225–234. Compare Frank Mitchell, "The Legal Effect of the Acquisition of the Philippine Islands," *American Law Register* 48, old series no. 4 (1900): 193–210. For an invaluable discussion of the application of the notion of "wardship" to American Indians, see David Wilkins, *American Indian Sovereignty and the U.S. Supreme Court* (Austin: University of Texas Press, 1997).

35. Carroll, *Report*, 56. Carroll reached his conclusions, in part, on the basis of a public gathering or "congress" held in San Juan on 30 October 1898. The group made recommendations for future government and submitted the results to Carroll, who passed them on to the president. The specific recommendations included the following: immediate establishment of civil government; "establishment of the Territorial system, with laws common to other Territories of the Union; a legislature in two branches; suffrage for male citizens of 21 years of age or over, the right to be sur-

rendered at the end of the first two years by those who do not know how to read and write; judicial reform; introduction of the jury system; autonomy for municipal governments; taxation on the basis of valuation; free and reciprocal commerce with the ports of the United States; aid for agriculture; obligatory and universal education; trade schools; savings banks" (56).

36. Ibid., 56–58.

37. Ibid., 57, 63–65. Carroll's specific recommendations included the following: the extension of the Constitution and laws of the United States; manhood suffrage (with subsequent literacy requirements); an executive branch headed by an appointed governor-general; a legislative branch of an elected senate and an elected assembly; a judicial branch consisting of a supreme court and district and municipal courts; an elected delegate to Congress; elected municipal councilmen and mayors; U.S. currency; and universal and obligatory free public schools "in which the English language shall be taught."

38. Davis, *Civil Affairs* (1899), 72, 76, 82. In choosing his comparisons and contrasts, Davis used several criteria: racial composition, population density, colonial experience, climate, soil, and religion.

39. Ibid., 81.

40. Ibid., 74–75. Davis commented that the "masses" were more interested in economic benefits—free trade, better wages, and general prosperity—than in the particular form of government.

41. Philippine Commission (Schurman), *Report*, vol. 1, 106. The commission also rejected the "Malayan" protectorate because it was too similar to a crown colony and the proposed "Tagalog" protectorate because it granted self-government to the Philippines under U.S. protection from foreign intervention. The commission was willing neither to accept self-government nor to offer U.S. protection in the absence of any external controls over local government. Also, note that the commission recommended that a representative be sent to the U.S. Congress. The organic act, however, provided for two resident commissioners who were entitled to governmental recognition in Washington but had no official standing in Congress.

42. Eblen distinguishes "district" from "territorial" government, following the legal scheme of the Northwest Ordinance of 1787. District government consisted of a skeleton staff of presidential appointees with no clear separation of powers. In contrast, territorial government included a fully or partially elected legislative branch in addition to appointed executive and judicial branches. By the end of the nineteenth century, Congress favored passing over the district phase and immediately establishing territorial governments. See Eblen, *The First and Second United States Empires;* Dávila, *Breakthrough from Colonialism,* vol. 1. Apparently, the commission's distinction of a "second-class" and a "first-class" government corresponds to Eblen's "district" and "territorial"

governments respectively. The lack of elected representation was the source of dissatis-
faction among the residents of the territories with district governments.

43. The child metaphor had been used previously to justify territorial governments in the United States. See Onuf, *Statehood and Nation*, 69–72. In the imperial
context it was elaborated further, albeit toward different ends.

44. Philippine Commission (Schurman), *Report*, vol. I, III. Congress modified
this recommendation somewhat by organizing a fully appointed upper house. The
commission also recommended that Filipinos fill civil service posts, especially lower-
level ones, whenever possible.

45. Cabranes provides a detailed analysis of the congressional debates over the
Puerto Rican bills; see Cabranes, *Citizenship and the American Empire*. Golay also briefly
discusses the importance of the "Puerto Rican precedent" in *Face of Empire*, 58–59.

46. Joseph Foraker, "Temporary Civil Government for Porto Rico," Committee
on Pacific Islands and Porto Rico, 56th Cong., 1st sess., 5 February 1900, Senate Report
249, 1–17.

47. In "Trade of Porto Rico," 56th Cong., 1st sess., House of Representatives, 22
February 1900, *Congressional Record* 33, nos. 3–5, 2100.

48. Beveridge, "Government for Porto Rico," appendix, 285. Compare Representative Bromwell, who stated, referring to Puerto Rico, "She came to us with open
arms." See "Trade of Porto Rico," 22 February 1900, 2043.

49. In "Trade of Porto Rico," 56th Cong., 1st sess., 19 February 1900, *Congressional Record* 33, nos. 1–2, 1946.

50. In "Trade of Porto Rico," 56th Cong., 1st sess., House of Representatives, 28
February 1900, *Congressional Record* 33, nos. 3–5, 2404.

51. The literature on Puerto Rico is vast. Two important recent contributions are
Pedro Cabán, *Constructing a Colonial People*, and Santiago-Valles, *"Subject People" and
Colonial Discourses*.

52. For details on the congressional bills, see Golay, *Face of Empire*, 47–89.

53. In "Civil Government for the Philippine Islands," 57th Cong., 1st sess., 25
April 1902, *Congressional Record*, 35, nos. 6–8, 4673.

54. Lopez, *The "Tribes" in the Philippines*. See also the message of Felipe Buencamino to Congress and the interview with Sixto Lopez reproduced in "Civil Government for the Philippine Islands," 57th Cong., 1st sess., 2 June 1902, *Congressional
Record*, 35, nos. 6–8, 6168–6187.

55. In "Civil Government for the Philippine Islands," 57th Cong., 1st sess., 31 May
1902, *Congressional Record*, 35, nos. 6–8, 6128.

56. The Foraker Act created a civil government for Puerto Rico. It was approved
on 12 April 1900. See "An Act Temporarily to Provide Revenues and a Civil Government for Porto Rico, and for Other Purposes," *U.S. Statutes at Large*, vol. 31, 77. The

civil government of the Philippines was created on 1 July 1902 by "An Act Temporarily to Provide for the Administration of the Affairs of Civil Government in the Philippine Islands," *U.S. Statutes at Large*, vol. 32, 691.

57. In Puerto Rico, the executive commission was known as the Executive Council; in the Philippines, as noted, it was known as the Philippine Commission. By law, both were composed of a European American majority.

58. The law abolished slavery, involuntary servitude, imprisonment for debt, and all titles of nobility. Some constitutional rights, such as the right to trial by jury and the right to bear arms, were excluded.

59. Trías Monge, *Historia constitucional*, vol. 1, 298–299; "An Act Making Appropriations for the Legislative, Executive, and Judicial Expenses of the Government for the Fiscal Year ending June Thirtieth, Nineteen Hundred and Seven," *U.S. Statutes at Large*, vol. 34 (22 June 1906), 417.

60. Kramer, *The Blood of Government*, 286.

61. According to the Foraker Act, Puerto Rico became a customs area of the United States with respect to international trade. However, the act also established temporary tariffs on trade between Puerto Rico and the United States in order to finance the Puerto Rican civil government for a limited time. The "internal" tariff was challenged on the grounds that it violated the principle of uniform taxes and tariffs within the United States. This case went to the Supreme Court, which established in *Downes v. Bidwell* (182 U.S. 287) that Puerto Rico "was a territory appurtenant and belonging to the United States, but not a part of the United States within the revenue clauses of the Constitution." The temporary internal tariff lasted until 1 March 1902, after which free trade was established between Puerto Rico and the United States. See *U.S. Statutes at Large*, vol. 31, 77.

62. Of the original nine Insular Cases, seven dealt with Puerto Rico, one with Hawai'i, and one with the Philippines. They became the legal precedents for territorial law, which was further refined in various additional cases decided from 1902 to 1922. See Efrén Rivera Ramos, "The Legal Construction of American Colonialism: The Insular Cases (1901–1922)," *Revista Jurídica Universidad de Puerto Rico* 65, no. 2 (1996): 240–241. These cases have been thoroughly analyzed, from a strictly legal standpoint, in several books and articles, and it would be redundant to go over this ground again on a case-by-case basis. In addition to Rivera, several earlier works deal with these cases: Juan Torruella, *The Supreme Court and Puerto Rico: The Doctrine of Separate and Unequal* (Río Piedras: Editorial de la Universidad de Puerto Rico, 1985); Trías Monge, *Historia constitucional*, vol. 1; Cabranes, *Citizenship and the American Empire*. For a fascinating study of the cases and their historical context, see Sparrow, *The Insular Cases*.

63. According to Sparrow, tariff issues were central to these cases. Sparrow, *The Insular Cases*.

64. Rivera, "Legal Construction." For a discussion of the history and contemporary relevance of the this case, as well as the other Insular Cases, see Christina Duffy Burnett, Burke Marshall, José A. Cabranes, and Mark S. Weiner, *Foreign in a Domestic Sense: Puerto Rico, American Expansion and the Constitution*. Durham, N.C.: Duke University Press, 2001.

65. In *Downes*, 278. The phrase "American Empire" is from Chief Justice John Marshall's ruling in *Loughborough v. Blake* (5 Wheat. 317), a contentious legal precedent for the Insular Cases. Herein, Marshall defined the "American Empire" as follows: "It is the name given to our great republic, which is composed of States and territories." At the time, the term did not refer to an overseas empire like that of the British Empire.

66. Justice Brown mentioned the cases of Louisiana, Mexico, Florida, Alaska, Puerto Rico, and the Philippines. The case of Alaska was notable in that citizenship would be granted to inhabitants who remained three years, "with the exception of uncivilized native tribes." In the case of Puerto Rico and the Philippines, the Treaty of Paris stated that "the civil rights and political status of the native inhabitants . . . shall be determined by Congress." In *Downes*, 279.

67. Ibid., 279–280.

68. Ibid., 281.

69. Ibid., 286.

70. Ibid.

71. Ibid., 283.

72. Ibid., 282–283.

73. Ibid., 283.

74. James Thayer, "The Insular Tariff Cases in the Supreme Court," *Harvard Law Review* 15, no. 2 (1901): 164–168.

75. In *Downes*, 295.

76. Ibid. In this way White opposed the "extension" principle of Justice Brown's ruling, even though he concurred with its conclusion. Brown ruled, in principle, that Congress had the power to rule in the possessions as long as it did not violate any universal rights. White, however, argued that Congress was always regulated by the Constitution. Thus, White avoided the unpleasant conclusion, implied by Brown's logic, that the Constitution did not necessarily apply in the territories or districts that were not states.

77. Ibid., 307–308.

78. Ibid., 341–342.

79. Ibid., 372.

80. Ibid., 373.

81. Cuba had uniformly governed provinces with equal participation in national government. Puerto Rico, Guam, and Hawai'i were not divided into provinces.

82. William McKinley, "Instructions of the President to the Second Philippine Commission." Letter to Elihu Root, secretary of war, 7 April 1900. Reproduced in Worcester, *The Philippines Past and Present*, vol. 2, 980–988.

83. Walter Williams argued that "Indian policy" provided the blueprint for all governmental policy in the Philippines in general. While suggestive, this argument failed to distinguish three different models of rule for different kinds of "tribes": the Mountain Province, the Moro Province (the two "special provinces"), and the "Christian" provinces. See W. Williams, "United States Indian Policy," 810–831.

84. "An Act Temporarily to Provide for the Administration of the Affairs of Civil Government in the Philippine Islands," *U.S. Statutes at Large*, 693–694. For a description by one of the imperial officials of the implementation of the various provincial governments, see Worcester, *The Philippines Past and Present*, chs. 12, 21–22.

85. Kramer, *The Blood of Government*, 212.

86. Contrary to McKinley's suggestion that Congress had permitted American Indians to retain their tribal organizations, Wilkins has argued that the years 1886–1903 saw a "policy era bent on the destruction of tribes as identifiable cultural, sociological, and religious bodies." See Wilkins, *American Indian Sovereignty*, 64.

87. David Barrows, "Report of the Chief of the Bureau of Non-Christian Tribes," in U.S. War Department, *Annual Reports of the War Department for the Fiscal Year Ended June 30, 1902: Report of the Philippine Commission*, 57th Cong., 2nd sess., 1903, appendix Q, 684.

88. Donna Amoroso reaches the same conclusion in "Inheriting the 'Moro Problem.'" Her contrast between British indirect rule and the U.S. model of direct rule is very instructive.

89. Sultans were aristocratic sovereigns who ruled through *panglima*s (personal representatives of the sultan) and local *datu*s (aristocrats). Several sultans, with their respective *panglima*s and *datu*s, ruled over the areas that would become Moro Province in 1903. See W. K. Che Man, *Muslim Separatism: The Moros of Southern Philippines and the Malays of Southern Thailand* (Manila: Ateneo de Manila University Press, 1990), 30–31, 46–55.

90. Peter Gowing, *Mandate in Moroland: The American Government of Muslim Filipinos, 1899–1920* (Quezon City: Philippine Center for Advanced Studies, University of the Philippines System, 1977), chs. 2–5. Only the main concentrations of Muslims on Mindanao and in the Sulu Archipelago were grouped into the "special" Moro Province. Areas with predominant Christian populations in northern Mindanao and on the island of Palawan were formed into regular provinces.

91. Ibid., chs. 6–8.

92. Howard Fry, *A History of the Mountain Province* (Quezon City: New Day Publishers, 1983), chs. 2 and 3. The Mountain Province included the former provinces of

Benguet and Lepanto-Bontoc along with large areas carved out of the adjacent prov-inces of Abra, Cagayan, Isabela, and Nueva Vizcaya. Paul Barclay argues that colonial discourse alone is insufficient to explain the character of rule in the mountains of Luzon and stresses the importance of the "global political economy." By comparing the actions of the Japanese in the mountains of Taiwan, where land and lumber exploita-tion prevailed, he concludes that the relatively benign paternalism in Luzon occurred in the absence of any definitive and overriding economic interest. See Paul Barclay, "They Have for the Coast Dwellers a Traditional Hatred: Governing Igorots in North-ern Luzon and Central Taiwan, 1895–1915," in Go and Foster, *The American Colonial State in the Philippines.*

93. Paul Kramer argues that this system of "dual mandates" was important in guaranteeing Christian Filipino collaboration in the colonial regime; see Kramer, *The Blood of Government*, ch. 3.

Chapter 6

Guam:
The Ship Metaphor and Military Rule

Establishment of a Naval Station

In January 1899, the commander of the collier *Brutus,* Lieutenant Vincedon Cottman, arrived in Guam and immediately set about to produce the first
official report for the secretary of the navy. Although it was never published
nor presented to Congress, this report would establish the basic principles and
justification for military rule.[1] Cottman's chief interest was the preparation of
Guam for use as an adequate naval station. Toward this end, he addressed the
issues of harbors, coaling stations, weather conditions, and navigation charts. In
addition, he dedicated much of the report to the health of the inhabitants, agricultural production, the character of the "natives," and the local government. He
expressed two fundamental concerns. First, the whole population was in need of
basic sanitation, hygiene, and health care. He recommended a number of measures to improve water supply and sewers and to provide doctors and medicines.
Clean water and sanitation would produce a healthful environment; medical
care would cure the ill; and among the worst cases, the sick should be isolated
from the healthy. He recommended that four doctors be sent to examine the
entire population, with the intent of deporting all lepers to the leper colony at
Molokai and the isolation of "syphilitics" from the rest of the population. The
navy should then establish a pharmacy to provide free medicine for those with
treatable illnesses. Quarantine also took on a moral dimension; social undesir-
ables, such as Spanish priests and Filipino ex-convicts, should be deported. Cottman referred to the former as "moral lepers" and noted that the latter were the
"only people who give any trouble" on the island with their particular propensity
to use machetes while fighting.[2]

Second, Cottman was concerned about local provisioning of food and labor for the naval station. When he arrived, he noted that the island did not even have a reliable food supply. He hoped that Guam might become self-supporting by means of agricultural improvement. He recommended an agricultural station in order to expand production for the local market and the naval station. The question of agricultural exports was entirely ignored. At the same time, the able-bodied should be educated and given practical instruction so that they would be both loyal to the naval command and productive contributors to the naval station. According to Cottman, general improvements were required in the local way of life since the population was not "accustomed to work," except for that required for basic household consumption. This deficiency was, in his opinion, the fault of the Spanish, who had set bad examples, imposed unfair taxation, coerced labor for public projects, and in general had not provided any incentives. Cottman also recommended compulsory public schooling and the establishment of an industrial school. He was confident that the natives would prove to be "adept pupils" if provided with the proper education and means to a "better condition of life" and would improve "their morals." Most important, education should be "beneficial and instructive to them and enable them to raise better crops, build better homes or boats, or raise more stock."[3]

Cottman's depiction of the character of the inhabitants, Chamorros, was generally positive, although he did complain about their indolence and morals. They did not steal but helped themselves to any foodstuffs that were "common property." They were both naïve and inconsistent in business and the use of money, at times giving things away, at times asking an exorbitant price, at times refusing to sell at any price. They were not quarrelsome and settled any minor disagreements by means of a fistfight. In general, he wrote, "The natives are quiet, orderly, and well behaved; they are generous and hospitable to strangers, taking pride in showing such hospitality as their means afford. In disposition, they are mild, sympathetic, and good natured."[4] He also noted that villages elected their officials every other year and were responsible for maintaining order, collecting taxes, and recruiting labor for public works. However, at no time did he suggest that the inhabitants were to become students or practitioners of self-government.

Throughout the report, Guam was portrayed as little more than a potential naval station. Indeed, this idea determined Cottman's recommendations: the proposed naval station must be healthy, well provisioned, and well served by a compliant local population. Likewise, the local population needed sanitation, doctors, agricultural improvement, and education. The island was still lacking in the basic resources to sustain a naval station, but the people were good natured, well behaved, and potentially more productive; they were primitive but not savage.[5] The Cottman report presumed military government; there was no mention of any plan to establish even limited self-government.

In August 1899, the first military governor, Captain Richard Leary, arrived with the handwritten report prepared by Cottman. Three days after his arrival, the new governor issued a proclamation that established the "naval government of Guam" under the authority of the United States. The proclamation asserted his "occupation and administration of this Island, in the fulfillment of the Rights of Sovereignty thus acquired [by the Treaty of Paris] and the responsible obligations of government thus assumed." In addition to immediately assuming plenary power, Leary soon created a number of new governmental offices manned by his appointees: the departments of government, medicine, treasury, post office, justice, prisons, education, and public works. The basic framework of municipal government, a holdover from Spanish rule, was retained. However, while the municipal governments in the Spanish administration had been elected, the naval governor now appointed all local officials. Most of the highest positions in the new departments were occupied by navy officers. Residents of Guam were employed principally as assistants, clerks, and inspectors. All appointees were answerable to the governor.[6]

Leary became simultaneously the commander of the naval station and the military governor of the island, with plenary jurisdiction over all military and civil matters. The proclamation guaranteed "the security of the persons and property of the people of the island" and "all of your private rights and relations." Furthermore, "all persons are enjoined to render prompt and cheerful obedience to the same in order that the blessings of good government, with the benefits of civilization and freedom, coupled with happiness and prosperity for the greatest good of the greatest number, may be the heritage of all the residents of the island, as worthy citizens of the island of Guam, under the free flag of the United States." All public lands became property of the United States. Existing laws that did not conflict with the provisions of the proclamation remained in effect until modified or annulled by executive order. The proclamation also abolished all political rights held by the Catholic clergy.[7]

Abolishing the clergy's political rights would be the first of a series of measures to eliminate Catholic influence in the public life of Guam. Shortly thereafter, all Spanish priests were ordered to leave Guam, which they did in September 1899. Only Father Palomo, who was a Chamorro and who had gained the respect of the governor's aide, William Safford, was permitted to stay. Executive Order 4 of 25 August 1899 prohibited "feast days of the patron saints of villages." Religious feast days could be celebrated in churches or private residences but not publicly. The tolling of bells to call parishioners to mass was also restricted by Leary's verbal order. The only public holidays would be Sundays and those authorized by the U.S. government.[8] In November of that same year the governor issued, in Spanish, a proclamation that established 30 November as the public holiday of Thanksgiving. The governor mentioned various things for which to be thankful, including health, happiness, peace, prosperity, protection, freedom of religion, and exemption from epidemics and hurricanes. In an indirect but clear reference to the expelled Catholic clergy the governor also gave thanks for the "liberation from the arrogant and tyrannical domination of the contemptible tutors." Finally, all religious instruction in the public schools was prohibited, although it was permitted in "the home circle, church, chapel, or Sunday school."[9]

Five of the fourteen executive orders issued by the first governor (numbers 1, 2, 8, 11, and 14) dealt directly with the problem of military discipline among the sailors and marines stationed on Guam. Public drunkenness, assaults upon civilians, the destruction of private property, the abandonment of the naval station, and interference with the functions of public officials were all addressed. Of particular interest was order 11, which prohibited men from referring to the civilian residents of Guam as either "damned dagoes" or "niggers." This order also referred to several incidents perpetrated by unidentified marines who had "ruthlessly destroyed private property, viciously violating the sanctity of native homes." The governor insisted that Chamorros were "law-abiding, respectful human beings" who were entitled to the same "courtesy, respect, and protection of life and liberty in their homes and in their occupations as are the best citizens of New York, Washington, or any other home city." Notwithstanding this comparison, the governor was not prepared to treat Chamorros as citizens of the United States. Apparently, his mission in Guam was another: "the preservation of the well-earned reputation of the American Navy as champions in succoring the needy, aiding the distressed, and protecting the honor and virtue of women."[10] Thus, he cast the navy men as courteous and respectful gentlemen, even though obviously many were not living up to the image, and Chamorros as "needy," as "distressed," or as "women" to be protected, but not as citizens with full political rights.

Evidently, there was a serious problem of military discipline at the naval station and on the island. In addition to Executive Order 11, Executive Order 14 ordered the punishment, by local officials, of anyone "who shall strike, maltreat, threaten, or in any other manner attempt to intimidate a resident of this island." In principle, this order referred to anyone, either civilian or military, but the problems of public order had been created by sailors and marines. Order 14 also dealt with sailors and marines who were absent without permission from the naval station. Apparently, many were living with local women without the sanction of marriage. Again, the metaphor of illness was applied broadly. The order prohibited military personnel from leaving the naval station and living among the local population because such a practice "incurs the risk of infection by dangerous fever or disease." All such persons were to return to the naval station and be placed in quarantine, not as a "punishment," but rather as a "sanitary precaution."[11] Leary, as well as successive governors, would attempt to segregate military personnel and Chamorro residents. Initially, at least, this was considered to be an issue of hygiene.[12]

Many of the first executive orders addressed the issue of financing the military government and provisioning the naval station. The orders regarding taxation, land distribution, agricultural production, and tariffs did not anticipate the development of commercial agriculture for export. Instead, they provided incentives for civilians to increase their agricultural surpluses in order to supply the military installation. These orders were consonant with the principle that a naval station should not be isolated from its land base, which should provide protection and support in times of war. Executive Order 6 prohibited the exportation of cattle, hogs, fowl, eggs, rice, corn, and sweet potatoes. Only copra exports were explicitly permitted. Visiting ships could be provisioned only with permission, and only enough food for subsistence for the departing voyage was allowed. In addition, according to Executive Order 7, all (male) inhabitants without a trade or occupation had to provide for their own subsistence (and that of their families) by planting corn, rice, cacao, sweet potatoes, or other fruits and vegetables. In addition, they had to maintain at least twelve hens, one cock, and one sow. Those who did not have land for this purpose could apply to the government for an allotment to be cleared, cleaned, and planted. Those that did not comply could be considered vagrants. A proclamation of 1 January 1900 abolished peonage on the island.[13]

Leary also articulated a discourse of hygiene and expressed his concerned for the health of the inhabitants and the lack of medical supplies. He reported that there were no medical supplies whatsoever on the island, with the exception of those belonging to the naval vessels. The inhabitants, he stated, were "seriously in want of medical attendance," and the services and supplies of the navy "will be carefully, judiciously but gratuitously given for the amelioration of their condition." The governor felt this was a simple "act of humanity." At the same time, the "improvement of the hygienic condition of the island" was necessary for the "protection of our own men."[14] Thus, Leary managed to portray his efforts as humanitarian and altruistic while safeguarding the interests of the naval station. One of the first orders of business, then, was to establish a hygienic and healthful environment for the commanders, sailors, and marines stationed in Guam. As indicated, this included a certain measure of segregation from the local population.

Shortly after issuing the first four general orders, Leary sent a short report to the Navy Department.[15] He noted, as others had before him, that the "inhabitants of Guam seem to be much pleased with our arrival and they have given many assurances that our control of the island will be very acceptable and agreeable to them." He expected them to be peaceful, and he anticipated their "most hearty co-operation and subordination in all matters pertaining to the Government."[16] The first military governor did not contemplate any measure at all of self-government for the local population. As noted, under Spanish rule, the towns had had a measure of municipal self-government: *gobernadorcillos*, literally "little governors," were elected to two-year terms, subject to the approval of the Spanish governor. Their duties consisted of maintaining order, collecting taxes, and supplying workmen for public projects organized by the governor. Under U.S. rule, these positions were appointed directly by the military governor. Leary's report, with its list of recently issued executive orders, expressed a new concern not evident in the earlier recommendations: the concern for military order over the entire island was now added explicitly to the previous ones of hygiene and self-provisioning.

Leary's harsh treatment of the Catholic priests and his disdain for Catholic customs resulted in protests among U.S. Catholics. General Otis, military governor of the Philippines, sent Joseph Wheeler, the famous brigadier general in the army, to inspect the conditions on Guam and report to the War Department in Washington. Notwithstanding some friction between the military governor and the general, Wheeler lent his full support to the military government and in his report concluded that "the governor and his aide, Lieutenant Safford, have used their best judgment in framing the orders which have become the laws of the island of Guam." He did admit, however, that the orders regarding religion were "evidently considered as a hardship and are distasteful to a majority of the people." Nevertheless, he did not make recommendations for any changes in the government of the island.[17]

Wheeler completed his tour of the six largest villages on horseback in less than four days, an indication of the relative smallness of Guam in contrast to the other island territories. He was favorably impressed by the order and neatness of the villages and the reception the townspeople offered him. In the town of Merizo, the locals came out to meet the general, flying flags, firing salutes with small arms, and ringing bells of welcome. They entertained the general's party with a "very good dinner." Much the same reception was found in Umata, which had a "clean and cheerful appearance." The townspeople of Agat fired a salute from "one little cannon" and several small arms. Bells were rung and a leading man of the town, a Spaniard, served them a "very nice luncheon." Again, the "streets, houses, and people all presented a very clean appearance." The reception at Ynarajan was marked with great "hospitality," and it was "touching to see the efforts of all the people to show respect to the American Government." The young son of the town governor accompanied the general's entrance into town to the music of his accordion. The general and his party were put up in the best house in town, where they were given an "excellent supper and were furnished comfortable beds with very clean, nice, snow-white sheets and pillowcases."[18] Wheeler summed up his discussion of the towns and their inhabitants in the following way:

> The people are very cordial and friendly. At every town we entered we were met by the leading men of the place, at two places with United States flags flying. White flags were upon many of the houses, bells were rung, and other efforts were made by the natives to manifest regard for the Americans. I saw a few people who I was informed were pure Chamorros, and they impressed me very favorably. Their features were regular, their forms erect, and they were in all respects fine physical specimens. The people seemed very desirous of establishing the kindest relations with the Americans, and their conduct impressed me with the idea that they hoped for and expected great advantages to come to the island from American rule.[19]

Wheeler's report included nineteen photographs, including the principal towns, churches, government buildings, roads, and scenes of the "jungle," but only one picture depicted Chamorros. The photograph in figure 6.1, according to the caption, showed Wheeler's "host and his family at his ranch near Santa Rosa peak," with a "bread fruit tree in background." The text did not mention the host's name or anything more about him or his family; they were reduced to impersonal figures of hospitality. The breadfruit tree, representing the agricultural bounty of the island, was as important as the host in the composition of the photograph.

In addition to his descriptions of the towns and the receptions given by the townsfolk, Wheeler appealed to two comparisons to briefly describe Chamorro culture. First, he contrasted the few immigrants from the Caroline Islands on Guam. These immigrants "preserve the native customs and methods of dress and have quite the appearance of American Indians," and "their civilization is very far behind that of the other inhabitants." Second, Chamorros "very much resemble the Tagals and the Visayos, but some writers contend that they are perhaps more indolent—a fault compensated for by good qualities, of which sobriety and unselfishness may claim notice."[20] Wheeler never went beyond the superficial repetition that all the local inhabitants were orderly, friendly, and receptive to U.S. rule. There was no discussion of language, history, or customs and not the slightest indication that the general interviewed any people about their recommendations, hopes, or aspirations regarding some form of civil government. Indeed, the population was reduced to the status of a welcoming party for the general and, by extension, U.S. military rule. This would be a persistent pattern in successive reports.

The second military governor, Seaton Schroeder, filed a report in 1901 in which he recommended allocations of funds for three projects. First was the acquisition of a schoolmaster to teach English. Second was the construction of a road from the capital city, Agana, to the outlying towns in order to promote agricultural production among smallholders, who often lived in town. Third was the construction of sewers and a dam to collect water upstream because the

Figure 6.1. Our Host and His Family. Wheeler, *Report on the Island of Guam.*

supply of fresh water in Agana was contaminated by sewage. The governor also hoped to collect a census of population, which in fact he did complete during the following year.[21] These three projects corresponded with the two principal concerns of the navy on the island: hygiene and provisioning.

In general, the locals showed a "friendly feeling for the American government, its flag, and its representative here." Nevertheless, some of "less thoughtful" still harbored a "feeling of uneasiness engendered by the detestable spirit of lawlessness displayed by a part of the Marine battalion." This problem had also been mentioned by the previous governor. Interestingly enough, the problem of the lack of order on Guam was not caused by the locals, who were "peaceable and law-abiding," but rather by the very marines under the command of the military governor and commander of the naval station.[22]

One year later, Schroeder reported that even without the requested financial assistance from Congress, his administration had commenced instruction in English in three schools under the direction of a certain Mr. Hiatt, his wife and daughter, two marine officers, and a "fairly competent young Chamorro woman." In addition, an excellent road from Agana to Piti was complete, although extensions to other towns were also planned. However, the water and sewage conditions in Agana were still "deplorable" and could not be improved without finances allocated by Congress. In addition, the administration had established a leper colony on the island and had otherwise offered medical services to the population. The governor had funded the projects by means of local taxation: customs, a land tax, and a personal tax.[23]

The report of 1903, written by William Sewell, was quite short. Again, it emphasized the growing necessity of "substantial aid from the home government" (i.e., Congress) since the island had not yet recovered from a devastating typhoon (November 1900) and a strong earthquake (September 1902). Due to the bleak conditions on the island and the lack of resources, all those attached to the naval station were assigned extra duties with no compensation. Skilled and common labor was in short supply. In addition, Sewell reported that there were no inducements for "Americans to settle in the island."[24]

The official report of 1904 made quite explicit the particular relationship that Governor George Dyer proposed between the naval station and the inhabitants of Guam. Dyer began with the affirmation that the island was of strategic value due to its location and good harbor. In addition, the particular conditions of the island were as follows. First, the island was small. Second, the people were agriculturalists but barely produced enough for subsistence. "The people are poor, ignorant, very dirty in their habits, but gentle and very religious. . . . Their methods of cultivation are the most primitive. Their wants are few, and they lead lives of Arcadian simplicity and freedom from ambition or the desire for change or progress. They are like children, easily controlled and readily influenced by example, good or bad." Third, the naval station was constrained by the condition of the natives, who in turn depended upon the naval station. "The one [navy], as an organization, cannot escape, or live far apart, from the other, and the efficiency of the first depends entirely on the welfare of the second." Therefore, the residents must be "kept healthy and free from contagion," and they must be "afforded practical instruction in their sole pursuit, agriculture." Furthermore, some must be educated to serve at the naval station as "clerks, mechanics, and intelligent laborers" since at present there is "no class from which to draw these." Even though the governor indicated that it was not his "intention to suggest an extreme paternalism," he concluded that the local inhabitants "must be taught at once to help themselves in ways to make them useful to us and to attain a higher grade of living, but their preliminary steps must be guided by us and they must be supplied with means to this end now entirely beyond their own resources."[25]

One year later, Dyer confirmed his assessment of 1904 and went on to establish the connection between the particular conditions he had noted and the continuation of the military government in Guam:

> With a view to recommending legislation which could establish a permanent government under the authority of Congress, I have made a constant study of the conditions prevailing in Guam in the past, and during the twelve months elapsed since the date of my last annual report. The convictions, there expressed, of the absolute interdependence of the native community and the American authorities composing the Naval Station, have been many times confirmed. The one cannot exist efficiently without the other. The area of the island is so limited, the means of the natives to get away so infrequent and inadequate, large centers of population so remote, that the one community cannot escape, nor live apart from the other. The Naval Station is entirely dependent upon the natives for mechanics, machinists, artisans of all kinds, laborers, and for some food supplies. The native population is entirely dependent on the Naval Station for medical assistance and medicine. Their protection against contagious diseases, and maintenance in proper physical condition, are necessary for the preservation of the health of the Americans and the consequent effectiveness of the Naval Station. . . . No Americans can be induced to live here permanently, therefore, the continuing employees of the Naval Station must be natives. Under intelligent direction they make efficient laborers and excellent artisans, and fill subordinate positions faithfully and well. In fact, we have here

a sober, intelligent, virile, and docile population of sufficient size to equip the Naval Station, at all times, and still leave enough to produce food for all.

For the foregoing reasons there should be no attempt to have two administrative organizations. The law should provide for the combination of all interests, as is actually the case at present, under the same executive head, the Commandant of the Naval Station. Otherwise there could be no harmony, and the real purpose of the retention of Guam by the United States would be impaired, if not defeated. *Guam may be aptly compared to a ship where the narrowness of the quarters and the object to be attained can only be accommodated by a single director.*

The whole island, therefore, should be legally considered and proclaimed as included in the Naval Station. This is now actually, and always has been, the case since its cession to the United States.

The natives are well pleased with the sovereignty of the United States and there is no sentiment amongst them for an independent government.[26]

In scarcely two pages, the governor outlined the relationship between the naval station and the local inhabitants and justified the indefinite continuance of the military government. First, the governor established a geographical determinant: the island was so small that the naval station and the locals were unavoidably thrown together in close contact. Second, the naval station depended upon Chamorros for food supplies and labor. Third, Chamorros were well suited for the auxiliary tasks required by the naval station. This estimation was based upon an assertion of their acceptance of the military government, a brief description of their character, and an evaluation of their potential. Fourth, Chamorros were dependent upon the naval station, especially for medical attention. Fifth, it would be counterproductive to have two different administrations, one civilian and one military. Here the Dyer compared Guam with a ship: only one captain could be authoritative and effective. This powerful metaphor summed up the logic that justified the military government in Guam. Finally, Chamorros were happy and content with this arrangement; they did not desire civil government.

Denial of Self-Government

The argument that the population of Guam did not desire civil government was clearly inaccurate. Several months before the arrival of Governor Leary in August 1899, some residents had formed a provisional government and attempted to organize a bicameral legislature. After the surrender of Guam to the U.S. Navy in June 1898, a single Spanish official continued to exercise authority through January 1899. At this time, a "pro-American" group of

residents, with the support of transient navy officials, formed a civilian government composed of an acting governor, a treasurer, a paymaster, an assessor, a
doctor, and a "general utility man," as well as an advisory council composed of
six leading residents. This provisional government was short lived, however;
it prevailed only in the temporary absence of the navy. Upon the arrival of the
navy once again in March 1899, the new commanding officer, Lt. Louis Kaiser,
removed the civilian officials of the provisional government and appointed an
associate of his as the new acting governor. In response, the residents organized
a bicameral legislature, which Kaiser immediately disbanded. A few weeks later,
Governor Leary arrived and definitively established military rule, thus ending
the "chaos" of the "interregnum."[27]

The establishment of naval government in 1899 dispossessed all residents
of political rights and defined them as "citizens of Guam"—in effect, wards of
the United States. In 1901, discontentment over the lack of political rights, civil
authority, and meaningful participation in local affairs led thirty-two prominent
residents to send a petition to Congress—by way of the (second) military governor, Seaton Schroeder, and the secretary of the navy, John Long—requesting
that a commission be formed to recommend a permanent civil government for
Guam. The residents identified themselves as "citizens of Guam, a dependency
of the United States." They emphasized that they had been "loyal, law-abiding,
and patient" and had supported the military government "morally and materi-
ally." However, "A military government at best is distasteful and highly repug-
nant to the fundamental principles of civilized government, and peculiarly so to
those on which is based the American Government; its only legitimate excuse
for existence is military necessity or as a provisional government until the newly
acquired territory can be properly brought under the scheme of government of
its new sovereign."[28]

The petitioners argued that the current military government was not a military necessity and the time was long past to organize an appropriate civil authority. The military government, they wrote, had "grave defects," among them the
"supreme power" of the governor in the "executive, legislative, and judicial
branches, with absolutely no limitations to his actions." The people of the island
had "no voice whatsoever in the formulating of any law or the naming of a single
official." In other words, they objected to a government that was not at all democratic; it was autocratic. It was not structured according to the constitutional
principle of the separation of powers; it recognized only the plenary power of
the appointed governor. Indeed, they protested, "fewer permanent guarantees
of liberty and property rights exist now than under Spanish dominion." In addition, the current legal code consisted of a disordered juxtaposition of the recent

military orders issued in English by the governor and the old Spanish code. The latter was entirely inappropriate because, first, it consisted of a copy of the previous Spanish laws created for the Philippines, and second, it was expressed in a language that was foreign to the navy governor. The petitioners concluded with the following specific appeal: "We respectfully and earnestly petition Congress to name and send a commission for the purpose of studying the situation and needs of our people, with instructions to formulate and present to Congress for its action such measures as it may deem advisable for the establishment of a permanent government in this island, that will enable us to mold our institutions to the American standard, and prepare ourselves and our children for the obligations and the enjoyment of the rights and privileges to which, as loyal subjects of the United States, we feel ourselves rightfully entitled."[29]

The petition appealed to Congress in its own language, the rhetoric of "civilized government" and the "American standard." Echoing the military reports, the petitioners represented themselves as "loyal subjects" who were entitled to democratic participation in stable civil government. They pointed out the contradiction of a democratic nation that maintained a military government overseas; they called attention to the paradox and sought a remedy from the highest legislative body of the republic. In response to the petition, the Senate passed a bill to commission a new government, but the House of Representatives never acted upon the bill, presumably because of objections in the Department of the Navy.[30] So Congress never sent a commission to Guam.

In 1904 the desire for civil government was still evident among the population. In that year, Lt. Leonard Cox, a civil engineer with the U.S. Navy, prepared a report in which he summarized his findings regarding the hopes and expectations of the residents Guam. He found that they expected the United States to establish a civil government similar to that of the territories and to extend U.S. citizenship to the residents of Guam. They also desired a civil legal code adapted to their circumstances, a revision of the judiciary system, and the right to appeal to U.S. courts. In addition, they hoped that the U.S. government would provide a regular budget for schools, an experimental agricultural station, improved roads, and the installation of water and sewage systems. While the first military governors would respond to the demands for betterment of infrastructure and education, the political demands were effectively ignored.[31]

In 1904, Cox also published a pamphlet entitled *The Island of Guam*. It was a public document designed to inform all interested parties of the current conditions on the island.[32] This pamphlet devoted much more attention to the history of Guam and a description of Chamorros. The detail was greater, but the basic content was quite consistent with other reports. First, Chamorros were an agricultural people with little concept of specialized trades. There were three classes: the "better class" (but not wealthy) of landowners; the "middle class" of smallholders; and the "lower classes." The better class furnished men for certain civilian offices, such as commissioners, judges, attorneys, or clerks. From the middle class came artisans who worked in the navy yard. From the lower classes came the common laborers. The men were described as "short of stature but well formed and strong in the legs." Cox asserted that they could carry heavy loads great distances in the hot sun. However, he also said they did not have "much strength in the arms and back, and are not good at lifting weights or striking hard blows." The women were "well formed, very erect in carriage, and almost without exception have beautiful black hair, of which they take great care and are very proud." The children, he asserted, were abandoning "native games" to play American games like baseball and marbles. Concerned about the supply of labor for the naval station, Cox complained that Chamorros had few needs, and this gave them little incentive to work; however, he was reluctant to call them lazy. He hoped that the supply of American products would induce them to seek out wage work in order to pay for them.[33]

Cox described Chamorros as a "race" or a "dependent people" but not as a "tribe," the common term for describing the peoples in the Philippines. He attributed the lawlessness and disorder of the marines stationed in Guam to their inexperience in colonial administration and their ignorance regarding other races. As we have seen above, the sailors and marines demonstrated both their ignorance and their disdain of the local population with the use of the pejorative terms "damned dagoes" and "niggers." Cox explained, "As in every case of change in sovereignty, the interregnum brought forth its crop of abuses with which the American governor had at once to deal. Our troops, new to conquest and familiar with only one race other than their own, needed a great deal of control and correction in matters unofficial and nonmilitary, and they were in many cases lawless and turbulent." Furthermore, the navy was not accustomed to colonial administration: "Colonies were a new thing to us, dependent peoples had previously formed no part of our scheme of things and we found the new work not easy." This, of course, was the author's way of posing the imperial problem: how to establish rule over "dependent peoples" in ways appropriate for them. Indeed, Cox suggested that the "education of ourselves as a ruling nation" was as important as the "education of new wards."[34] However, this education was not to be political tutelage as in the Philippines and Puerto Rico. Instead, it was to train the residents to be healthy, productive, and orderly employees and providers for the naval base. Unlike Cox's earlier report, the public pamphlet completely ignored the political aspirations of the residents and placed the responsibility of government exclusively upon the navy. In this sense, the pamphlet, as well as most of the other official reports on Guam, elided the citizens' manifest desire for political participation and focused upon strictly administrative matters of hygiene, provisioning, and maintenance of order for both the military and civilian populations. Self-government, it was understood, could not directly address these priorities.

During the first years of the twentieth century, the navy consolidated its military government of Guam. The island retained its traditional administrative division of four districts, each one with an appointed *gobernadorcillo* (called a commissioner after 1905) to deal with village affairs. The Spanish legal code remained in force, although the military governor had the authority to abolish or modify all existing laws by means of executive order, which had the force of law. Members of the Insular Patrol (established in 1905 and composed of enlisted marines), policed the island, served as game wardens, and also taught English and served as principals in the village schools. In addition, a small civilian police force served Agana. The chief of police, a marine officer, provided leadership and authority for both the military and the civilian police forces. The Court of the First Instance (established in 1903) had only one judge, and no appeals or juries were permitted. In 1910, the judicial system was modified slightly. The new Island Court comprised two judges, but juries or appeals were still not permitted. Since Guam did not have a civil government, it was legally an "unorganized territory" under the sovereignty of the president of the United States, who appointed the military governor, and the Congress, which could legislate for the island as it saw fit.[35]

* * *

In his report of 1904, Governor Dyer stated that "the conditions [in Guam] are entirely dissimilar from those in any of the other island possessions of the United States, with all of which I am somewhat familiar, having been an interested observer, on the spot, for long intervals in Hawaii, Cuba, and the Philippines."[36] While the United States established important naval bases within all of these sites, as well as in Puerto Rico, only on Guam did the naval station overwhelm the geographical and social terrain. From the beginning, Guam was not considered to be anything but a naval base: no immigration, no capital investment, no agricultural exports, no manufacturing, and no civil government were contemplated. The metaphor of a ship, expressed explicitly for the first time in 1904, provided the underlying logic and justification of these strategies.

The military governors treated civilians as auxiliary to the naval station and subordinate to its interests. They were described as agriculturists and common laborers, as adept students of industrial arts and the English language, but also as suffering from disease and the lack of hygiene. Thus, Chamorros would provide agricultural products and labor and in return would receive the benefits of medicine and sanitation. They were seen as a simple people, neither desirous nor deserving of any but the barest minimum of political rights. The official reports consistently described them as friendly and hospitable people who embraced the establishment of the U.S. rule. They were, in effect, reduced to the status of a welcoming committee without any particular culture or historical narrative worthy of consideration. In spite of attempts of the local population to organize a civil government (1899) and regardless of their formal petition for a commission to do the same (1901), the Department of the Navy objected to any and all such proposals. More than in any other site, local culture and politics were effectively treated as matters secondary to military concerns. Rogers, in his discussion of the ship metaphor, writes that "until World War II, the island would be administered as if it were a ship, the 'USS *Guam*,' with the governor as the captain, U.S. military personnel as crew, and Chamorros as mess attendants."[37] Self-government on the "USS *Guam*" was out of the question. Only a military government would suffice.

The U.S. Navy reports reveal the deployment of three interlocking strategies of rule in Guam. The first was the establishment of infrastructure and the introduction of programs of sanitation and health care. In this context, the metaphor of hygiene was fundamental in the diagnosis of the situation and conceptualization of solutions. The second was the creation of the conditions for a self-provisioning naval base, with the bulk of the foodstuffs and labor derived from the native population. In this context, we find the importance of the image of the docile, cooperative, politically passive native. Vocational and technical education, but not political tutelage, figured central. The third was to establish order over the entire population, both military and civilian. In this context, the metaphor of a ship commanded by a captain was central. Chamorros both resisted and adapted to this new regime by means of political and social tactics to advance local interests while accepting the general proposition of U.S. sovereignty. This form of resistance stressed the enhancement of the political status of Chamorros (especially full citizenship rights) within the U.S. system and the quest for civil government at both the municipal and island levels. Chamorros adopted the basic rhetoric and tactics of the U.S. political system, pointing out the contradictions of military rule in a territorial possession of a self-professed republic. Through the years, Chamorro culture has shown considerable resilience and adaptability in asserting its self-identity within the U.S. political system.[38] Chamorros had long lived in the shadow of the Spanish empire, and the new regime, although it offered less immediate political participation, provided for some modest improvement in material conditions, especially the water supply, medical care, and roads.[39] Confronting the overwhelming power of the navy, the local residents adopted a tactic of appeal, petitioning the empire for civil authority and citizenship in its own rhetorical language of the promise of democracy.

Notes

1. Vincedon Cottman, *Description of Island of Guam*, handwritten letter to the secretary of the navy, 20 February 1899, National Archives, Washington, Record Group 80, Secretary of the Navy, General Correspondence, 1897–1915, File 9351 (35). A very detailed narrative of the first years of navy rule, with extracts from official reports and facsimiles of proclamations, may be found in Henry Beers, *American Naval Occupation and Government of Guam, 1898–1902* (Washington: Office of Records Administration, Navy Department, 1944); Administrative Reference Service Report 6. For a tragicomic narrative of the comings and goings of the U.S. Navy during and after the Spanish-American War, see Rogers, *Destiny's Landfall*, ch. 7.

2. Ibid., passim. Anne Perez Hattori shows how the navy's health care regime in Guam was an important mechanism of U.S. colonial power and moral authority over Chamorros. She studies four defining episodes: the exile of Chamorro leprosy patients to a leper colony in the Philippines, the hookworm programs for children, the regulation of native midwives and the education of nurses, and the creation and operation of a hospital for women and children. See Hattori, *Colonial Dis-Ease: U.S. Navy Health Policies and the Chamorros of Guam, 1898–1941* (Honolulu: University of Hawai'i Press, 2004).

3. Cottman, *Description of Island of Guam*, passim.

4. Ibid., 9.

5. Julian Go has found that for Guam and Samoa a "romanticized scheme" was dominant, in contrast to the "Lamarckian scheme" for the Philippines. See Go, "Racism and Colonialism."

6. Beers included a facsimile of Leary's proclamation in *American Naval Occupation*, 22. See also Rogers, *Destiny's Landfall*, ch. 7.

7. In Beers, *American Naval Occupation*, 22.

8. Joseph Wheeler, *Report on the Island of Guam* (Washington: Government Printing Office, 1900), 38–39; War Department, Adjutant-General's Office, Document No. 123. This report included the full text of three proclamations and the first fourteen executive orders.

9. In ibid., 41–42. The key phrase of the proclamation was *"soltura de la arrogante y tiránica dominación de indignos preceptores."* The term *preceptores*, which means

"tutors," was directed at the priests, who were responsible for the secular and religious instruction of the inhabitants.

10. Ibid., 48.

11. Ibid., 49.

12. Executive Order 5 prohibited concubinage in general because it was "repulsive to the ideas of decency, antagonistic to moral advance, incompatible with the generally recognized customs of civilized society, a violation of the accepted principles of Christianity, and a most degrading injustice to the innocent offspring." Ibid., 40. In 1907, marriage between military personnel and Chamorros was prohibited. See the discussion in Rogers, *Destiny's Landfall*, 130.

13. Wheeler, *Report*, 40–41, 46–47.

14. Richard Leary, *Report of the Governor of Guam*, Typewritten letter to the Navy Department, Washington, 28 August 1899, 5. William Wuerch at the Micronesian Area Research Center, University of Guam, Mangilao, provided me with copies of the official reports from the first several years of the military government.

15. Leary, *Report*. Compare letter of naval commander Edward D. Tausig to the secretary of the navy, Navy Department, Washington, 1 February 1899.

16. Leary, *Report*, 1.

17. Wheeler, *Report*, 35.

18. Ibid., 26, 28, 34.

19. Ibid., 16.

20. Ibid., 17, 20.

21. Seaton Schroeder, *Report of the Governor of Guam*. Typewritten letter to the Navy Department, Washington, 8 July 1901, 4–9.

22. Ibid., 10.

23. Seaton Schroeder, *Report of the Governor of Guam*. Typewritten letter to the Navy Department, Washington, 16 July 1902, passim.

24. William Sewell, *Report of the Governor of Guam*. Typewritten letter to the Navy Department, Washington, 30 June 1903, 2–4.

25. George Dyer, *Report of the Governor of Guam*. Typewritten letter to the Navy Department, Washington, 21 June 1904, 2–5.

26. George Dyer, *Annual Report of Naval Station, Island of Guam*. Typewritten letter to the Navy Department, Washington, 30 June 1905, 2–3. Emphasis added.

27. Beers, *American Naval Occupation*.

28. *Petition Relating to Permanent Government for the Island of Guam*, 57th Cong., 1st sess., House of Representatives, 26 February 1902, House Document 419; U.S. Serials 4361: 1–4.

29. Ibid.

30. It should be noted, however, that Governor Schroeder endorsed the petition, which he received and forwarded with his "cordial approval and recommendation." Ibid., 3–4. Rogers states that the Department of the Navy opposed this petition, but he does not elaborate; see *Destiny's Landfall*, 125.

31. This section of Cox's report is summarized in Beers, *American Naval Occupation*, 52, and Rogers, *Destiny's Landfall*, 126.

32. Leonard M. Cox, *The Island of Guam* (Washington: Government Printing Office, 1917). Originally published in 1904; rewritten by E. J. Dorn, 1910; revised by K. C. McIntosh, 1911; revised and enlarged by M. G. Cook, 1916. I have not located the original document. I trust that the principal changes made subsequently to the 1904 pamphlet were to update the information and that the more general observations about Chamorros did not change substantially.

33. Ibid., 52–55.

34. Ibid., 43–44.

35. Rogers, *Destiny's Landfall*, 127–132; Laura Thompson, "Crisis on Guam," *Far Eastern Quarterly* 6, no. 1 (1946): 5–11.

36. Dyer, *Report*, 1904, 14. Dyer referred specifically to the lack of agricultural exports, the absence of any local manufacturing, and the extremely high cost of living due to the dependence upon imports from the United States.

37. Rogers, *Destiny's Landfall*, 126.

38. Michael Perez, "Contested Sites: Pacific Resistance in Guam to the U.S. Empire," *Amerasia Journal* 27, no. 1 (2001): 97–114; Ronald Stade, *Pacific Passages: World Culture and Local Politics in Guam* (Stockholm: Stockholm Studies in Social Anthropology, 1998); Vicente Diaz, "Simply Chamorro: Tales of Demise and Survival in Guam," *Contemporary Pacific* 6, no. 1 (1994): 29–58.

39. Hattori described the complicated, contradictory effects of the health care regime in Guam, with emphasis on its variable impact on Chamorros according to age, sex, and class. In addition, she documented some of the experimental, ill-conceived, and erroneous practices. See Hattori, *Colonial Dis-Ease*.

Conclusion

THE SYMBOLIC REPRESENTATIONS and narrative expositions—the imaginary, if you will—were not capricious fantasies about exotic peoples. These representations—frequently expressed in gender, infantile, and racial vocabularies—and narratives—which told of the past, present, and a projected future—were fundamental to the creation of different governments throughout the imperial archipelago. The many participants—travel writers, photographers, lawyers, colonial administrators, legislators, and judges—produced a complex archive of imperial discourse, comprising illustrated travelogues, official reports, legal studies, congressional debates, legislation, and Supreme Court decisions. The operative principle of this imperial discourse was that the multiple imperial subjects were to be ruled differently, according to their level of civilization and capacity for self-government. Imperial discourse, then, articulated two dimensions: on the one hand, the symbolic and narrative representations of imperial subjects, and on the other, the conception, establishment, and justification of different forms of rule. These representations were neither fantastic misrepresentations nor objective descriptions. They were practical and creative engagements with local peoples that resulted in the establishment of new governments. They were sensitive to differences as well as to similarities. The metaphors of women, children, and races were both very general and quite specific, as colonial administrators sought both to establish the overall legitimacy of their expansionist enterprise and to forge specific policies for the different peoples of the imperial archipelago. Thus, the descriptive question—What kind of women, children, or races were these?—was intimately related to the practical political question—How should they be ruled? The attention to difference provided a means—comparative knowledge—to establish rule over the diverse peoples of the imperial archipelago.

Table 2 summarizes the different representations and their correspondence to the forms of rule. These representations constituted strategic interpretations of the cultural, social, and political conditions of each site, and they established the logic and practice of imperial rule. These representations—articulated within the framework of narratives—were not precision instruments for making policy and writing legislation. They provided a rough guide, an overall comparative outlook, for the further development and deployment of the minutia of imperial rule. In addition, there were often disputes over the adequacy of these representations. These disputes corresponded to different political projects; counternarratives with contrasting political agendas challenged the hegemony of the predominant ones. These disputes, both within the United States and the territories, over the proper narrative representations were part and parcel of the political controversies about imperialism and resistance against it. More than mere empty rhetorical polemics, these representations helped produce political outcomes. These discourses, here characterized as narrative representations, were not, of course, purely unmediated linguistic determinants of the forms of rule. Rather, they provided the means to examine and evaluate the local conditions. In particular, imperial discourse mediated the realities of these sites in three general areas of interest, concern, and evaluation: the legacy of European settlement, the development of national unity, and the forms of resistance and collaboration. The discursive engagements with these social conditions resulted in the establishment of the particular governments, their justification, and normalization throughout the imperial archipelago.

The difference between the U.S. settler colony, Hawai'i, and the former Spanish colonies corresponded to both a historical legacy and a discursive distinction of primary importance. The principal representations of Hawai'i stressed the Americanization of a beautiful, attractive paradise inhabited by exotic women and passive men. The principal narrative recounted the transition from the native monarchy to a democratic republic led by the European American elite. This narrative validated the claims of both the local and the congressional annexationists for the establishment of self-government of Hawai'i as a territory of the United States. Nevertheless, the portrayal of Hawai'i as a white settler colony was open to debate. On the one hand, in the United States there was concern about the complex racial composition of the islands. Opponents to annexation questioned the character of the many Japanese and Chinese inhabitants, especially their capacity for self-government, their loyalty to the United States, and their possible migration to the continental states or territories. On the other hand, many Hawaiians protested the usurpation of the monarchy and challenged the legitimacy of the annexation. These Hawaiians, however, were but a subordinate minority in their own country.

Table 2   Representation and Rule in the Imperial Archipelago

	REPRESENTATIONS	GOVERNMENT
Cuba	White educated elite; uneducated black and mulatto masses; military rebellion against Spanish, collaboration with United States in war; strong national sentiments; pretty and patriotic women. Principal narrative: the struggle for national independence with U.S. help and guidance.	Formally independent government; protectorate (according to the provisions of the Platt Amendment and permanent treaty).
The Philippines	Christian Malay elite; armed resistance to U.S. military presence; not a nation, but rather a collection of diverse tribes, ranging from the most primitive to the most advanced; women unattractive and hateful. Principal narrative: the evolution of diverse tribes.	Imperial government; economic and judicial separation from United States; provincial governments according to religion.
Puerto Rico	Weak elite; racially mixed population, becoming "whiter"; needy children; pretty and hard-working women; all welcomed U.S. presence. Principal narrative: the liberation of a poor, uneducated, and passive people.	Imperial government; economic and judicial integration with United States; uniform local government.
Hawai'i	Excellent public education in English; Euro-American elite (haoles); active statehood movement; Euro-American hegemony in context of cultural diversity maintains harmony; exotic, beautiful women. Principal narrative: transition from monarchical to democratic government led by Euro-American settlers.	Territorial government; Chinese and Japanese excluded from citizenship; internal frontier for Chinese migration.
Guam	A people without history or culture; welcomed U.S. presence. Principal metaphor: Guam is like a ship.	Military rule by naval officers; unorganized territory.

The counternarrative portrayed a legitimate constitutional monarchy that had been illegally deposed and replaced by a republic of non-Hawaiian, foreign interlopers. This counternarrative had little resonance in the Republican, expansionist Congress. For one thing, Congress had few sympathies for monarchies in general (having been founded upon a revolution against the British monarchical rule) and even less for the Hawaiian monarchy in particular. For another, a number of clauses in the organic act deflected the concern over Japanese and Chinese immigration: limitation or exclusion of their future migration to Hawai'i, or from Hawai'i to the mainland, and denial of citizenship. In the end, members of Congress accepted the narrative of their "kith and kin"—that is, European Americans—successfully establishing a republic in an idyllic, tropical, yet not so distant land. The hegemonic settlers (and their progeny) prevailed, and two years after annexation in 1898, Congress provided for Hawai'i a standard territorial government, according to the model it had already used in the recent continental territories, including New Mexico, Arizona, and Oklahoma. Of the insular territories, only Hawai'i approximated the continental experience of European American settlement and local hegemony. For this reason, Hawai'i was the only new territory to be incorporated into the United States and eventually (1959) admitted as a state. Hawai'i, then, was a distant frontier of European American settlement, and this distinguished it from the former Spanish colonies acquired in 1898.

The presence and recognition of a strong, long-standing, and militant nationalist culture distinguished Cuba from the other former Spanish colonies. The principal narratives of Cuba emphasized the struggle of the population for national independence from Spain. Cuban men had heroically struggled and so had earned the right of manhood: political independence. Nevertheless, the problems of Cuba—poverty, limited education, racial mixing, and inadequate defense from foreign aggression—were greater than what the elites could handle on their own. Accordingly, Cuba was seen as a fledgling state that would require the constant vigilance, protection, and intervention, when necessary, of the United States.

At the end of war, the Cuban Army of Liberation was still intact and controlled vast areas of the central provinces, but it was exhausted and broke and had not gained control of the central state apparatus. The U.S. military authorities found it necessary to appease the leaders and the armed forces. Since economic concerns were pressing, they immediately began to promote Cubans to civil positions, offering them the economic security of employment and expecting loyalty in return. In the period immediately after the war, military authorities looked to the Cuban elites, especially returning exiles who were sympathetic to the United States, to occupy positions in public administration and to create networks of support and ties of patronage. With the support of the Cuban military leaders, the United States disbanded the revolutionary army and created a rural guard under control of the provisional government.

In the end, the Cuban elites negotiated a deal; they would gain power, privilege, and profit in exchange for political concessions to the United States by way of the Platt Amendment, which was included in the Cuban constitution. Although Cuba gained its formal independence in 1902, according to provisions in the Cuban constitution and a subsequent permanent treaty, the United

States had legal justification for military intervention into the internal affairs of Cuba and, in fact, intervened in 1906. The United States also secured the right to establish coaling stations and naval bases on Cuban soil. Finally, Cuba was prohibited from making any treaty or compact with any other country that would impair its independence or authorize the establishment of foreign military or naval bases on the island. In effect, Cuba became a protectorate of the United States.

In contrast to Cuba, neither Puerto Rico nor the Philippines nor Guam showed *both* a strong, compact national culture—understood in terms of unity of language, religion, customs, and traditions—*and* the political will and capacity to engage in protracted armed struggle. They would not become protectorates. In contrast to Hawai'i, none of these three sites had been or was conceivably a site for European American settlement. They would not receive traditional territorial governments. Between the two extremes—a formally independent protectorate and an incorporated territory—Puerto Rico, the Philippines, and Guam occupied a middle ground that, until then, had no clear constitutional status or political definition: they became possessions legally constructed as unincorporated territories. These territories belonged to, but were not a part of, the body politic of the republic. This determination followed from the conclusion that the people of these islands were of fundamentally different "races," were not familiar with U.S. culture and government, and did not constitute modern nations. The absence of European American settlement and nationhood, articulated discursively as a basic alterity and a fundamental lack, inspired a new legal distinction (the unincorporated territory), unique legislation (the organic acts for Puerto Rico and the Philippines), and for the first time in U.S. history, an extended military government in an overseas possession, Guam.

Nevertheless, both the Philippines and Puerto Rico were deemed capable of limited degrees of self-government under the strict tutelage of the United States. Their governments were adaptations of the territorial model used in the continental territories and Hawai'i, but their organic laws marked a shift in U.S. expansionism: from colonization via settlement to imperialism via political dominion. The basic structure of these imperial governments resembled that of a territorial government, but one firmly under the control of appointed European American administrators, especially in the executive and legislative branches. The executive branch comprised a presidentially appointed governor and an appointed executive commission. The legislative branch was composed of the same executive commission, which functioned as the upper house, and a lower house of elected representatives. At this level, then, the governments of Puerto Rico and the Philippines were similar: European Americans controlled the executive branch and shared power with the locally elected lower house in the legislative branch. In both cases, a strict separation of powers between the two branches was not established.

However, while Congress fully integrated Puerto Rico into the commercial and judicial systems of the United States, it excluded the Philippines. This followed from the conclusion, as clearly expressed in the narrative representations, that Puerto Rico might somehow become "Americanized" but that the Philippines could never be assimilated. Strictly from a commercial point of view, Puerto Rico became a domestic port, and the U.S. dollar became the official currency. Regarding the judicial system, Puerto Rico became a jurisdiction in the district court system, and all U.S. statutes automatically applied. Although the island retained a parallel local judicial system, it was subject to the ultimate authority of the U.S. Supreme Court. In contrast, the Philippines remained a foreign port, subject to trade agreements and tariffs. In addition, Congress established a new official currency, the Philippine peso. Regarding the judicial system, the organic act established a local court system independent of the U.S. district courts, although the U.S. Supreme Court had ultimate authority over the Philippine Supreme Court. Congress retained the right to enacted special legislation as it deemed necessary, but the Philippines was not automatically subject to U.S. statutes. One unique feature of the Philippine organic act was the exclusion of "Moros and other non-Christian tribes" from representative self-government; it led to the creation of two special provinces: Moro Province and Mountain Province.

The representations of Puerto Rico—primarily images of women and children—stressed the weakness and helplessness of the people and their lack of leadership. Still, there existed some sympathy for the Puerto Ricans, and they seemed both capable of and disposed to some degree of cultural assimilation. As a people, they were both very poor and ignorant of democratic institutions, but they were not considered either "savage" or "barbarian" tribes. The narrative of Puerto Rico stressed the backwardness of a simple people oppressed by centuries of Spanish mismanagement. The story continued with the noble, long-suffering people, who welcomed the presence of the United States. This narrative representation was consistent with the organic act, which established a government with appointed colonial administrators in the executive branch and the upper legislative body (the executive commission), a lower house of elected legislators, and elected municipal officials. The integration of Puerto Rico into the commercial and judicial systems of the United States left open the possibility of further assimilation through "Americanization" via capital investment, commercial development, public education, and political tutelage.

The alternate narrative stressed the easy assimilation of the Puerto Rican people, and it suggested the appropriateness of even greater local self-government and autonomy, along the lines of a conventional U.S. territory. This alternate narrative was not oppositional but rather suggested disagreements regarding the meaning, extent, and timing of autonomous self-government and assimilation. Peaceful autonomist, not militant nationalist, politics were pervasive in late-nineteenth-century Puerto Rico, even if there were unmistakable signs of a national culture. The Puerto Ricans had actively resisted Spanish rule at various moments during the nineteenth century, especially during the armed independence rebellion in 1868. Nevertheless, Puerto Rican politics had mostly favored accommodation, local self-government, and autonomy, which Spain granted just prior to the war of 1898. The Puerto Rican elites, and the population in general, received the U.S. military with open arms, believing that an equal or greater measure of autonomy would be granted and that access to new markets would be economically advantageous. The elites shared with the discourse of empire many ideas regarding the importance of material development and the lack of capacity of the common, uneducated masses for self-government. They understood that in their role as local leaders, the existing patronage system of political control and influence would persist in their favor. Accommodation and collaboration were the order of the day, although not without political conflicts and misunderstandings over the meaning and practice of autonomy and self-government. Conflicts arose principally when military, and later civilian, colonial administrators treated the elites as corrupt and inept inferiors. Nevertheless, these conflicts played out in the normal sphere of electoral party politics and within the context of imperial government institutions and administration.

In contrast, the representations of the Philippines—primarily portrayed as an aggregate of tribes—stressed its backwardness, cultural heterogeneity, and lack of nationhood. The analogy of tribes, which originally suggested a rough equivalence of the North American tribes and those of the Philippines, provided a powerful justification for U.S. hegemony in general. Nevertheless, the analogy quickly underwent changes as colonial officials sought to delineate the more "civilized" tribes with leadership capacities to supervise them in the paths of self-government. The principal narrative was of the evolution of various tribes in widely disparate levels of development, from the most primitive to the high standard of European civilization. On the one hand, the assimilation of these diverse tribes to the United States was impossible. On the other hand, at present no single tribe was capable of governing all of the others. These judgments of cultural heterogeneity resulted in a structure of a strong central government in the control of colonial administrators and legislators and largely appointed provincial governments, along with special provinces for the "non-Christian tribes." In addition, the impossibility of future assimilation led to the judicial and economic separation of the Philippines from the United States. The elites of the Philippines were to be tutored and nurtured until they could successfully manage self-government.

The counternarrative stressed the similarity between Cuba and the Philippines and suggested a similar political solution: a protectorate. The analogy of the tribes was hotly contested by those who saw the Philippines as a nation and who argued in favor of a quick transition to independence. Only in the Philippines did a revolutionary government and its organized armed forces directly challenge and tenaciously resist the imposition of the imperial regime. When this resistance was exhausted by military defeat and devastation of civilian populations, many sectors of the elite found ways to accommodate themselves in the new government and reestablish the system of patronage they had known under the Spanish regime. Filipinos had demonstrated an ardent desire for independence and were willing to fight and die for it, but the nation was fragmented by geography, language, culture, and religion. The militancy of the Filipinos led to a promise of eventual independence, already contemplated in the earliest of the congressional debates. However, that independence was contingent upon the capacity both to maintain a stable central government, as determined by the United States, and to establish national traditions, under the tutelage of colonial administrators and overseen by Congress. Thus began a long period characterized by a politics of accommodation in which the elites sought to reestablish their relations of patronage and to be recognized by colonial administrators as the rightful leaders of a self-governing nation.

In Guam, the interests of the Department of the Navy prevailed over all other considerations. Government officials considered the local people to be hospitable and eager to accept U.S. sovereignty, while they largely ignored the inhabitants' language, culture, and history. A people without history could not expect to develop self-government. Unlike the other sites of the imperial archipelago, Guam was not afforded a narrative, only a static simile: under control of the navy, the island was like a ship under the command of a captain. Guam fell into the same legal category as Puerto Rico and the Philippines—an unincorporated territory—but was denied even the minimum opportunity for local self-government. Instead, the Department of the Navy established a government simultaneously in charge of civil and military affairs. Guam had shown considerably less outright political resistance to the Spanish empire than either revolutionary Cuba or autonomist Puerto Rico; it did not openly challenge the new regime with a force of arms as in the Philippines. Although municipal leaders had been elected in the Spanish regime, national party politics had not developed. The residents of Guam expected an expansion of democratic and civilian rule with the change of sovereignty. During the short period between empires, they organized a civil government and hoped to have political rights and duties in the new regime. They were sorely disappointed, however, with the arrival of the military governor. Resistance took the form of appeals to Congress to honor Guam's own democratic traditions, but these fell upon deaf ears for several decades. The local population accommodated itself as best it could in the overwhelming presence of the U.S. Navy.

Thus, three local factors—the history of settlement, the development of national culture, and the forms of resistance or collaboration—were the basic materials for the elaboration of discursive practices in the imperial archipelago. These historical conditions acquired importance by means of discursive strategies that established their truth as essential realities, evaluated the state of affairs, and produced an eventual result, the varied forms of rule. The processes of description, by means of representations and narratives, and of evaluation, through the application of normative standards, were translated into law, which was simultaneously legitimized by these same means. Study, judge, and rule: these were the discursive practices that led to the establishment of governments in Cuba, Guam, Hawai'i, the Philippines, and Puerto Rico.

BIBLIOGRAPHY

Primary Sources

National Archives

Record Group 350, Bureau of Insular Affairs. College Park, Maryland

Record Group 80, Secretary of the Navy, General Correspondence. Washington, D.C.

Micronesian Area Research Center, University of Guam

Cox, Leonard M. *The Island of Guam*. Washington: Government Printing Office, 1917. Originally published in 1904; rewritten by E. J. Dorn, 1910; revised by K. C. McIntosh, 1911; revised and enlarged by M. G. Cook, 1916. Photocopy from Micronesian Area Research Center, University of Guam.

Dyer, George. *Annual Report of Naval Station, Island of Guam*. Typewritten letter to the Navy Department, Washington, 30 June 1905. Photocopy from Micronesian Area Research Center, University of Guam.

———. *Report of the Governor of Guam*. Typewritten letter to the Navy Department. Washington, 21 June 1904. Photocopy from Micronesian Area Research Center, University of Guam.

Leary, Richard. *Report of the Governor of Guam*. Typewritten letter to the Navy Department, Washington, 28 August 1899. Photocopy from Micronesian Area Research Center, University of Guam.

Schroeder, Seaton. *Report of the Governor of Guam*. Typewritten letter to the Navy Department, Washington, 8 July 1901. Photocopy from Micronesian Area Research Center, University of Guam.

———. *Report of the Governor of Guam*. Typewritten letter to the Navy Department, Washington, 16 July 1902. Photocopy from Micronesian Area Research Center, University of Guam.

Sewell, William. *Report of the Governor of Guam*. Typewritten letter to the Navy Department, Washington, 30 June 1903. Photocopy from Micronesian Area Research Center, University of Guam.

Tausig, Edward D. *Letter to the Secretary of the Navy*, 1 February 1899. Photocopy from Micronesian Area Research Center, University of Guam.

Official Documents and Reports, Congressional Debates, and U.S. Statutes

Barrows, David. "Circular of Information: Instructions for Volunteer Field Workers." Manila: Bureau of Non-Christian Tribes, 1901. National Archives, Record Group 350, 3833.

———. "Report of the Chief of the Bureau of Non-Christian Tribes." In U.S. War Department, *Annual Reports of the War Department for the Fiscal Year Ended June 30, 1902: Report of the Philippine Commission*. 57th Cong., 2nd sess., 1903, appendix Q.

Beveridge, Albert J. "Government for Porto Rico," *Congressional Record*, 56th Cong., 1st sess., Senate, 29 March 1900. Vol. 33, nos. 6–8, appendix.

Carroll, Henry. *Report on the Industrial and Commercial Condition of Porto Rico*. Washington: Government Printing Office, 1899.

"Civil Government for the Philippine Islands." 57th Cong., 1st sess., 25 April, 31 May, and 2 June 1902. *Congressional Record* 35, pts. 6–8.

Davis, George W. *Report of Brig. Gen. Geo. W. Davis, U.S.V., on Civil Affairs of Puerto Rico, 1899*. Washington: Government Printing Office, 1900.

———. *Report of the Military Governor of Porto Rico on Civil Affairs*. In U.S. War Department, *Annual Reports of the War Department for the Fiscal Year Ended June 30, 1900*. 56th Cong., 2nd sess., House of Representatives, House Document 2. U.S. Serials 4088: 1–819. Washington: Government Printing Office, 1902.

de Quesada, Gonzalo. *Cuba*. Washington: International Bureau of the American Republics, 1905.

Edwards, Clarence. *Annual Report of the Chief of the Division of Insular Affairs to the Secretary of War*. Washington: Government Printing Office, 1901.

———. *Report of the Chief of the Bureau of Insular Affairs to the Secretary of War*. Washington: Government Printing Office, 1902.

Foraker, Joseph. "Temporary Civil Government for Porto Rico." Committee on Pacific Islands and Porto Rico, 56th Cong., 1st sess., 5 February 1900. Senate Report 249.

Griffin, A. P. C. *List of Books Relating to Cuba: Including References to Collected Works and Periodicals*. 55th Cong., 2nd sess., Senate, 1898. Senate Document 161. U.S. Serials 3600: 1–61.

———. *List of Books Relating to Hawaii*. Washington: Government Printing Office, 1898.

———. *List of Books (with References to Periodicals) on Porto Rico.* 56th Cong., 2nd sess., Senate, 2 March 1901. Senate Document 222. U.S. Serials 4176: 1–55.

———. *List of Books (with References to Periodicals) on the Philippine Islands in the Library of Congress.* 56th Cong., 2nd sess., Senate, 1903. Senate Document 74, pt. 1. U.S. Serials 4423: 1–397.

———. *List of Books, with References to Periodicals, Relating to the Theory of Colonization, Government of Dependencies, Protectorates, and Related Topics.* 57th Cong., 1st sess., House of Representatives, October 1901. House Document 15, supplement. U.S. Serials 4313: 1567–1626.

Hawaiian Commission. *Report of the Hawaiian Commission.* 55th Cong., 3rd sess., Senate, 1898. Senate Document 16. U.S. Serials 3727: 1–95, appendix.

Jenks, Albert. *Philippines: The Bontoc Igorot.* Manila: Department of the Interior, Ethnological Survey, 1904.

Magoon, Charles, *Report on the Legal Status of the Territory and Inhabitants of the Islands Acquired by the United States during the War with Spain, Considered with Reference to the Territorial Boundaries, the Constitution, and Laws of the United States.* 56th Cong., 1st sess., Senate, 12 February 1900. Senate Document 234. U.S. Serials 3858: 1–72.

"Monthly Summary of Commerce and Finance of the United States, Colonial Administration, 1800–1900." 57th Cong., 1st sess., House of Representatives, October 1901. House Document 15, pt. 4. U.S. Serials 4313: 1197–1631.

Petition Relating to Permanent Government for the Island of Guam. 57th Cong., 1st sess., House of Representatives. 26 February 1902. House Document 419. U.S. Serials 4361: 1–4.

Philippine Commission (Schurman). *Report of the Philippine Commission to the President.* 4 vols. 56th Cong., 1st sess., Senate, 31 January, 15 May, and 20 December 1900. Senate Document 138. U.S. Serials 3885

Philippine Commission (Taft). *Reports of the Taft Philippine Commission.* 56th Cong., 2nd sess., Senate, 1901. Senate Document 112. U.S. Serials 4040: 1–333.

Taft, William. "Address by Taft in Manila before the Union Reading College, Manila, 17 December 1903." 58th Cong., 2nd sess., 1904. Senate Document 191.

"Trade of Porto Rico." 56th Cong., 1st sess., House of Representatives, 19, 22, and 28 February 1900. *Congressional Record* 33, nos. 1–5.

U.S. Bureau of the Census. *Census of the Philippine Islands, Taken under the Direction of the Philippine Commission in the Year 1903.* 4 vols. Washington: Bureau of the Census, 1905.

U.S. Congress. 55th Cong., 2nd sess., 1898. *Congressional Record,* 31, pts. 6–7.

———. 56th Cong., 1st sess., 1900. *Congressional Record,* 33, pts. 1–2, 6–8.

———. 57th Cong., 1st sess., 1902. *Congressional Record,* 35, pts. 3–8.

U.S. Department of the Interior. "Report of the Commissioner of Education." In *Annual Reports of the Department of the Interior for the Fiscal Year Ended 30 June 1900; 56th Cong., 2nd sess., House of Representatives, 1901, House Document 5, vols. 1–2, chapter 29; U.S. Serials 4114–4115: xl.

U.S. *Statutes at Large.* "An Act Providing a Civil Government for Alaska." Vol. 23 (17 May 1884), 24–28.

———. "Joint Resolution to Provide for Annexing the Hawaiian Islands to the United States." Vol. 30 (1898), 750.

———. "An Act Temporarily to Provide Revenues and a Civil Government for Porto Rico, and for Other Purposes." Vol. 31 (1900), 77.

———. "An Act to Provide a Government for the Territory of Hawaii." Vol. 31 (1900), 141.

———. "An Act Temporarily to Provide for the Administration of the Affairs of Civil Government in the Philippine Islands." Vol. 32 (1902), 691.

———. "An Act Making Appropriations for the Legislative, Executive, and Judicial Expenses of the Government for the Fiscal Year Ending June Thirtieth, Nineteen Hundred and Seven." Vol. 34 (1906), 417.

———. "An Act to Create a Legislative Assembly in the Territory of Alaska, to Confer Legislative Power Thereon, and for Other Purposes." Vol. 37 (24 August 1912), 512–518.

U.S. War Department, Division of Insular Affairs. *The People of the Philippines.* 56th Cong., 2nd sess., Senate, 26 February 1901. Senate Document 218. U.S. Serials 4043: 1–76.

———. *Report of the United States Insular Commission to the Secretary of War, upon Investigations Made into the Civil Affairs of the Island of Porto Rico with Recommendations.* Washington: Government Printing Office, 1899.

———, Office Director Census of Cuba. *Report on the Census of Cuba, 1899.* Washington: Government Printing Office, 1900.

———, Office Director Census of Porto Rico. *Report on the Census of Porto Rico, 1899.* Washington: Government Printing Office, 1900.

Wheeler, Joseph. *Report on the Island of Guam.* Washington: Government Printing Office, 1900. War Department, Adjutant General's Office, Document No. 123.

Wilcox, W. B., and Leonard Sargent. *Affairs in the Philippine Islands.* 56th Cong., 1st sess., Senate, 9 January 1900. Senate Document 66. U.S. Serials 3850: 1–44.

Period Books and Articles

Adams, Elmer. "The Causes and Results of Our War with Spain from a Legal Standpoint." *Yale Law Journal* 8, no. 3 (1899): 119–133.

Baldwin, James. *Our New Possessions: Cuba, Puerto Rico, Hawaii, Philippines.* New York: American Book, 1899.

Baldwin, Simeon. "The Constitutional Questions Incident to the Acquisition and Government by the United States of Island Territory." *Harvard Law Review* 12, no. 6 (1899): 393–416.

———. "The People of the United States." *Yale Law Journal* 13, no. 4 (1899): 159–167.

Beach, John. "Constitutional Expansion." *Yale Law Journal* 8, no. 5 (1899): 225–234.

Boyce, William. *U.S. Colonies and Dependencies.* Chicago: Rand McNally, 1914.

Browne, George Waldo, ed. *The New America and the Far East: A Picturesque and Historic Description of These Lands and Peoples.* 8 vols. Boston: Marshall Jones, 1907.

Bryan, William S., ed. *Our Islands and Their People, as Seen with Camera and Pencil.* St. Louis: Thompson Publishing, 1899.

Buel, James William, and Harry P. Mawson, eds. *Leslie's Official History of the Spanish-American War: A Pictorial and Description Record of the Cuban Rebellion, the Causes That Involved the United States, and a Complete Narrative of Our War with Spain on Land and Sea; Supplemented with the Fullest Information Respecting Cuba, Porto Rico, the Philippines and Hawaii.* Issued by subscription by the War Records Office, Washington, and *Leslie's Weekly,* 1899.

Chamberlain, Frederick. *The Philippine Problem, 1898–1913.* Boston: Little, Brown, 1913.

Church, A. M., ed. *Picturesque Cuba, Porto Rico, Hawaii, and the Philippines: A Photographic Panorama of Our New Possessions.* No. 168 in the Farm and Fireside Library. Springfield, Ohio: Mast, Crowell, and Kirkpatrick, 1898.

Comisión General de España. *Exposición universal de Chicago de 1893, adición al catálogo de la sección española comprende las islas de Cuba, Puerto-Rico y Filipinas.* Madrid: Imprenta de Ricardo Rojas, 1894.

Coudert, Frederic, Jr. "Our New Peoples: Citizens, Subjects, Nationals or Aliens." *Columbia Law Review* 3, no. 1 (1903): 13–32.

"The Cuban Census." *National Geographic Magazine* 11, no. 5 (1900): 205.

Dana, Richard. *Two Years before the Mast: A Personal Narrative of Life at Sea.* New York: Harper and Brothers, 1840.

Dewell, James. *Down in Porto Rico with a Kodak.* New Haven, Conn.: Record Publishing, 1898.

Dinwiddie, William. *Puerto Rico: Its Conditions and Possibilities.* New York: Harper and Brothers, 1899.

Edwards, Clarence. "The Work of the Bureau of Insular Affairs." *National Geographic Magazine* 15, no. 6 (1904): 239–255.

Everett, Marshall, ed. *Exciting Experiences in Our Wars with Spain and the Filipinos.* Chicago: Book Publishers Union, 1899.

Fernald, James. *The Imperial Republic*. New York: Funk and Wagnalls, 1898.

Fisher, Horace. *Principles of Colonial Government Adapted to the Present Needs of Cuba and Porto Rico, and of the Philippines*. Boston: L. C. Page, 1899.

Foreman, John. *The Philippine Islands: A Historical, Geographical, Ethnographical, Social and Commercial Sketch of the Philippine Archipelago and Its Political Dependencies, Embracing the Whole Period of Spanish Rule*. London: Sampson Low, Marston, Searle and Rivington, 1890.

Halstead, Murat. *The History of American Expansion*. N.p.: United Book Publishers of America, 1898.

———. *Pictorial History of America's New Possessions*. Chicago: Dominion, 1899.

Hamm, Margherita Arlina. *Manila and the Philippines*. London: F. Tennyson Neely, 1898.

———. *Porto Rico and the West Indies*. London: F. Tennyson Neely, 1899.

Hartwell, Alfred. "The Organization of a Territorial Government for Hawaii." *Yale Law Journal* 9, no. 3 (1899): 107–113.

Hermann, Karl Stephen. *From Yauco to Las Marias, Being a Story of the Recent Campaign in Western Puerto Rico by the Independent Regular Brigade, under the Command of Brigadier-General Schwan*. Boston: R. G. Dadger, 1900.

Hill, Robert. "Cuba." *National Geographic Magazine* 9, no. 5 (1898): 193–242.

———. *Cuba and Porto Rico with the Other Islands of the West Indies*. New York: Century, 1898.

Jiménez de la Romera, Waldo. *Cuba, Puerto-Rico y Filipinas*. Barcelona: Daniel Cortezo, 1887.

Jones, Rosalie. *The American Standard of Living and World Cooperation*. Boston: Cornhill Publishing, 1923.

Kidd, Benjamin. *The Control of the Tropics*. New York: Macmillan, 1898.

Lala, Ramón Reyes. *The Philippine Islands*. New York: Continental Publishing, 1899.

Langdell, C. C. "The Status of Our New Territories." *Harvard Law Review* 12, no. 6 (1899): 365–392.

Lopez, Sixto. *The "Tribes" in the Philippines*. Boston: New England Anti-Imperialist League, 1900.

Lowell, Abbott. "The Status of Our New Possessions: A Third View." *Harvard Law Review* 13, no. 3 (1899): 155–176.

March, Alden. *The History and Conquest of the Philippines and Our Other Island Possessions, Embracing Our War with the Filipinos in 1899, Together with a Complete History of Those Islands from the Earliest Times to the Present*. Philadelphia: John C. Winston, 1899.

Mitchell, Frank. "The Legal Effect of the Acquisition of the Philippine Islands." *American Law Register* 48, old series no. 4 (1900): 193–210.

Morris, Charles. *Our Island Empire: A Handbook of Cuba, Puerto Rico, Hawaii, and the Philippine Islands.* Philadelphia: J. B. Lippincott, 1899.

Neely, F. Tennyson. *Neely's Color Photos of America's New Possessions.* New York: F. Tennyson Neely, 1899.

———. *Neely's Panorama of Our New Possessions.* New York: Neely Publishing, 1898.

———. *Neely's Photographs: Panoramic Views of Cuba, Porto Rico, Manila and the Philippines.* New York: F. Tennyson Neely, 1899. Neely's Educational Library, no. 10.

Ober, Frederick. *Puerto Rico and Its Resources.* New York: Appleton, 1899.

Pierce, Edward. *The "Single Tribe" Fiction.* Chicago: Anti-Imperialist League, 1900.

Powers, Lilian, and H. C. Phillips, eds. *Report of the Lake Mohonk Conference of Friends of the Indians and Other Dependent Peoples.* Lake Mohonk, N.Y., 1909.

Randolph, Carman. "Constitutional Aspects of Annexation." *Harvard Law Review* 12, no. 5 (1898): 291–315.

Rector, Charles H. *The Story of Beautiful Puerto Rico: A Graphic Description of the Garden Spot of the World by Pen and Camera.* Chicago: Lind and Lee, 1898.

Robinson, Albert Gardner. *The Porto Rico of Today: Pen Pictures of the People and the Country.* New York: Charles Scribner's Sons, 1899.

Roosevelt, Theodore. "The Strenuous Life." Speech presented at the Hamilton Club, Chicago, 10 April 1899. Retrieved on 14 September 2001 from the Theodore Roosevelt Association Web page: www.theodoreroosevelt.org.

Snow, Alpheus. *The Administration of Dependencies: A Study of the Evolution of the Federal Empire, with Special Reference to American Colonial Problems.* New York: Knickerbocker Press, 1902.

Taft, William. "The Philippines." *National Geographic Magazine* 16, no. 8 (1905): 361–375.

Thayer, James. "The Insular Tariff Cases in the Supreme Court." *Harvard Law Review* 15, no. 2 (1901): 164–168.

———. "Our New Possessions." *Harvard Law Review* 12, no. 7 (1899): 464–485.

Thurston, Lorrin Andrews. *A Handbook on the Annexation of Hawaii.* St. Joseph, Mo.: A. B. Morse, 1897.

White, Trumbull. *Our New Possessions.* Boston: Adams, 1898.

Wilfley, Lebbeus R. "How Great Britain Governs Her Colonies." *Yale Law Journal* 9, no. 5 (1900): 207–214.

Willets, Gilson, Margherita Arlina Hamm, and Burr McIntosh. *Photographic Views of Our New Possessions.* Chicago: Waverly Publishing, n.d.

Willoughby, William. *Territories and Dependencies of the United States: Their Government and Administration.* New York: Century, 1905.

Wood, Leonard, William Taft, Charles Allen, Perfecto LaCoste, and M. E. Beall. *Opportunities in the Colonies and Cuba.* New York: Lewis, Scribner, 1902.

Worcester, Dean. "Field Sports among the Wild Men of Northern Luzon." *National Geographic Magazine* 22, no. 3 (1911): 215–267.

———. "Head-Hunters of Northern Luzon." *National Geographic Magazine* 23, no. 9 (1912): 833–930.

———. "The Non-Christian Peoples of the Philippine Islands: With an Account of What Has Been Done for Them under American Rule." *National Geographic Magazine* 24, no. 11 (1913): 1157–1256.

———. "Notes on Some Primitive Philippine Tribes." *National Geographic Magazine* 9, no. 6 (1898): 284–301.

———. *The Philippines Past and Present*, 2 vols. New York: Macmillan, 1914.

Youth's Companion. *Greater America: The Latest Possessions*. Boston: Perry Mason, 1902.

Secondary Sources

Adas, Michael. *Dominance by Design: Technological Imperatives and America's Civilizing Mission*. Cambridge, Mass.: Belknap Press, 2006.

Ahmad, Aijaz. *In Theory: Classes, Nations, Literatures*. London: Verso, 1992.

Alloula, Malek. *The Colonial Harem*. Minneapolis: University of Minnesota Press, 1986.

Álvarez Curbelo, Silvia. "La batalla de los signos: La invasión norteamericana de 1898 y la vida cotidiana en Puerto Rico." *Revista Mexicana del Caribe* 1, no. 2 (1996): 202–215.

Amoroso, Donna. "Inheriting the 'Moro Problem': Muslim Authority and Colonial Rule in British Malaysia and the Philippines." In Go and Foster, *The American Colonial State in the Philippines*.

Barthes, Roland. *Image, Music, Text*. New York: Hill and Wang, 1977.

Bederman, Gail. *Manliness and Civilization: A Cultural History of Gender and Race in the United States, 1880–1917*. Chicago: University of Chicago Press, 1995.

Beers, Henry. *American Naval Occupation and Government of Guam, 1898–1902*. Washington: Office of Records Administration, Navy Department, 1944. Administrative Reference Service Report No.6.

Bell, Roger. *Last among Equals: Hawaiian Statehood and American Politics*. Honolulu: University of Hawai'i Press, 1984.

Bhabha, Homi. *The Location of Culture*. London: Routledge, 1994.

Buck, Elizabeth. *Paradise Remade: The Politics of Culture and History in Hawai'i*. Philadelphia: Temple University Press, 1993.

Burnett, Christian Duffy, Burke Marshall, José A. Cabranes, and Mark S. Weiner. *Foreign in a Domestic Sense: Puerto Rico, American Expansion and the Constitution*. Durham, N.C.: Duke University Press, 2001.

Cabán, Pedro. *Constructing a Colonial People: Puerto Rico and the United States, 1898–1932*. Boulder: Westview Press, 1999.

———. "Subjects and Immigrants during the Progressive Era." *Discourse* 23, no. 3 (2001): 24–51.

Cabranes, José. *Citizenship and the American Empire: Notes on the Legislative History of the United States Citizenship of Puerto Ricans*. New Haven, Conn.: Yale University Press, 1979.

Castro, Edgardo. *El vocabulario de Michel Foucault: Un recorrido alfabético por sus temas, conceptos y autores*. Buenos Aires: Universidad Nacional de Quilmes, 2004.

Chaterjee, Partha. *The Nation and Its Fragments*. Princeton, N.J.: Princeton University Press, 1993.

Che Man, W. K. *Muslim Separatism: The Moros of Southern Philippines and the Malays of Southern Thailand*. Manila: Ateneo de Manila University Press, 1990.

Chrisman, Laura. "The Imperial Unconscious? Representations of Imperial Discourse." In *Colonial Discourse and Post-Colonial Theory: A Reader*, ed. Patrick Williams and Laura Chrisman. New York: Columbia University Press, 1994.

Corpuz, O. D. *The Roots of the Filipino Nation*. 2 vols. Quezon City: AKLAHI Foundation, 1996.

Crespo, Jorge. *Puerto Rico 3D: 100 años de historia a través de la estereoscopía*. Gurabo: Centro de Estudios Humanísticos, Universidad del Turabo, 2003.

Cubano, Astrid. *El hilo en el laberinto: Claves de la lucha política en Puerto Rico (siglo XIX)*. Río Piedras: Ediciones Huracán, 1990.

Cullinane, Michael. *Ilustrado Politics: Filipino Elite Response to American Rule, 1898–1908*. Quezon City: Ateneo de Manila University Press, 2005.

Dávila Colón, Luis. *Breakthrough from Colonialism: An Interdisciplinary Study of Statehood*. 2 vols. Río Piedras: Editorial de la Universidad de Puerto Rico, 1984.

Daws, Gavan. *Shoal of Time: A History of the Hawaiian Islands*. Honolulu: University of Hawai'i Press, 1974.

Dery, Luis Camara. *The Army of the First Philippine Republic and Other Historical Essays*. Manila: De La Salle University Press, 1995.

Desmond, Jane. "Picturing Hawai'i: The 'Ideal' Native and the Origins of Tourism, 1880–1915." *Positions: East Asia Cultures Critique* 7, no. 2 (1999): 459–501.

Diaz, Vicente. "Simply Chamorro: Tales of Demise and Survival in Guam." *Contemporary Pacific* 6, no. 1 (1994): 29–58.

Dominguez, Virginia. "When the Enemy Is Unclear: U.S. Censuses and Photographs of Cuba, Puerto Rico, and the Philippines from the Beginning of the 20th Century." *Comparative American Studies* 5, no. 2 (2007): 173–203.

Doyle, Michael. *Empires*. Ithaca, N.Y.: Cornell University Press, 1986.

Dreyfus, Hubert, and Paul Rabinow. *Michel Foucault: Beyond Structuralism and Hermeneutics.* Chicago: University of Chicago Press, 1983.

Duany, Jorge. *Puerto Rican Nation on the Move: Identities on the Island and in the United States.* Chapel Hill: University of North Carolina Press, 2002.

Eblen, Jack. *The First and Second United States Empires: Governors and Territorial Government, 1787–1912.* Pittsburgh: University of Pittsburgh Press, 1968.

Edwards, Elizabeth, ed. *Anthropology and Photography, 1860–1920.* New Haven, Conn.; and London: Yale University Press in association with the Royal Anthropological Institute, 1992.

Erman, Sam. "Meanings of Citizenship in the U.S. Empire: Puerto Rico, Isabel González, and the Supreme Court, 1898–1905." *Journal of American Ethnic History* 27, no. 4 (2008): 5–33.

Fabian, Johannes. *Time and the Other.* New York: Columbia University Press, 1983.

Foner, Philip. *The Spanish-Cuban-American War and the Birth of American Imperialism.* 2 vols. New York: Monthly Review Press, 1972.

Frederickson, George. *Racism: A Short History.* Princeton, N.J.: Princeton University Press, 2002.

Fry, Howard. *A History of the Mountain Province.* Quezon City: New Day Publishers, 1983.

García, Gervasio Luis. "I Am the Other: Puerto Rico in the Eyes of North Americans, 1898." *Journal of American History* 87, no. 1 (2000): 39–64.

Gatewood, Willard. *Black Americans and the White Man's Burden, 1898–1903.* Urbana: University of Illinois Press, 1975.

Gibson, Arrell Morgan. *Yankees in Paradise: The Pacific Basin Frontier.* Albuquerque: University of New Mexico Press, 1993.

Gittinger, Roy. *The Formation of the State of Oklahoma (1803–1906).* Berkeley: University of California Press, 1917.

Go, Julian. *American Empire and the Politics of Meaning: Elite Political Cultures in the Philippines and Puerto Rico during U.S. Colonialism.* Durham, N.C.: Duke University Press, 2008.

———. "Chains of Empire, Projects of State: Political Education and U.S. Colonial Rule in Puerto Rico and the Philippines." In Go and Foster, *The American Colonial State in the Philippines.*

———. "The Provinciality of American Empire: 'Liberal Exceptionalism' and U.S. Colonial Rule, 1898–1912." *Comparative Studies in Society and History* 49 (2007): 74–108.

———. "Racism and Colonialism: Meanings of Difference and Ruling Practices in America's Pacific Empire." *Qualitative Sociology* 27, no. 1 (2004): 35–58.

Go, Julian, and Anne Foster, eds. *The American Colonial State in the Philippines: Global Perspectives.* Durham, N.C.: Duke University Press, 2003.

Golay, Frank Hindman. *Face of Empire: United States-Philippine Relations, 1898–1946.* Quezon City: Ateneo de Manila University Press, 1997.

Gould, Stephen Jay. *The Mismeasure of Man.* New York: Norton, 1981.

Gowing, Peter G. *Mandate in Moroland: The American Government of Muslim Filipinos, 1899–1920.* Quezon City: Philippine Center for Advanced Studies, University of the Philippines System, 1977.

Hall, Stuart, ed. *Representation: Cultural Representations and Signifying Practices.* Thousand Oaks, Calif.: Sage Publications, 1997.

Hardt, Michael, and Antonio Negri. *Empire.* Cambridge, Mass.: Harvard University Press, 2000.

Hattori, Anne Perez. *Colonial Dis-Ease: U.S. Navy Health Policies and the Chamorros of Guam, 1898–1941.* Honolulu: University of Hawai'i Press, 2004.

Hawley, Charles. "You're a Better Filipino Than I Am, John Wayne: World War II, Hollywood, and U.S.-Philippines Relations." *Pacific Historical Review* 71, no. 3 (2002): 389–414,

Healy, David. *Modern Imperialism: Changing Styles in Historical Interpretation.* Washington: American Historical Association, 1967.

Hobson, J. A. *Imperialism: A Study.* Ann Arbor: Anchor Books, 1965. Originally published 1902.

Hoganson, Kristin. *Fighting for American Manhood: How Gender Politics Provoked the Spanish-American and the Philippine-American Wars.* New Haven, Conn.: Yale University Press, 1998.

Holt, Elizabeth Mary. *Colonizing Filipinas: Nineteenth-Century Representations of the Philippines in Western Historiography.* Honolulu: University of Hawai'i Press, 2002.

JanMohamed, Abdul. "The Economy of Manichean Allegory: The Function of Racial Difference in Colonialist Literature." *Critical Inquiry* 12, no. 1 (1985): 59–87.

———. *Manichean Aesthetics: The Politics of Literature in Colonial Africa* (Amherst: University of Massachusetts Press, 1983).

Johnson, John. *Latin America in Caricature.* Austin: University of Texas Press, 1980.

Kahn, Joel. *Culture, Multiculture, Postculture.* London: Sage, 1995.

Kaplan, Amy. *The Anarchy of Empire in the Making of U.S. Culture.* Cambridge, Mass.: Harvard University Press, 2002.

Kaplan, Amy, and Donald Pease, eds. *Cultures of United States Imperialism.* Durham, N.C.: Duke University Press, 1993.

Karnow, Stanley. *In Our Image: America's Empire in the Philippines.* New York: Random House, 1989.

Karpiel, Frank, Jr. "Mystic Ties of Brotherhood: Freemasonry, Ritual, and Hawaiian Royalty in the Nineteenth Century." *Pacific Historical Review* 69 (2000): 357–397.

Kramer, Paul. *The Blood of Government: Race, Empire, the United States, and the Philippines.* Chapel Hill: University of North Carolina Press, 2006.

Krishnaswamy, Revathi. *Effeminism: The Economy of Colonial Desire.* Ann Arbor: University of Michigan Press, 1998.

Lenin, V. I. *Imperialism: The Highest Stage of Capitalism.* New York: International Publishers, 1939. Originally published 1917.

Lewinski, Jorge. *The Camera at War: A History of War Photography from 1848 to the Present Day.* New York: Simon and Schuster, 1978.

Loke, Margarett, ed. *The World as It Was, 1865–1921: A Photographic Portrait from the Keystone-Mast Collection.* New York: Summit Books, 1980.

Love, Eric. *Race over Empire: Racism and U.S. Imperialism, 1865–1900.* Chapel Hill: University of North Carolina Press, 2004.

Lutz, Catherine, and Jane Collins. *Reading National Geographic.* Chicago: University of Chicago Press, 1993.

Marcus, Lisa. *Tender Violence: Domestic Visions in the Age of U.S. Imperialism.* Chapel Hill: University of North Carolina Press, 2000.

Maxwell, Anne. *Colonial Photography and Exhibitions: Representations of the "Native" and the Making of European Identities.* London: Leicester University Press, 2000.

McClintock, Anne. *Imperial Leather: Race, Gender, and Sexuality in the Colonial Contest.* New York: Routledge, 1995.

Merry, Sally Engle. *Colonizing Hawai'i: The Cultural Power of Law.* Princeton, N.J.: Princeton University Press, 2000.

Missal, Alexander. *Seaway to the Future: American Social Visions and the Construction of the Panama Canal.* Madison: University of Wisconsin Press, 2008.

Mommsen, Wolfgang. *Theories of Imperialism.* New York: Random House, 1980.

Moore-Gilbert, Bart. *Postcolonial Theory: Contexts, Practices, Politics.* London: Verso, 1997.

Morillo Alicea, Javier. "Looking for Empire in the U.S. Colonial Archive: Photos and Texts." *Historia y Sociedad* 10 (1998): 23–47.

———. *The Routledge Companion to Historical Studies.* London: Routledge, 2000.

———. "Uncharted Landscapes of 'Latin America': The Philippines in the Spanish Imperial Archipelago." In Schmidt-Nowara and Nieto-Phillips, *Interpreting Spanish Colonialism.* Munslow, Alun. *Deconstructing History.* London: Routledge, 1997.

Mykkänen, Juri. *Inventing Politics: A New Political Anthropology of the Hawaiian Kingdom.* Honolulu: University of Hawai'i Press, 2003.

Naranjo Orovio, Consuelo, Miguel Angel Puig-Samper, and Luis Miguel García Mora, eds. *La nación soñada: Cuba, Puerto Rico y Filipinas ante el '98.* Aranjuez, Spain: Ediciones Doce Calles, 1995.

Okihiro, Gary. *Cane Fires: The Anti-Japanese Movement in Hawaii, 1865–1945.* Philadelphia: Temple University Press, 1992.

Onuf, Peter. *Statehood and Nation: A History of the Northwest Ordinance.* Bloomington: Indiana University Press, 1987.

Osorio, Jonathan Kay Kamakawiwoʻole. *Dismembering Lāhui: A History of the Hawaiian Nation to 1887.* Honolulu: University of Hawaiʻi Press, 2002.

Osterhammel, Jürgen. *Colonialism: A Theoretical Overview.* Princeton, N.J.: Markus Wiener, 1997.

Pérez, Louis, Jr. *Cuba between Empires, 1878–1902.* Pittsburgh: University of Pittsburgh Press, 1983.

———. *Cuba in the American Imagination: Metaphor and the Imperial Ethos.* Chapel Hill: University of North Carolina Press, 2008.

———. *The War of 1898: The United States and Cuba in History and Historiography.* Chapel Hill: University of North Carolina Press, 1998.

Perez, Michael. "Contested Sites: Pacific Resistance in Guam to the U.S. Empire." *Amerasia Journal* 27, no. 1 (2001): 97–114.

Picó, Fernando. "Las construcciones de lo español entre los militares norteamericanos en Puerto Rico, 1898–99." *Revista de Indias* 57, no. 211 (September–December 1997): 625–635.

Porter, Dennis. "Orientalism and Its Problems." In *Colonial Discourse and Post-Colonial Theory: A Reader,* ed. Patrick Williams and Laura Chrisman (New York: Columbia University Press, 1994).

Pratt, Mary Louise. *Imperial Eyes: Travel Writing and Transculturation.* London: Routledge, 1992.

Raffucci de García, Carmen. *El gobierno civil y la ley Foraker.* Río Piedras: Editorial Universitaria, 1981.

Rivera Ramos, Efrén. "The Legal Construction of American Colonialism: The Insular Cases (1901–1922)." *Revista Jurídica Universidad de Puerto Rico* 65, no. 2 (1996): 225–328.

Rogers, Robert. *Destiny's Landfall: A History of Guam.* Honolulu: University of Hawaiʻi Press, 1995.

Russ, William Adam. *The Hawaiian Republic (1894–98) and Its Struggle to Win Annexation.* Selinsgrove, Pa.: Susquehanna University Press, 1961.

———. *The Hawaiian Revolution (1893–94).* Selinsgrove, Pa.: Susquehanna University Press, 1959.

Rydell, Robert. *All the World's a Fair: Visions of Empire at American International Expositions, 1876–1916.* Chicago: University of Chicago Press, 1984.

Said, Edward. *Culture and Imperialism.* New York: Vintage Books, 1994.

———. *Orientalism.* New York: Pantheon, 1994.

———. *The World, the Text, and the Critic.* Cambridge, Mass.: Harvard University Press, 1983.

Santiago-Valles, Kelvin. *"Subject People" and Colonial Discourses: Economic Transformation and Social Disorder in Puerto Rico, 1898–1947.* Albany: State University of New York Press, 1994.

Schmidt-Nowara, Christopher, and John Nieto-Phillips, eds. *Interpreting Spanish Colonialism: Empires, Nations, and Legends.* Albuquerque: University of New Mexico Press, 2005.

Scott, Joan. *Gender and the Politics of History.* New York: Columbia University Press, 1988.

Silva, Noenoe. *Aloha Betrayed: Native Hawaiian Resistance to American Colonialism.* Durham, N.C.: Duke University Press, 2004.

Slotkin, Richard. *Gunfighter Nation: The Myth of the Frontier in Twentieth-Century America.* New York: Atheneum, 1992.

Sparrow, Bartholomew. *The Insular Cases and the Emergence of the American Empire.* Lawrence: University of Kansas Press, 2006.

Spurr, David. *The Rhetoric of Empire: Colonial Discourse in Journalism, Travel Writing, and Imperial Administration.* Durham, N.C.: Duke University Press, 1993.

Stade, Ronald. *Pacific Passages: World Culture and Local Politics in Guam.* Stockholm: Stockholm Studies in Social Anthropology, 1998.

Stocking, George. *Race, Culture, and Evolution: Essays in the History of Anthropology.* Chicago: University of Chicago Press, 1962.

Tagg, John. *The Burden of Representation: Essays on Photographies and Histories.* Amherst: University of Massachusetts Press, 1988.

Takaki, Ronald. *Pau Hana: Plantation Life and Labor in Hawai'i, 1835–1920.* Honolulu: University of Hawai'i Press, 1984.

Thomas, Nicholas. *Colonialism's Culture: Anthropology, Travel, and Government.* Princeton, N.J.: Princeton University Press, 1994.

Thompson, Lanny. "'Estudiarlos, juzgarlos y gobernarlos': Conocimiento y poder en el archipiélago imperial estadounidense." In Naranjo Orovio et al., *La nación soñada.*

———. "The Imperial Republic: A Comparison of the Insular Territories under U.S. Dominion after 1898." *Pacific Historical Review* 71, no. 4 (2002): 535–574.

———. "Representation and Rule in the Imperial Archipelago: Cuba, Puerto Rico, Hawai'i, and Philippines under U.S. Dominion." *American Studies Asia* 1, no. 1 (2002): 3–39.

Thompson, Laura. "Crisis on Guam." *Far Eastern Quarterly* 6, no. 1 (1946): 5–11.

Todorov, Tzvetan. *Symbolism and Interpretation.* Ithaca, N.Y.: Cornell University Press, 1982.

Torruella, Juan. *The Supreme Court and Puerto Rico: The Doctrine of Separate and Unequal.* Río Piedras: Editorial de la Universidad de Puerto Rico, 1985.

Trask, Haunani-Kay. *From a Native Daughter: Colonialism and Sovereignty in Hawai'i.* Monroe, Maine: Common Courage Press, 1993.

Trías Monge, José. *Historia constitucional de Puerto Rico.* 4 vols. Río Piedras: Editorial Universitaria, 1980.

————. *Puerto Rico: The Trials of the Oldest Colony in the World.* New Haven, Conn.: Yale University Press, 1997.

Ugarte, Eduardo. "'Qualifications Most Necessary to Rule': The Amok in the Construction of Filipino and American Identities." *American Studies Asia* 1, no. 1 (2002): 41–73.

van Dijk, Teun. *Ideology: A Multidisciplinary Approach.* London: Sage, 1998.

Vergara, Benito. *Displaying Filipinos: Photography and Colonialism in Early 20th Century Philippines.* Quezon City: University of Philippines Press, 1995.

Weber, Max. *The Methodology of the Social Sciences.* Translated and edited by Edward Shils and Henry Finch. New York: Free Press, 1949.

————. *The Protestant Ethic and the Spirit of Capitalism.* New York: Charles Scribner's Sons, 1958.

Weston, Rubin. *Racism in U.S. Imperialism: The Influence of Racial Assumptions on American Foreign Policy, 1893–1946.* Columbia: University of South Carolina Press, 1972.

Wilkins, David. *American Indian Sovereignty and the U.S. Supreme Court.* Austin: University of Texas Press, 1997.

Williams, Eric. *From Columbus to Castro: The History of the Caribbean.* New York: Vintage Books, 1970.

Williams, Patrick, and Laura Chrisman, eds. *Colonial Discourse and Post-Colonial Theory: A Reader.* New York: Columbia University Press, 1994.

Williams, Walter. "United States Indian Policy and the Debate over Philippine Annexation: Implications for the Origins of American Imperialism." *Journal of American History* 66 (1980): 810–831.

Wilson, Norman. *History in Crisis? Recent Directions in Historiography.* Upper Saddle River, N.J.: Prentice Hall, 1999.

Young, Robert. *White Mythologies: Writing, History and the West.* London: Routledge, 1990.

Zimmerman, Warren. *First Great Triumph: How Five Americans Made Their Country a World Power.* New York: Farrar, Straus and Giroux, 2002.

INDEX

Page numbers in **boldface** refer to illustrations.
Page numbers in *italics* refer to tables.

ABOUT THE AUTHOR

LANNY THOMPSON is professor and director of graduate studies in the Department of Sociology and Anthropology at the University of Puerto Rico, Río Piedras. He has published several articles in books and journals in the United States, Spain, the Philippines, and Puerto Rico on the theme developed in this volume. His most recent article, published in *Pacific Historical Review* (vol. 71, no. 4), won two prizes: the James Madison Prize for its outstanding contribution to the history of the U.S. government and the Louis Knott Koontz Award, granted by the American Historical Association.